NORTHWEST BOUNTY

Text by Schuyler Ingle and
Recipes by Sharon Kramis

◆

Foreword by Marion Cunningham

Simon and Schuster
New York   London   Toronto   Sydney   Tokyo

Simon and Schuster
Simon & Schuster Building
Rockefeller Center
1230 Avenue of the Americas
New York, New York 10020

SIMON AND SCHUSTER and colophon are registered trademarks
of Simon & Schuster Inc.

Designed by M. B. Kilkelly/Levavi & Levavi
Manufactured in the United States of America

1   3   5   7   9   10   8   6   4   2

Library of Congress Cataloging-in-Publication Data
Ingle, Schuyler.
Northwest bounty/text by Schuyler Ingle and recipes by Sharon Kramis;
foreword by Marion Cunningham.
p.   cm.
Includes index.
1. Cookery, American—Pacific Northwest style.   I. Kramis,
Sharon.   II. Title.
TX715.2.P32I54   1988
641.59795—dc19   88-18752
CIP
ISBN 0-671-62537-3

Dedicated to the memories of
James Beard
Barry Farrell
Theo Caldwell
Fr. Mike Schmidt
cook, writer, back-country wanderer, servant of the poor:
Northwest boys, each one; each one leading the way.
Breaking trail.

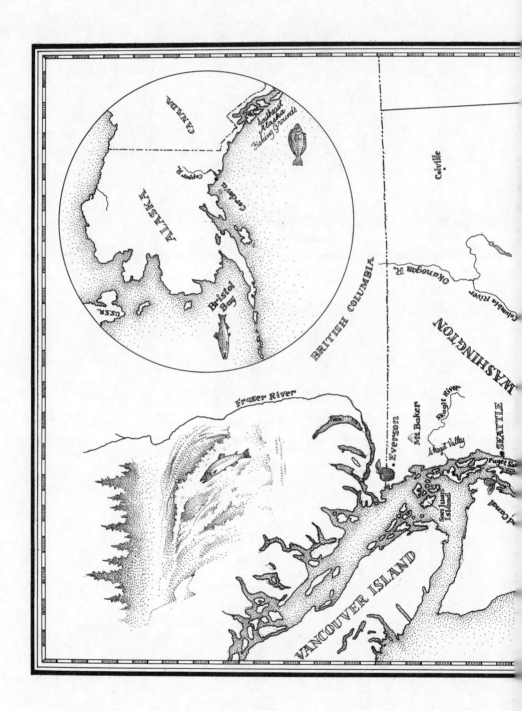

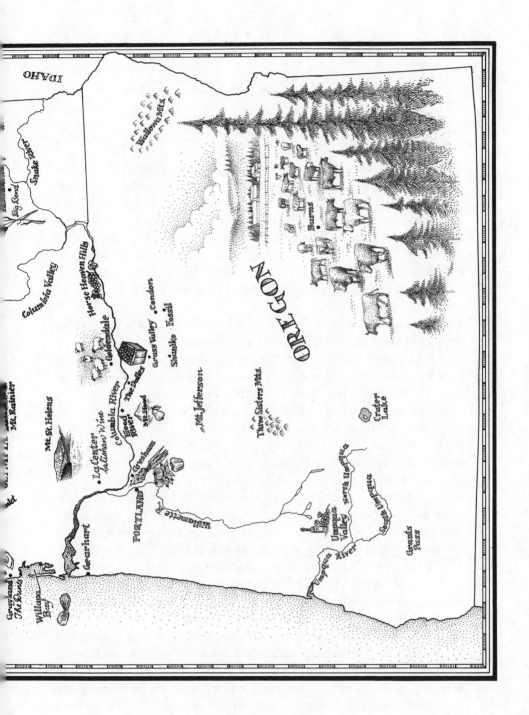

ACKNOWLEDGMENTS

I doubt I would find myself writing about Pacific Northwest food and the people who make it happen were it not for a magnificent editor in Seattle, Ann Senechal. Ann forced me to look hard at my interest in food, and to admit that that interest was more than a passing fancy. Then she took my best work and made me do better. I learned about writing during the editing process, an experience any writer will tell you is rare. Ann Senechal will never understand how fortunate I feel to have spent a little time under her wing.

The people who have shared their knowledge of Pacific Northwest food with me are simply too numerous to name, which I hope they understand. I thank them all. In particular I want to thank Jon Rowley, who infected me with his enthusiasm for fish and shellfish. Mark Musick has done much the same with fruit and produce and with small-scale farming. The Pacific Northwest is lucky to have both of these advocates working and living in the region. Judy Lew, director of the Uwajimaya supermarket cooking school in Seattle, and Paul Nagasawa, produce manager for Uwajimaya, were a big help in identifying the Asian vegetables that have become common in the Northwest. Sue Gilbert, advertising and promotions assistant for the Pike Place Market Preservation and Development Authority, was more than gracious with her time, her boss's office and her vegetable and fruit files. I am indebted to Alec Bayless and Larry Stone for sharing with me their knowledge of the wines of the Pacific Northwest.

I have discovered with this enterprise the tremendous labor that writing a book can be. Carole Lalli, my editor at Simon and Schuster, has made the job a pleasure with her humor, her prodding, her insight and her well-sharpened pencil. Her assistant, Kerri Conan, deserves a Mother Theresa award for the way she dealt with all my demands on her time. I thank her for not simply swatting me away like some miserable nuisance. But no manuscript would ever have ended up on Carole Lalli's desk had my agent, Sallie Gouverneur, not shown consummate patience over the years with this recalcitrant writer. I am sure lesser souls would have given up on me long ago, what with all the whining. But not Sallie. I think of her as a dear, close friend. And I think I am very lucky that she is negotiating from my side of the table.

When my disk drives failed, when my printer broke down, when I had to bankroll a road trip and couldn't come up with ready cash, my parents, John and Joyce Ingle, were right there, ready to lend a hand, and I can't thank them or love them enough. Their support over the years has been steady and unwavering. Now that I am a parent I only hope I can do for my own son what they have done for me.

Farrell was born just about the time I started working on *Northwest Bounty*. I don't recommend becoming a new parent and tackling a book project all at once. My wife, Tamara Moats, made my book-writing endeavors possible in the midst of the glorious, exhausting chaos that comes with being new parents. This book is as much hers as it is mine. Thank you, Tamara, for making it happen.

Schuyler Ingle
Spring, 1988

A special thank-you to my father who taught me to love to eat, to my mother who taught me to love to cook, and to my husband and children—Joe, Tom and Julie—who love to eat what I cook.

And for their support and help in completing this project: Marion Cunningham, Janey Matheson, Dean Pugh, Anthony's Homeport Restaurants, Restaurants Unlimited, Larry and Sally Brown, The James Beard "Master Class" and Robin Klingberg.

Sharon Kramis
Spring, 1988

CONTENTS

FOREWORD

I don't know when I've been as inspired by a cookbook as I am by *Northwest Bounty*. Schuyler Ingle and Sharon Kramis have created a remarkable book. Schuyler and Sharon are sensitive and talented, Schuyler as a first-rate writer and Sharon as a fine home cook.

Schuyler has written about a group of rugged individuals, today's pioneers, who with great spirit, struggle and success are responsible for some of the best regional food in the Pacific Northwest: Duane Fagergren, who has saved the wondrous Olympia oyster; Bruce and Kathy Gore, whose frozen salmon often outshine the best of the fresh; Peter Chan, who plants a backyard vegetable garden each summer that attracts 1,000 visitors; Gwen and Theo Caldwell, who raised pure-bred sheep; Carl Woestendiek and Shery Litwin, who formed edible landscapes; Ann Franklin, who grows perfect berries; and Tom and Cheryl Thornton, who grow treefruit on their Cloud Mountain Farm. These idealists have changed and improved the quality of the food both in restaurants and in home kitchens in the best and only true way—through excellence of ingredients. Schuyler and Sharon partake of this same idealism, and it is this which gives this book its magic.

Sharon is one of the best cooks I know. We met around 1972 in one of James Beard's first cooking classes in Seaside, Oregon. We became great friends and have shared many good times over the years. I am impressed with her boundless curiosity and her sense of the roots of our culinary traditions. She has a fine, critical palate that is never persuaded by fad or high-fashion food. Her recipes generally have few ingredients, are easy to fix, and are delicious. I recently asked Sharon what she thought her special talent was with food, and without thought she answered, "I know what a dish should taste like, and I always know when it is wrong." James Beard recognized Sharon's talent and indeed he was right. Schuyler Ingle and Sharon Kramis have created a splendid book that genuinely represents Pacific Northwest food and cooking.

Marion Cunningham

INTRODUCTION

My wife Tamara and I moved to Seattle in winter from Los Angeles where we had lived long enough to leave without so much as looking back over our shoulders. Winter is the best time to move to Seattle. The city is dark and wet, day and night. While there are moments in an overcast, drizzling day when the shades of light in the sky produce remarkable layers of grays and near blue blacks, the winter sky for the most part is the color of old crumbling sidewalks and it weighs in on the spirit. A Scandinavian melancholia of hallucinatory quality is a most appropriate mid-winter mood. If the new arrival can make it through winter (and most of spring), he is likely to stop wondering when it will clear up, and he will stay.

Tamara and I had the advantage of having grown up in Seattle, and what might have seemed wet and miserable to some seemed normal to us. Besides, we had both become exhausted by California skies of one dimension and palette, of weather reports that droned on day after day with the same dull information. A wet winter in Seattle felt refreshing, rejuvenating.

By the time we arrived in the city, the local farmers selling their goods in the Pike Place Market had all but finished for the year. One wrinkled old prune of a man held on with the last of his potatoes, yellow Finns. Knobby little things. I remember taking the potatoes home without thinking much about them, then boiling them for dinner. I put them in a bowl, poured melted butter over them, sprinkled them with kosher salt and chopped chives and an afterthought dash of cumin, and set them on the table. When Tamara and I cut into them we discovered flesh the color of the Yellow Pages. The potatoes had a full, round flavor, and they were sweet, incredibly sweet.

We ate them all. And when we went back for more, they were all gone. And then the farmer disappeared as well. By the time he returned in spring we weren't sure which one of the many old wrinkled prunes he might be. So we have never found the same potato. And we ate our opportunity to plant and preserve the strain.

That first spring we watched the land come alive at the Pike Place Market. Market farmers and gardeners piled their tables with greens and root crops. As summer approached, so too did the berries. Soon enough we found ourselves out on a blueberry farm picking fruit to freeze for the coming year. And then we did the same with raspberries.

We wouldn't have dreamed of harvesting our own fruit in southern California. The drive alone would kill off any interest in the labor. But in Seattle these things are in reach. Within twenty minutes of downtown one can be picking berries at the most idyllic blueberry farm imaginable.

Our connection to food changed. It became much more direct, more relaxed, more real. We came to know the people growing our food at the Pike Place Market. We started growing our own at home. And what we didn't grow we began to seek out and harvest. Over the years that has turned into family camping trips that cleverly mask food expeditions to the east side of the Cascade Mountains in search of vine-ripened sauce tomatoes and peppers of every description, of peaches and apricots, all of it to put up in jars for winter.

The Pacific Northwest fails on several food fronts. It fails to be frantic about food the way California seems to be if I read the magazines right. But that's the Northwest: relaxed, easygoing, shuffling along. Where mid-winter raspberries might bring a thrill to the Los Angeles diner, in the Northwest people know those berries belong to summer and look for something else on the menu.

As interesting as the growing restaurant scene in the Pacific Northwest might be, the real food of the region happens at home. There's no regional cuisine in the Pacific Northwest the way there is in New Orleans or Santa Fe. But there is a style, a way with food not hounded by tradition. Everybody but the Indians arrived in the Pacific Northwest too recently for regional traditions of any great meaning to have taken hold. So European-based cuisine gets kind of jumbled up with Asian ingredients and cooking techniques. It all depends on who's in the kitchen and who did the shopping.

The recipes Sharon Kramis has accumulated and developed for this book reflect the style of the Pacific Northwest. They are straightforward, simple, flavorful, and they will be as relevant in fifty years as they are today.

By the time I had met Sharon Kramis and we had agreed that a Pacific Northwest cookbook was indeed a good idea, I had banged around on both sides of the Cascade Mountains, in Washington and Oregon, in Idaho and British Columbia, and I had met the kinds of people who lend themselves to long-winded essays. Food people. That is, the kind of people who make food happen: sheep breeders, apple farmers, oyster growers, vegetable gardeners.

I thought the opportunity existed to define the style of the Pacific Northwest with recipes; and I thought the same opportunity existed to illuminate the texture of the Pacific Northwest with essays that would give a sense of people and place. It is all too easy to think the sum total of the Pacific Northwest is the rainy weather in Seattle. It is also too simple a thing to think that all we eat in this corner of the country is Pacific salmon.

The cowboy choking on alkali dust while moving cattle from winter to summer range in southeastern Oregon; the Croatian fisherman heading north out of Puget Sound for Alaskan fishing grounds; the Scandinavian loggers; Italian miners; Basque shepherds; Scots wheat farmers; Dutch orchardists; Tarheel millworkers; Asian truck farmers; and the young viticulturalists newly arrived on land that has seen farms come and go, forests rise and fall—and the people who have been here forever, the Indians of the Coast, of the Rivers, of the Interior Plains, the ones who embrace modern logging and sawmill and aquaculture technology, and the ones who retain the Old Ways, who each year celebrate the coming of First Salmon, First Berry, First Nut, First Root, First Deer: These people are the Pacific Northwest.

Oregon, Washington, Idaho, British Columbia. Mountains, rivers, rain forests, islands, deserts, prairies. Cattle, sheep, apples, wheat, oysters, salmon, potatoes, wild mushrooms. Rain that lasts forever, and sun that burns late into the night. The Pacific Northwest is all of this, too.

So it didn't seem realistic to simply publish a book of recipes and call it "The Pacific Northwest." Nor could essays do it alone. Sharon Kramis and I think this is the answer: a book you can cook with and read.

SEAFOOD

T hough many fine fish can be pulled from the ocean waters of the Pacific Northwest and Alaska—ling cod, halibut, various rockfish, black cod, among others—salmon is the fish that attracts the most attention. If there is a mystic core to the Pacific Northwest, salmon swims at its center. For numberless centuries Indians on major rivers in the region have waited for the return in spring of First Salmon. Those with their traditions still intact celebrate the event with a ritualistic feast that functions much like the taking of the Eucharist. The sacred songs the Indians sing to welcome home First Salmon honor the fish like a relative, which may not be so far from the truth. The fish that return to their place of birth to spawn and die are the direct descendants of salmon that did much the same 10,000 years before. And the Indian who nets and kills that fish and preserves it by drying it on racks or smoking it in a shed for the time when food is scarce is following an ancient forefather who did much the same. No other salmon fishermen in the Pacific Northwest can make such a claim. No other fishermen feel, as many Pacific Northwest Indians do, that if they stop fishing, the salmon will no longer return to the rivers.

Though I grew up in the Pacific Northwest, my exposure to salmon was somewhat more ordinary. The fish never represented the difference between subsistence or hunger to me. The first fresh salmon, a late-winter chinook netted in the Columbia River, didn't come to the table as an old, trusted friend. It came instead as the harbinger of spring. That first salmon meant the dull flavor of winter would soon give way. Strawberries weren't too far off, or asparagus, or sweet onions from Walla Walla, or the first runs of king and silver salmon caught in the cold waters off Alaska.

The sacred words that passed over the fish in the house of my childhood were basic at best, though well intentioned. My mother spoke a simple refrain, like a grace, when she served salmon. "Watch out for the bones," she would say while passing the plates around the table.

I can remember my father returning home with silver salmon from Neah Bay out near the northwest tip of the Olympic Peninsula where the Strait of Juan de Fuca channels Pacific Ocean water into Puget Sound. Each year he would join with colleagues from the teaching staff of the University of Washington School of Dentistry, exchanging his white lab coat for old weekend clothes to go off and fish the late summer run. Silver salmon caught outside Neah Bay have just begun to turn away from salt water and to head for fresh water spawning grounds. They have been feeding hard on shrimp and herring, laying on thick layers of oily fat full of Omega-3, the fatty acid that's good for the heart. The closer the fish get to fresh water, the less they eat. And when they are in fresh water they use their own bodies for fuel, burning up the energy in their fat and flesh to get upstream and spawn. To compensate for weight loss they absorb water, which softens their flesh. A king or silver salmon caught at Neah Bay is close to perfection in terms best understood at the dinner table. The flesh is as firm as it will ever be, the color deep orange-red. The flavor bursts in the mouth because so much fat and oil is marbled into the meat. Lean salmon, by contrast, has a pitiful taste and texture.

·I remember my father and his fishing partners rolling out of the station wagon with their weekend growths of beard, their stories spilling together at once. Their old trousers, messy with fish blood and slime, winked in the sun in places where the salmon scales had stuck fast. The men laid out the salmon on the lawn with the biggest at one end, the smallest at the other. Some of the fish were so long my place would have been somewhere in the middle had I stretched out on the lawn among them.

By evening the biggest of the fish had been butterflied open and trapped between two pieces of chicken wire. Our first barbecue was a pit underneath the swing set and the salmon was suspended from a complicated, jury-rigged frame of wire and rebar above a bed of charcoal that had burned until a gray, powdery surface covered the briquettes. That pit was later replaced by a barbecue made from the curved bottom of a small boiler. Pacific Northwest Indians simply trap a butterflied salmon between the tight arms of a partially split stake driven into the ground at a slant to an alder-wood fire. Thin cross pieces of wood pierce the salmon flesh and hold the fish spread out before the heat. The result is a perfectly cooked fish with an undercarriage of sweet smoke.

The salmon would cook in minutes in my parents' backyard, first on the flesh side, then skin side down. The moment two men flipped the fish my mother moved in with a pot of her barbecue sauce, a savory concoction of melted butter and catsup with garlic, Worcestershire sauce, mustard, and lemon juice intermingling in the pot, sopping it up with a paintbrush, then stroking it onto the seared flesh. Dinner guests edged closer to the buffet table.

There is good reason I can still smell those salmon cooking, the fat falling in the fire in small explosions of smoke and sizzle. The warm flavor had a tangible shape and presence in my young mouth. The fish were much closer to the sea, to a state of living perfection, than anything available in city fish markets of the day —the difference between the exalted and the ordinary. Some rudimentary steps had been taken by my father and his friends to maintain the quality of the fish. I remember chunks of dry ice left smoking on the lawn after the catch had been divided among the fishermen. It is remarkable what ice can do for the quality of fish. Even though much more is understood today about keeping fresh fish at peak quality than was known thirty years ago when my father and his friends drove off to Neah Bay, there are fishmongers in the Pike Place Market in Seattle who still fail to cover their salmon with shaved ice.

Jon Rowley used to howl like a prophet in the wilderness about just such fish abuse, and it seemed for a time that no one would listen. His point was simple: If the public is made aware of how good the best fish can be, it won't settle for less; consumers will be willing to pay more for top quality, calling it a better value. Rowley, at one time a commercial fisherman, knew the difference. He knew what fish tasted and felt like when it was pulled from the water right into the pan. There was no reason, he believed, that the same experience couldn't be delivered to market. And he has been proven correct, though it has taken close to a decade.

In 1987 Jon Rowley was inducted into the *Cook's* magazine and *Restaurant Business* magazine's *Who's Who in Cooking in America,* one of the few Pacific Northwest recipients of the honor. His contribution to the food world is evident throughout Seattle, a city where the consumer can buy fish in the supermarket with every expectation of taking home the highest quality product. Seattle restaurants and markets actually compete with each other to present to the public fish that is so good it was thought not to exist only a few years back. The fish was always there, of course. It simply took consumer demand to see it to the marketplace. And it took cherub-cheeked Jon Rowley, his benign monomaniacal enthusiasm for seafood in full toot, to wake up the consumer.

Rowley understood the process for bringing the best-quality fish to market, and worked with fishermen who would use it. The Scandinavians base the fine reputation of their fishery on it. The process begins with the fish in the water at the side of the boat. It is caught on hook and line, not in a net. Net-caught fish fight themselves to exhaustion when they discover they are trapped. They pump their flesh full of adrenalin. A hook-and-line-caught fish can be pulled in to the side of the boat and dispatched without a struggle.

It takes a whack on the head, a sound crack with the handle of a gaff hook, to stun a fish. A stunned fish won't flop around on the deck of a fishing boat, bruising itself in a fruitless, frantic struggle that breaks capillaries and spills traces of blood into the flesh. Patches on a fish where scales are missing suggest those scales were knocked free by just such a struggle, not a good sign. Blood spoils before anything else in any kind of fish. It is blood going off that gives up the first faint odor we call "fishy." Good fish should have an ocean scent about them, something of the sea breeze, not the sewer. Blood going off also taints fish with a metallic flavor.

To rid the stunned fish of as much blood as possible, the fisherman sticks it with a knife at the throat latch to sever a main artery. The process, called live bleeding—the heart pumps the blood out of the fish—is common in the Scandinavian fishing industry. Were it not for live bleeding, those snow white cod fillets from Norway and Iceland would have a rosy tinge.

Some fish can simply be iced down once they have been live bled. The various rockfish—yellow-eye, quillback, canary—the ones steamed in Pacific Northwest Chinese restaurants and sold as rock cod, are like that. Salmon is a different story. Salmon must be eviscerated as quickly as possible. They have remarkable digestive acids that begin eating through the stomach as soon as the fish dies. It isn't uncommon to find salmon in the marketplace with patches of "belly burn" visible in the abdominal cavity, a sign that the fish wasn't cleaned immediately. The digestive acids then leaked out and burned through the membrane lining the belly walls. That and a layer of fat on the belly flaps starting to go rancid are the two greatest inhibitors of optimum flavor in salmon. The gills have to go as well; fish-spoiling bacteria are particularly drawn to gills.

Cooling down a fish as fast and as soon as possible slows a build-up of bacteria on the skin that if left unchecked turns a prime-quality fish into something fit for the dumpster and the alley cat. The closer to 32 degrees the better. Cooling also slows and pro-

longs *rigor mortis,* an important factor in determining the best possible texture in the cooked fish. A fish that is immediately iced will
take hours to enter *rigor* and will then stay in it for days if kept cold
enough. The fish will then gradually relax out of the state, which
makes it seem like it has just been pulled from the water. Days can
pass and a properly iced fish can still deliver an optimum culinary
experience. The opposite effect, a mushy-textured fish, is often a
result of improper cooling. The fish that rapidly enters *rigor,* suddenly seizing up tight like a fist, then just as suddenly letting go,
turns into a flaccid, dead thing with little to be said for either its
texture or flavor.

The fishmonger's shaved ice has a distinct purpose. It keeps the
fish at an optimum temperature and, as it melts, it washes away
the constant bacteria buildup on the skin. At home a whole fish can
be iced and refrigerated in a poaching pan with the rack inverted to
elevate the fish above the bottom of the pan where the melt-off
collects.

The result of all this care is a fish ready for cooking that shines
with a deep luster. The flesh will have a translucent look to it, will
appear alive and radiant, and will be resilient, springing back when
pressed with the fingertips. The skin will have the same kind of
slime on it that the fish has in the ocean, almost like an aspic. And
the smell will bring to the home memories of the most pleasant
walks along the seashore. There are those who say the eyes of fresh
fish must shine, but this is true only of certain—not all—fish. A
salmon can be in a far from ideal state and still have bright eyes; so
judging quality by eyes alone is not a good idea.

Not all commercial fishermen, of course, would care to listen to
a Jon Rowley going on and on about live bleeding and immediate
cleaning and icing. Commercial fishermen get set in their ways. If
they have treated fish in one fashion, cleaning them when they
have time, say, icing them down only if they happen to have ice,
and the market doesn't seem to mind if they don't, then why
change? It could only mean more work.

Bruce and Kathy Gore, two of the best commercial salmon fishermen to work off the coast of southeastern Alaska, had reached a
point of maximum frustration a dozen years ago with a salmon
processing and distribution system that encouraged a poor quality
product. By nature alone Bruce Gore always does the best he can,
no matter what the job. He and Kathy would gillnet salmon, treat
their catch with care, and deliver to the dock premium-quality fish.
Then they would watch their salmon go into a pile of fish that had

never seen ice. "All Kathy and I were doing with our fresh catch," Gore says, "was raising the overall quality of the pack."

Most commercial fishing in the United States is an anonymous endeavor. The fisherman brings his catch to the dock where he is paid so much a pound, good fish or bad. He takes his money and goes back to sea. There is never a connection between the fish in the market and the individual fisherman. The fish brokers get on the phone and sell to buyers, and neither party ever actually looks at the quality of the catch. Until very recently, quality hasn't much mattered. Fish need only be "wholesome," which is to say not toxic to humans, to pass FDA muster as fresh and be labeled as such. Fresh fish isn't necessarily good.

A fisherman who makes every effort to produce the best quality fish is paid the same as the fisherman who is too busy killing fish to care about live bleeding or icing down his catch, so there is little incentive within the system to improve or change. "Before we started freezing our catch we were killing lots of fish," Bruce Gore explains, "but we weren't making much of a living. What we needed to do was increase the value of each fish we caught, not catch more."

To that end the Gores had to figure out a way around the salmon processing and distribution system, and freezing their catch at sea seemed to be the best answer. The Canadians were working with the system, and the French were paying top dollar at the time, flying the frozen salmon back to France to cure and smoke. There was little competition in Europe back then from the Norwegian farm-raised Atlantic salmon industry.

The Gores have been freezing at sea hook-and-line-caught salmon for the last ten years on their 44-foot troller, *Triad*. *Triad* salmon are some of the best to come out of Alaskan waters. When properly handled, thawed and cooked, these frozen salmon are so good, culinary luminaries like Julia Child have selected them over fresh product in blind taste tests.

The Gores take live bleeding to remarkable extremes. They have honed their technique with experience that has included monitoring their product from the time it is frozen until it is served in a restaurant to a customer. Typically, Bruce Gore stuns a fish before pulling it aboard *Triad*. He lays it on the deck and sticks it with his dressing knife; depending on the size of the salmon, it will take anywhere from five to thirty minutes to bleed out and die. Bruce then cuts the head off, eviscerates it, and cleans the belly cavity of all membrane and pockets of blood. By cutting the salmon at the anterior end of the backbone, Bruce Gore exposes the kidney and applies the deck hose. The pressurized water floods into the arteries along the back and in the tail of the fish, draining into the belly cavity. Flipping the fish belly side down into a trough, Bruce massages the back of the salmon, rubbing along the lateral line, the slight pressure and gravity combining to drain out more blood. Finally, he rubs down the veins in the belly cavity on the belly flap, squeezing out what blood he can. When rushed, Bruce can process a fish a minute.

Kathy Gore established *Triad* quality control. Once Bruce finishes with a salmon, he passes it to Kathy who then continues applying the hose to the backbone, massaging the fish, checking the belly cavity for any remaining membrane, scraping down the veins in the belly cavity with a spatula, and checking the salmon for its cosmetic look. When the salmon is as drained of blood as it will ever be, Kathy lays it on deck under wet burlap bags to cool down.

The salmon don't stay there long. The Gores have discovered over time that they achieve a better end-product when they freeze the salmon before it enters *rigor mortis,* this in spite of the industry standard of freezing fish after they have passed through *rigor.* When the Gores have about twenty salmon under burlap, enough time has passed that *rigor* is close. So Kathy begins to lower the fish down to Bruce in the freezer hold where the temperature is a steady −35 degrees Fahrenheit.

Most freezer boats maintain temperatures of between −5 and −10 degrees Fahrenheit, but the Gores have found that at these temperatures salmon freeze too slowly. Ice crystals form, expand, and puncture the walls of the individual cells that make up the flesh of the fish. When a fish frozen at these temperatures thaws, it characteristically releases liquid from those damaged cells and the resulting flesh has little or no resilience. It's mushy. The Gores' salmon is frozen so fast at −35 degrees Fahrenheit that ice crystals can't form and expand. The fish freeze to the core within twenty-four hours, and it probably takes a month for them to enter and pass through *rigor.* Bruce Gore thinks of the process as stopping the biological clock. In a final stage the salmon are submerged several times in a sugar-water solution which glazes and seals them from any air. A plastic tag bearing Bruce Gore's name is attached to each fish. That, in and of itself, is something of a revolution in the fishing industry.

When the Gores first tagged each of their frozen salmon, they suddenly became visible, unlike any other fishermen in the industry. If something was wrong with the fish, the consumer knew where to turn. The name of the fisherman was right there. If the quality was significantly better and consistent, however, the Gores expected a premium price. Today they get it.

It was fortunate that the best efforts of the Gores coincided with Jon Rowley's labors in the Pacific Northwest to bring high-quality seafood to the consumer. It is a long way from the freezer to the marketplace, and the path is heavily pitted with ingrown resistance to frozen seafood. It still is, for that matter, and not without good reason.

Jon Rowley got the management and the chef at Ray's Boathouse in Seattle to try the Gores' frozen salmon. The reputation of Ray's, as well as much of its business, had been built on the fine piece of salmon it serves. This always remained a problem in winter when few fresh wild salmon are available in the market. There is a winter troll fishery in Alaska, but the numbers of the catch are small. The only real alternative, as many restaurants have discovered, has been farm-raised salmon, available all year long.

The Ray's Boathouse kitchen staff spent over a month testing the Gores' frozen salmon before putting it on the menu with a note explaining that rather than always trying to get fresh fish, it might be better to look for the best fish. And the best might sometimes be a frozen product. Once the waitstaff at Ray's became confident with the frozen salmon, diners began ordering it. And all it really takes is one bite. When one of Bruce and Kathy Gore's salmon thaws out, it shines with a brilliance seldom seen in fresh product. The fish looks alive, as if it has just slipped out of the water to lie on the cutting board. And in one sense it has. Once the biological clock begins ticking again, the Gore salmon is only two hours out of the water. And there's no fresh salmon served or sold anywhere that can support a similar claim.

The fortunes of Gore frozen salmon and Jon Rowley's seafood consulting firm, Fish Works!, have increased side by side. Rowley took the experience of Ray's—that a good fish product increases profits—and sold it to several Seattle-area supermarkets. His program went well beyond the Gores' frozen salmon and included teaching supermarket buyers how to set parameters of acceptability for seafood, and turn back at the door anything that didn't measure up. In most cases this meant the markets had to designate a seafood buyer on the staff. But once word got out about great fish in a supermarket, the overall fortunes of the stores that had come under Rowley's tutelage increased. Those shoppers who came to the market for good fish seemed to fill their shopping carts while they were there. And in winter they discovered they could buy salmon—the Gores' frozen product—every bit as good as the fresh salmon they enjoyed in the spring and summer.

The Gores remained selective about the restaurants they would work with. Having a unique product makes business for restaurants, and the Gores respect that. Plus they only want to work with restaurants they know will take extra effort to properly handle the frozen product. Supermarkets are another bowl of chowder. When it comes to retail, everyone has to have the latest product. So the Gores have grown over the years, balancing the demands of the retail and the restaurant markets for their product, always failing to meet the demand by a healthy 20 percent, growing slowly and carefully, never allowing demand to interfere with the consistent quality of the frozen salmon tagged with their name. Each year they have sold their catch before they even go fishing.

Seven freezer boats now fish under the *Triad* umbrella, producing 200,000 pounds of frozen-at-sea salmon a year, all of it tagged, all of it coming up to the standards set by Bruce and Kathy Gore. Other commercial fishermen are following the Gores' marketing concept. The Makah Indian fishery in Washington State has begun a tagging program where the best-quality salmon carry the name of the tribe to market and receive a premium price. Some Norwegian pen-raised Atlantic salmon are beginning to get the same attention. An Oregon salmon troller collective has been working on what they call a Signature Salmon marketing program. And the Alaska Seafood Marketing Institute has launched a Premium Quality labeling initiative for Alaska salmon aimed at the restaurant industry. The significance of all this turns on an enhanced appreciation of quality, both among the fishermen and the consumers. The benefits are of mutual value. The consumer gains access to a top-quality product, and the fisherman, becoming visible in the market, can take pride in the results of his labors as the exaltations of satisfied diners rise above the general din.

When the Gores switched to freezing salmon they made a philosophical commitment to produce the highest quality rather than the greatest quantity of salmon. The fishermen who now sell their frozen salmon under the *Triad* tag have had to come around to the same conceptual adjustment. "I've become so involved in the food end of the business, the restaurants and supermarkets," Bruce Gore explains, "that I think of myself in the food business, not the fish killing business. It is possible to kill more fish than you can properly handle, and it can be tempting when the fish are really hitting fast. But the first time you compromise your quality for production, and somebody gets a salmon that's not up to the standards Kathy and I have established under our name, it will come back and haunt us." To keep track of the fish and to be able to identify any problems in the system, Gore color-codes the fish tags according to the freezer boat of origin. When the salmon are graded and boxed before being shipped in freezer vans from Sitka to Seattle, the boxes are marked to indicate the run. "You put a salmon with the *Triad* tag in my hands," Bruce Gore says, "and I can tell you where it was caught."

The ever-growing alternative to Pacific salmon, whether frozen-at-sea or premium-grade fresh, is Norwegian pen-raised Atlantic salmon. Restaurateurs like the product because it is dependable and available year-round and, Bruce Gore salmon aside, a frozen fish product is a tough sell. The major salmon fishing season in Alaska starts in May and ends in September. With no fresh wild salmon available through winter, Bruce Gore's frozen product has only its farm-raised cousin as a competitor. Consistency is the key. The Gores have been able to do with a wild fish—achieve a consistent, marketable, bankable quality—what the Norwegians are busy perfecting with a farm-raised Atlantic salmon, though Atlantic salmon is more like a big trout than a Pacific salmon. There are certain basic advantages to the Gores' approach. Wild salmon aren't fed massive doses of antibiotics to keep them healthy. Atlantic salmon taste muddy if their commercial feed isn't of the highest quality. And if that feed doesn't contain ground shrimp and herring, pen-raised Atlantic salmon don't produce the Omega-3 fatty acids that lower body cholesterol in humans.

In the end, the wild salmon will always be better than pen-raised salmon simply for being untamed, for being free. As young fry, salmon swim backwards down rivers to the sea, coming out of the mystic core of the Pacific Northwest like ghost dancers, then disappearing into such a vastness we can only think of it as oceanic. Their return years later to the exact place of their birth is one of the great ongoing miracles and mysteries in the world. Fishermen like the Gores are not just proud of the remarkable job they can do catching and bringing to market so magnificent a fish as a king or silver salmon in the prime of life, they are proud of the fish itself and they do what they can to bring it to the table in the finest state. Respect is part of the equation because in the end, it is salmon worth praying over, whether in sacred song cycles, or in the simple incantation of a Pacific Northwest mom: "Watch out for the bones."

Seafood of the Pacific Northwest

Pacific cod: Known as "true cod." Excellent for fish and chips. Most of the harvest is processed and frozen at sea.

Ling cod: One of the best eating fish on the West Coast. Not a ling or a cod, but actually a greenling. Nice flavor and reasonably priced. Be sure to ask for longline-caught—fish that have been individually bled, gutted and iced (or frozen) on board the boat. You will pay more, but it's worth it. Don't be put off by the slight greenish color of this fish's flesh. It cooks a beautiful white color.

Black cod: Not an actual cod. Its true name is sablefish. Soft white flesh, rather oily. A favorite way of presenting it is lightly smoked, or cooked outdoors on the barbecue.

Salmon: There are five species of salmon that come to the market each year. It's important to know the different qualities of each species in order to cook them properly.

Silver (also known as coho): pastel salmon color. When cooked, it doesn't flake, but tears, leaving a jagged edge. A moist fish, but it can become dry if not cooked properly; the best method is oven-baked or poached.

King: ranges in size from 1 to 120 pounds. It is available fresh the year round. The color ranges from red to white. The Columbia River is the first to harvest in mid-February, and the last local harvest is from the Strait of Juan de Fuca, at the end of September. October through January all kings are harvested from Alaskan waters during winter troll fishing. This is the best salmon to barbecue.

Sockeye: brightest red of all the species. Availability is excellent nationwide. The Copper River Run in late May starts the season, which then finishes in August with the Puget Sound run. Sockeye is available "fresh frozen" the year round. The best method of cooking is oven-broiling or baking.

Chum (also known as fall or silver-brite salmon): it is absolutely critical to look for "hot pink" meat color. As the color of chum grows paler, the quality of its taste diminishes. Silvery skin is essential as is firm flesh. Southeast Alaska is the best source.

American shad: A delicious fresh water fish that takes great skill to bone. It is a member of the herring family. The roe is a delicacy fried and served with strips of bacon. Columbia River shad appears sporadically in the markets in May and June.

Smelt: February brings fresh smelt into the markets. Smelt are sold whole and average 3 inches to 8 inches in length. The euchalon, also called Columbia River smelt, is the major commercial species on the West Coast. These smelt are so rich in oil, Indians used them as "candles," drying them out and inserting cedar sticks for wicks.

Sole: Authentic sole is imported fresh or frozen to the United States from England or France. In the Northwest the seafood markets offer a variety of "sole" which are actually small flounder. The most popular and the best quality of the Pacific flounder marketed under the "sole" name is Petrale sole. Other flounder available in the markets of the Pacific Northwest are sold as Rex sole (too thin to fillet, so it is cooked whole and then boned at the table), English sole (small fillets, bland in taste), Butter sole, and Sand sole.

Pacific halibut: Firm white meat, usually sold in fillets or steaks. Halibut cheeks are a real delicacy. This is a fish that is available frozen most of the year, but watch for the brief openings in the early spring and summer for fresh halibut. Once you have eaten the fresh fish, it's difficult to enjoy the frozen. There is a remarkable difference in the texture.

Pacific sand dab: A small flounder with nice texture and good flavor. A wonderful pan-fried fish.

Rainbow trout: The trout you see in the seafood markets is usually "farm-raised." A good buy, but not as delicious as fresh-caught river or lake trout. The flesh is not as firm or as flavorful. However, it is available year-round in the markets and makes a nice dinner.

Steelhead: A sea-run rainbow trout. There are many rivers and streams with annual runs of steelhead in the fall and winter. This is the sportfisherman's dream fish and is delicious. A more muscular flavor than rainbow trout.

Sturgeon: The white sturgeon of the Columbia River is an excellent eating fish. It has a very firm texture so it holds up to grilling and has thus become more and more popular in the last few years. It is often seen on restaurant menus in Seattle and Portland. Sturgeon is also smoked, both "cold-smoked" and "hot-smoked." Columbia River sturgeon caviar is highly acclaimed. The demand far exceeds the supply.

Rockfish: More than 200 rockfish species can be found off the Pacific Coast. There is a great deal of confusion over the names given to the different species available in the markets. The most misleading is the term "red snapper." True red snapper is found only in the Atlantic Ocean and does not resemble the Pacific Coast rockfish which range from the 1-pound Rosethorn that the Chinese steam whole, to the giant 60-pound Yelloweye that goes into the sashimi market.

Surfperch: Usually caught by recreational fishermen. Sometimes available in the markets. (Ocean perch sold in the seafood markets is not really perch, but rockfish.) Both fish are usually marketed in 1- to 1½-pound size and are very good cleaned and oven-broiled.

How to select fresh seafood

The number one rule is: *consider the source*. I am fortunate to have access to an excellent seafood store where the quality of the fish is the best I have found. I strongly recommend that you take the time to find the best one in your neighborhood and then cultivate the people there. It is also exciting to see that retail grocery stores all over the country are upgrading the quality of the seafood for sale. Here are a few tips for picking out fish.

1. Fresh fish should never smell. In a good seafood store you should never smell fish; this goes for restaurants too. If you have any doubt, don't hesitate to give a fish a good, up-close sniff. A briny, "ocean" smell is good; a "fishy" smell is not.

2. If the skin looks too big for the fish, it's old fish. The skin should have 80 percent or more scales still on and should not have any exterior scars or marks.

3. Press the fish behind the head along the backbone: the flesh should be firm to the touch. Run your hand along the rib cage to make sure it's firmly attached to the flesh of the fish. If the fish is old, the flesh will have started to separate from the bones.

4. Fish fillets should have a translucent, glistening look. They shouldn't look dry; the flesh should be smooth and even, with no separations on its surface.

5. If possible, buy shellfish from a market that holds supply in live tanks or, at least, from one that gets fresh supplies every two days or so.

6. Buy scallops with your nose. A truly fresh scallop will smell like a fresh ocean breeze. As a scallop ages, it loses all of its smell. A scallop that is spoiled smells just like a wet dog.
   Good-sized scallops to buy are 20 to 30 to a pound.

DEFINING THE PACIFIC NORTHWEST STYLE

*Bruce Naftaly and Robin Sanders of Restaurant Le Gourmand
are two of the best cooks working in the Pacific Northwest.
Few chefs match Bruce Naftaly's abiding interest in and support of local food producers. Few pastry chefs in the Pacific
Northwest can do much better than Robin Sanders. Together
they have raised cuisine in this region to its highest level.*

Poached Fillet of
Copper River King Salmon
with Wind-Dried Salmon
and Sorrel

The king salmon that return each spring to Alaska's Copper
River have a flavor and color and texture against which all
other salmon must be measured, and fall short. The king
salmon are harvested for a brief time in late spring, appearing
for three or four weeks in markets and restaurants, and then
they are gone until the next year. The wind-dried salmon used
in this recipe comes from Indians who dry the salmon on racks
in the hot summer winds that blow through British Columbia's Fraser River Canyon. No more ancient ingredient exists
in the Northwest kitchen.

> *4 8-ounce Copper River king salmon fillets*
> *1 cup dry white wine*
> *1 quart white wine fish stock (see recipe below)*
> *1½ cups heavy cream*
> *1½ ounces shredded wind-dried salmon (dry-smoked
> kippered salmon may be used instead, though this
> will add a smoky quality to the sauce rather than the
> rich salmon flavor that comes from the wind-dried
> fish)*
> *Salt and freshly ground white pepper*
> *¾ cup fresh sorrel, cut roughly (chiffonade, see note on
> p. 119)*

To poach the fillets, place in a skillet to fit in 1 layer and pour in the white wine, adding cold water to cover if necessary. Bring to a simmer. Cover. Poach at slowest simmer for about 10 minutes.

Meanwhile, make the sauce. Reduce fish stock in non-aluminum pan to ½ cup. Add cream and dried salmon. Simmer until the sauce is thickened and of a smooth consistency. The dried salmon will expand as it is cooked. Correct seasoning with salt and white pepper. Five minutes before serving, add sorrel.

Remove the fish from poaching liquid, drain, and serve immediately with sauce.

Serves 4

DEFINING THE PACIFIC NORTHWEST STYLE

> ### *Poached White King Salmon with Gooseberry and Dill Sauce*

The white king salmon often sells for less because salmon customers expect red, not white, flesh from salmon. But white king, sometimes called ivory king salmon, is every bit as good as its red-fleshed cousin. The difference is in genetic makeup. White king salmon simply hail from a slightly altered gene pool.

> *4 8-ounce fresh white king salmon fillets*
> *1 cup dry white wine*
> *1 quart white wine fish stock (see recipe below)*
> *1 cup whipping cream*
> *½ cup gooseberry puree (½ cup gooseberries cooked slowly in non-aluminum pan with 2 tablespoons fish stock until berries are soft; puree and strain)*
> *¼ cup fresh dill, chopped*
> *Salt and freshly ground white pepper to taste*
> *½ cup gooseberries, topped and tailed*

Poach salmon fillets in the wine for 5 to 10 minutes; do not overcook. To make sauce, reduce fish stock to ½ cup. Add cream and reduce by half. Add gooseberry puree and dill. Check seasoning (salt and pepper) and consistency; the sauce should be thickened and smooth. Add whole berries and simmer until they are just done and still holding their shape. Serve each fillet on a pool of the sauce.

Serves 4

DEFINING THE PACIFIC NORTHWEST STYLE

White Wine Fish Stock

Use halibut trim from your fishmonger or an equivalent clean, pure, white fish trim for the best taste. Do not use salmon or rockfish trim.

> *1 tablespoon butter*
> *1 large leek, cut in small pieces*
> *1 large onion, cut in small pieces*
> *3 cups dry white wine*
> *1 pound halibut trim, cut in small pieces*

Melt butter and add leek and onion. Add 1 cup dry white wine, cover and steam onion and leek until they are translucent. Add the fish and the remaining 2 cups of wine and simmer for 10 minutes. Then add cold water just to cover. Bring to a boil, uncovered, then skim. Simmer at a gentle boil for 20 to 25 minutes, skimming regularly. Strain through fine chinois or cheesecloth.

Yield: 1 quart

Oven-Broiled Salmon

My favorite way to cook salmon steaks or fillets indoors is by oven-broiling. This method combines broiling and high-heat baking. Normally, during broiling in an oven, the door is left slightly open; however, here the door is closed completely. This creates the interior heat that glazes the fish and seals in the moisture. This method is for electric or gas broilers mounted inside an oven.

> *4 ounces butter*
> *1 tablespoon Worcestershire sauce*
> *Juice of 1 lemon*
> *4 6–8 ounce salmon fillets*

Preheat the broiler. Melt the butter in a small saucepan. Stir in the Worcestershire sauce and the lemon juice.

Place the salmon fillets on a broiler pan with a wire rack. Lightly oil the rack. Brush the salmon generously with the lemon butter. Sprinkle with salt and pepper. Position broiling pan so that the fish is 6–7 inches away from the direct heat. Close the oven door and broil-bake for 5 minutes. Brush with more lemon butter and cook 2 to 3 minutes longer.

Serves 4

DEFINING THE PACIFIC NORTHWEST STYLE

> ### *Szechuan Pepper-Broiled Salmon with Cilantro Sour Cream Sauce*

Greg Higgins, chef at the Heathman Hotel in Portland, leaves nothing to chance. He bakes his own breads, smokes his own fish and makes his own sausage. This is his very original preparation for fresh salmon steaks.

> *4 tablespoons Szechuan brown peppercorns*
> *4 tablespoons coarse-cracked black peppercorns*
> *1 pound butter, softened*
> *½ cup shallots, minced*
> *4 teaspoons garlic, minced*
> *Salt and pepper to taste*
> *2 cups bread crumbs*
>
> *4 6-ounce salmon steaks or fillets (one per person)*

Mix together all ingredients except fish and brush generously on salmon.

> Sauce:
> *Juice of 2 limes*
> *1 cup pinot gris*
> *2 ounces bay shrimp (usually marketed cleaned and*
>   *cooked)*
> *8 ounces sour cream*
> *1 bunch cilantro, finely chopped*
> *Salt and pepper to taste*

Combine lime juice and pinot gris in a small saucepan. Bring to a moderate boil and simmer until the wine is reduced by about half. Add the bay shrimp and remove from the heat.

While the salmon broils, combine the pinot gris and bay shrimp mixture with the sour cream and cilantro. Adjust the seasoning with salt and pepper to taste, mix thoroughly. Pour over broiled salmon.

Serves 4

Whole Baked Salmon with Cucumber Sauce

My favorite way to cook a 5- to 6-pound salmon is to bake it whole. It's easy and makes a nice entrée for a company dinner.

> *1 5- to 6-pound whole salmon (ask to have it boned)*
> *1 yellow onion, sliced*
> *1 large lemon, sliced*
> *1 orange, sliced*
> *¼ pound butter, cut into 6 pieces*

Preheat the oven to 400°. Lay the salmon on its side on a large piece of foil. Fill the cavity with the sliced onion, lemon and orange. Place the pieces of butter evenly along the inside of the fish from end to end. Fold the foil over, but don't seal it; leave it open along the cavity of the fish. Pinch both ends of the foil to close and place the wrapped fish on a baking sheet. Bake in the oven for 1 hour. You will have a perfectly cooked salmon.

Serves 8

> Cucumber Sauce:
> *1 English or burpless cucumber, peeled and cut in half*
> *1 cup water*
> *1 tablespoon salt*
> *¼ cup sugar*
> *⅓ cup white vinegar*
> *1 cup sour cream*
> *1 teaspoon fresh dill*

Remove seeds from cucumber, and cut across into thin slices. In a mixing bowl, combine water, salt, sugar, and vinegar. When sugar and salt are dissolved, add cucumber. Refrigerate for 1 hour before serving. When ready to serve, drain cucumber and fold into sour cream. Sprinkle with fresh dill.

DEFINING THE PACIFIC NORTHWEST STYLE

> ### *Bamboo-Steamed King Salmon Café Sport*

Chef Tom Douglas at Café Sport specializes in the freshest of Pacific Northwest ingredients prepared in a straightforward and delicious way. His unique style weaves the Pacific Rim influence in our cuisine through the seasonal availability of products.

2 7–8-ounce king salmon fillets
½ cup dry Riesling
1 cup water
12 sprigs lemongrass
3 star anise
2 ounces sliced ginger

Place salmon fillets in bamboo steamer (or place on rack in pan and cover). Combine Riesling, water, lemongrass, anise and ginger in a 10-inch sauté pan. Bring to a boil. Place steamer basket over boiling liquid and steam salmon until medium rare—6 to 8 minutes.

While fish is steaming, make the sauce.

Sauce:
1 cup dry Riesling
½ ounce ginger, sliced into julienne strips
3 sprigs lemongrass
1 cup fish fume
2 tablespoons butter

Combine all ingredients except butter in 8- to 10-inch shallow pan. Reduce to medium syrup and add butter. Serve with salmon.

Serves 2

Gravlax

This is the Scandinavian method for curing fresh salmon. It is delicious served with small cooked new potatoes and baby peas, and makes an excellent lunch served with Swedish rye bread and a special Mustard Sauce.

2½ pounds whole fresh salmon (or 2 center-cut fillets, same weight)
½ cup fine table salt
¼ cup sugar

20 coarsely crushed peppercorns
2 ounces chopped fresh dill, about ½ cup
Lemon slices
Gravlax Mustard Sauce (recipe follows)

If the fish is whole, bone it and cut it down the middle into two pieces, leaving the skin on. Wipe the fish dry. Score the surface of the skin in several places.

Mix salt and sugar together. Sprinkle ¼ cup of the salt mixture in a glass baking dish. Place half of the salmon, skin side down, in the dish and sprinkle generously with crushed peppercorns, the dill, and ¼ cup of the salt mixture. Place the other piece of fish, skin side up, on top and sprinkle with remaining ¼ cup of salt mixture. Cover with plastic wrap and a light weight. Refrigerate for at least 48 hours or up to 3 days. Turn the salmon over twice every day. Remove from the brine and rinse under cold water. The cured salmon will keep for 1 to 2 weeks in the refrigerator. To serve, slice thinly on the bias toward the tail at a 45° angle, freeing the salmon from the skin. Garnish with lemon slices and serve with the mustard.

Serves 8

Gravlax Mustard Sauce:
3 tablespoons oil
3 tablespoons prepared mustard (yellow mustard is usually used for this because of the flavor and color, but I prefer a Dijon-style)

1 tablespoon red wine vinegar
1 tablespoon sugar
½ teaspoon salt
2 tablespoons finely chopped dill

Shake or beat together all the ingredients except the dill and store in the refrigerator. Add the dill just before serving.

Smoked Salmon and Pecan Spread

Lynnie Ludtka, a young friend who is a cook by profession, serves this. It is a terrific appetizer, and a great snack to serve anytime.

½ cup finely chopped white onion
6 ounces hard-smoked salmon, broken into small chunks
8 ounces cream cheese
2 tablespoons cream-style horseradish
1 tablespoon lemon juice
Salt to taste
½ cup chopped pecans
1½ tablespoons butter

Chop onion in food processor. Remove to a mixing bowl. Blend the salmon and cream cheese together in food processor until well mixed. Add the horseradish, lemon juice and salt. Stir the salmon mixture into the onion and then transfer to serving bowl.

Sauté pecans in melted butter until lightly toasted. Sprinkle over the top of the salmon spread. Serve with toasted French bread or crackers.

Note: Hard-smoked salmon is smoked at a higher temperature than Nova Scotia-style cured salmon or lox and is more flavorful in this recipe.

Yield: 2 cups

Creamy Scrambled Eggs
with Smoked Salmon

This is a very good dish for brunch or for a light supper. Serve with a green salad and toasted sourdough bread. Slow cooking is essential to produce the luxuriously creamy eggs.

4 ounces butter
12 eggs, beaten with a fork
Salt and pepper
½ cup chopped green onion
⅓ pound thin-sliced cold-smoked salmon

Melt 1 ounce of the butter in a double boiler or a heavy saucepan and pour the eggs in. Stir the mixture gently and continuously over low heat until the eggs begin to coagulate. Add the rest of the butter, bit by bit. When eggs are creamy, but not dry, put immediately on a heated platter and sprinkle with salt, pepper and green onion. Lay the slices of smoked salmon across the eggs. Serve right away.

Serves 6

DEFINING THE PACIFIC NORTHWEST STYLE

Barbecued Salmon

While it is perfectly appropriate to grill salmon steaks over charcoal, the best way to barbecue salmon is a side at a time. Steaks have a tendency to dry out. Buy a whole fish and have the fishmonger remove the head, then bone and butterfly it.

Charcoal should be going just off its peak, the coals hot and covered with grey ash. Measure the width of the salmon side at its thickest and figure 10 minutes to the inch. Start the salmon, flesh side down to sear, and cook for half the allotted time. Flip salmon, cover with barbecue sauce and continue to cook until done.

Salmon Barbecue Sauce

Joyce Ingle doesn't claim this sauce is something of her own invention; she thinks she found it in a newspaper years ago. But she recognized a classic and in the process has indelibly defined for her family what the flavor of barbecued salmon should be.

> ½ pound butter
> 1 clove garlic, minced
> ¼ cup catsup
> 4 tablespoons soy sauce
> 2 tablespoons prepared mustard
> 1 tablespoon Worcestershire sauce
> 1 tablespoon fresh lemon juice
> Freshly cracked pepper

Melt butter with garlic. Mix in all of the remaining ingredients and warm over very low heat to keep the sauce from separating.

Yield: 2 cups

DEFINING THE PACIFIC NORTHWEST STYLE

Salmon with Lemon Verbena and Tuberous Begonia Sauce

The Herbfarm is located 30 miles east of Seattle at Fall City. Lola Zimmerman began this lovely place as a hobby and now it has grown into a mecca for food lovers—400 varieties of herbs, 120 species of succulents, greenhouses, llamas, doves, turkeys, and a restaurant serving beautiful and unique 6-course lunches. The Herbfarm also offers an extensive list of cooking and gardening classes. People from all over the country are sharing this "secret garden."

Tuberous begonia petals have a citric tang ideally complimented by the lemon scent and flavor of lemon verbena. Combined, they create a salmon sauce fit for royalty.

> 24 ounces salmon fillets
> Salt and cayenne pepper; a few drops of lime juice
>
> 2 shallots, minced
> 1 lime
> 6 tablespoons butter
> 2½ tablespoons lime juice
> 1½ tablespoons white port
> 1½ tablespoons white wine
> 3 lemon verbena leaves
> 3 tablespoons cream
> Salt, white pepper and cayenne
> 1 tuberous begonia blossom

To prepare the salmon: Preheat the oven to 500°. Remove bones from fillets with pliers. Cut diagonally into 4 equal serving pieces about ¾-inch thick.

Place salmon on half of a 24-inch-wide piece of aluminum foil set atop a baking sheet. Season salmon lightly with salt and a tiny amount of cayenne. Sprinkle with a few drops of lime juice—rub to spread around. Fold over foil. Fold edges twice to seal.

To prepare the sauce: Pick lemon verbena leaves and 1 tuberous begonia blossom (unsprayed). Mince shallots. Squeeze juice from 1 lime. Cut butter into several pieces.

In a small, heavy pan, melt 1 tablespoon butter and soften shallots (don't brown). Add lime juice, port, wine, and verbena leaves. Boil gently to reduce to a thick syrup.

Remove leaves. Add cream. Return to boil. Turn off heat. Whisk in butter 1 tablespoon at a time, making sure each pat melts before adding the next. Season with salt, pepper, a tiny amount of cayenne and more lime juice if needed.

With scissors, snip tuberous begonia blossom into thin threads, allowing them to fall into sauce. Stir.

To cook the salmon: Place baking sheet with salmon in oven and cook just until foil starts to puff up—about 4½ to 5½ minutes. Remove from oven. Serve on warmed plates with sauce.

Serves 4

Trail Creek Pan-fried Trout with Caper Butter

At Sun Valley, Idaho, you can ride horse-drawn sleighs to Trail Creek Lodge and have delicious trout.

> Caper Butter:
> *2 tablespoons capers*
> *Juice of 1 lemon*
> *4 ounces of butter, softened*
> *2 tablespoons chopped parsley*

Prepare several hours in advance. Mash capers lightly with a fork. Squeeze in lemon juice. Mix with soft butter until well blended. Stir in parsley. Wrap in foil and shape into a roll about 1½ inches in diameter. Refrigerate for several hours. When ready to serve, cut into ¼-inch slices and place 2 slices on top of each of the hot trout.

> *4 fresh trout*
> *Milk*
> *1 cup flour seasoned with salt and pepper*
> *¼ cup cornmeal*
> *½ cup clarified butter*
> *2 lemons, cut into wedges*

Dip trout in milk, then in seasoned flour mixed with cornmeal. Heat clarified butter in 10-inch frying pan—butter should be hot when trout are added. Cook trout until golden on one side; turn and cook quickly the other side and transfer to a heated serving dish. Serve the fish with the caper butter slices on top and lemon wedges.

Serves 4

Grilled Whole Trout with Peppered Bacon

Grilling whole fish outdoors on a barbecue results in a crisp skin and moist, tender meat inside. I have lots of mint growing near my barbecue, so I add it to the trout. I like to use a hinged square metal rack to grill small whole fish. It makes turning the fish easier.

Peppered bacon gives this trout an extra snap. I first tasted peppered bacon in Oregon, but have since had it in Washington and British Columbia. Peppered bacon is dry-cured bacon that has had crushed pepper pressed into the fat side. The resulting bacon has a lovely piquancy.

> *4 fresh trout*
> *Olive oil*
> *4 sprigs fresh mint*
> *4 slices peppered bacon, or thick sliced bacon*
> *2 lemons, cut in wedges*

Brush trout lightly with olive oil. Place a mint sprig inside each fish. Wrap with a strip of bacon. Place in the hinged grill and cook over medium-hot coals, 5 minutes per side.

Serve with the lemons.

Serves 4

Salted and Broiled Fresh Small Fish

Mrs. George Tsutakawa is a wonderful cook who generously shared her time with me to show me how to cook various types of fresh seafood in the Japanese style. I had never before bought small whole fish (1 to 2 pounds), buying fillets instead. Now, having learned how to cook the whole fish, I find them hard to resist.

Have the fish cleaned or if you are fishing and catch your own, clean it carefully, leaving the fins and tail on. Perch, in particular, is delicious cooked this way.

Make 3 diagonal slashes into the outside flesh of the fish on each side. This allows the fish to cook faster and have more flavor. Generously salt the skin sides of the fish. Lightly sprinkle the inside. If possible, salt the fish 15 minutes in advance of cooking.

If cooking indoors, preheat broiler. Place fish on a foil-lined baking pan about 8 inches from the heat source and broil for 5 minutes. Turn and cook 5 minutes longer. Place the fish in a warm shallow serving dish. The skin should be crisp and the flesh should pull away from the bone easily.

If you are cooking outdoors, simply cook the fish on the grill over moderate heat for 5 minutes on each side.

Note: If your broiler is mounted inside your oven, cook the fish with the oven door closed.

Yield: allow one 1- to 1½-pound fish for each

Fried Smelt with Parsley Butter

In February, in La Conner, Washington, 2,000 to 3,000 people arrive to "jig" for smelt, a small silvery, slightly oily fish. "Jigging" refers to the method used for catching smelt. The fishing line has 10 to 11 hooks and a weight at the end of the line, so you can cast. The line is then pulled back in a jerky motion, basically snagging the fish.

> *6 smelt per serving*
> *Salt and pepper*
> *Flour*
> *¼ cup butter*
> *¼ cup vegetable oil*
> *Lemon wedges*

To clean the smelt: Make a cut from the top of the neck straight down through the backbone, being careful not to sever the throat. Then, grabbing the body in one hand and the head in the other, with a quick twisting and pulling motion, you will remove the insides of the fish.

To cook the smelt: Sprinkle the smelt with salt and pepper and roll in flour. Heat butter and vegetable oil in a heavy frying pan. When the oil is hot, add the smelt in batches. Pour out the oil–butter mixture and replace it with fresh when it starts to fill with flour particles.

Serve with parsley butter and lots of fresh lemon to squeeze over. This method is equally satisfactory with store-bought smelt.

> Parsley Butter:
> *½ cup butter*
> *3 tablespoons minced parsley*
> *3 tablespoons lemon juice*

Heat butter over low heat, until just melted. Stir in parsley and lemon juice and drizzle over the hot fried smelt.

Serves 4

Pickled Herring

Our Scandinavian heritage in the Northwest is felt strongly in our fishing and in our baking. Pickled herring is traditional during the holiday season. (I can eat pickled herring for breakfast with lots of white onions and soda crackers. A good Norwegian friend of mine adds 5 cocktail onions to each jar—for the martinis that go with the pickled herring!)

> *10 pounds salted Icelandic herring, filleted (salted herring from*
> *Iceland are larger fish and have a higher oil content)*
> *2 cups white sugar*
> *1 gallon water*
> *½ gallon white vinegar*
> *5 large white onions, cut in quarters and sliced*
> *2 ounces pickling spices*
> *Brine*
> *4 tablespoons chopped fresh dillweed*

Place the fillets in a 5-gallon bucket in a deep sink. Let the cold water run continuously, overflowing slowly. Stick your hand in and stir around from time to time. Keep the fresh water running through for 2 hours. The herring will taste salty, but once it goes into the pickling brine it will balance out. Remove the herring and drain in a colander. Cut into bite-sized chunks.

Heat sugar and water to dissolve the sugar. Cool. Add vinegar to complete the brine. In a large, heavy 5-gallon crock or plastic container with a lid, layer herring, then onions, sprinkle with pickling spices, and repeat until all ingredients are used.

Pour in brine to cover and shake the crock to eliminate any air pockets; sprinkle generously with the fresh dillweed. Cover and store in a cool place. After two weeks, the herring will be ready to eat. I like to pack it in large canning jars with hinged lids to give to friends. At this point, the herring should be refrigerated.

Note: You can obtain 5-gallon crocks or containers at restaurant supply stores.

Yield: enough for a large crowd

Yelloweyed Rockfish

Generally sold whole, this fish must be bled immediately after catching to be of the highest quality. To check, look at the left gill palate for white membrane that shows it has been bled. If it has been prepared properly, the quality of yelloweye merits the cost. Filleted yelloweye is unique for flavor and texture.

Ask the fishmonger to cut the fish in half, one filleted, the other with the skin on and bone in. Cut the piece with the bone into 2-inch strips, crosswise. (Always take the head with you.) A 2- to 2½-pound whole fish can be cut up to yield two firm, fresh fillets and two nice collar pieces which can be used to make a very good soup. The fillets can be steamed or sliced thinly for sashimi.

This makes a good first course.

> *½ cup Japanese soy sauce*
> *2 tablespoons mirin or sake*
> *3 teaspoons sugar*
> *2 slices fresh ginger, cut into thin strips*
> *Additional soy sauce*
> *Wasabi (Japanese horseradish powder)*

Mix together the soy sauce, mirin or sake, sugar and ginger in a 2-quart saucepan. Bring the mixture to a boil. Add the bone-in strips of fish, skin side up. Cover and cook over moderate heat (the mixture should be just barely bubbling) for 3 minutes. Turn fish over and continue to cook for 3–4 minutes longer. Turn off heat, but leave the fish in the pan, covered, for 5 minutes before serving. This allows the flavors of the cooking sauce to be absorbed into the fish. Serve the fish skin side up in individual serving dishes with a little sauce spooned over. Serve the uncooked filleted half of the fish as sashimi, by cutting it into thin pieces and serving with soy sauce and wasabi.

Yield: 4 appetizer servings

*Alderbrook Inn
Fresh Halibut Steaks
in Caper Sauce*

The Alaskan coast's fresh halibut season is measured in hours, the amount of fish caught is measured to the closest million pounds and the amount shipped out fresh is limited only by the number of planes that are available to fly out. What can't be flown out is brought down by Sea-Land refrigerated vans, each one holding 35,000 pounds, and they come down by the hundreds. The best halibut of all is out of Alaska, and the farther north, the better the fish. The Alderbrook Inn Resort on Hood Canal, Washington, one of many pleasant resorts in the Northwest, takes advantage of this Alaskan bounty with the following recipe.

> *2 8-ounce halibut fillets (½-inch thick)*
> *½ cup flour, seasoned with 1 teaspoon salt and ½ teaspoon*
> *   pepper*
> *2 whole eggs, well beaten*
> *2 tablespoons butter*
> *2 tablespoons salad oil*
> *½ cup dry white wine*
> *3 tablespoons butter*
> *1 tablespoon fresh lemon juice*
> *1 tablespoon capers*

Dip halibut fillets into seasoned flour, coating lightly on both sides. Dip into beaten eggs. Heat butter and oil. Sauté halibut until golden (3–4 minutes on each side). Transfer to a heated platter. Pour off cooking oil. Pour wine into the pan used for cooking the fish and bring to a boil. Boil for 1 minute. Remove from heat and stir in butter, lemon juice and capers. Pour sauce over the fish and serve.

Serves 2

DEFINING THE PACIFIC NORTHWEST STYLE

> *Cheri Walker's*
> *Grilled Fillet of White Sturgeon*
> *with Chanterelles and*
> *Cranberry–Port–Cream Sauce*

Cheri Walker is the chef at the Shoalwater Restaurant in Seaview, Washington, part of the charming Shelburne Inn on the coast.

> *4 cups fish stock*
> *6 cups cranberries (reserve a few raw*
> * berries for garnish)*
> *2 cups port wine*
> *¼ cup sugar*
> *½ cup brandy*
> *1 pound fresh chanterelle mushrooms*
> *2 cloves garlic (1 teaspoon minced)*
> *1 tablespoon tarragon*
> *5 ounces butter*
> *2 ounces red wine vinegar*
> *½ teaspoon salt*
> *⅛ teaspoon pepper*
> *2 ounces heavy cream*
> *8 7–ounce white sturgeon fillets*

Combine fish stock, berries, port, sugar, brandy, 8 ounces finely chopped chanterelles, garlic and tarragon in large saucepan. Bring to boil, then simmer 20 minutes or until berries have popped. Mash the berries slightly to release juice. Strain through a fine-mesh sieve, pressing lightly to purée the fruit. Resieve through cheesecloth if juice is cloudy with seeds. Reduce the 4 cups of juice to 3 cups.

In a separate saucepan, melt 2 ounces of butter. Add the remaining 8 ounces of chanterelles and sauté until heated through. Deglaze with the vinegar, add salt and pepper and let simmer until liquid is almost absorbed.

To the three cups of reduced stock, add the cream and let simmer until sauce clears slightly. Add 3 ounces of cold butter in bits, stirring until sauce thickens and clears. Add the mushrooms and vinegar reduction. Keep sauce warm in *bain marie* as you grill sturgeon.

Grill sturgeon fillets approximately 5 minutes on first side; turn over and grill approximately 3–4 minutes on second side, or until just firm to the touch.

To serve, ladle 3 ounces of sauce on a platter. Top with grilled sturgeon. Garnish with sprigs of fresh tarragon and a few raw cranberries.

Serves 8

Beer Batter Fish and Chips

I like the moist, flaky ling cod the best for this. The Seattle waterfront offers a number of opportunities to buy fish and chips and sit by the water on a nice day. High-quality, hook-and-line-caught cod that is bled at sea is also wonderful baked.

> 1 cup flour
> 1 teaspoon baking powder
> 1 egg, beaten
> 2 tablespoons salad oil
> 1 cup light beer
> Peanut oil for deep frying
> 1½ pounds ling cod fillets, cut into 2-inch pieces
> Tartar sauce
> Lemon wedges

Mix flour, baking powder, egg, salad oil and beer together, using a wire whisk. Heat peanut oil in deep fat fryer to 375°. Coat fish with batter and drop 2 to 3 pieces at a time into the oil. Fry until golden brown, turning once. Drain well on paper towels. Serve with tartar sauce, lemon wedges and chips.

Chips:
2 large russet potatoes

Scrub potatoes well. Cut into matchstick pieces about ¼-inch thick. Rinse in cold water and pat dry. Drop into the hot fat (375°) when the fish has finished cooking. Sprinkle with salt and serve hot.

Serves 4

Parchment-Baked Ling Cod with Chive–Tarragon Butter

This is an easy way to cook any white fish that is ½- to ¾- inch thick. The parchment seals in the flavors and steams the fish nicely.

4 8-ounce fillets of ling cod
Kosher salt
4 ounces butter
4 tablespoons chopped chives
1 tablespoon fresh tarragon
4 lemon slices
Strips of carrot and celery, julienned
4 pieces of parchment
1 egg white, lightly beaten

Preheat the oven to 400°. Sprinkle fillets with kosher salt. Mix butter with chives and tarragon. Divide butter mixture into 8 pieces. Place two pieces on each fillet. Place a lemon slice on each fish and lay vegetable strips across top.

Place fish on parchment, fold over and seal by brushing edge with egg white and then twisting and rolling to seal. Bake in the oven for 10 to 12 minutes.

Serves 4

Black Cod in Swiss Chard with Lemon Butter Sauce

Black cod is an oily fish that is gaining acceptance locally. The very best black cod is caught at the mouth of the Juan de Fuca Strait and is called Cape Blackcod. Most of this catch is shipped to Japan. Many people have developed a liking for the velvety texture of this fish, and when cooked and served properly it can be a real treat. It is often sold at fish markets lightly smoked, which adds flavor and texture to the fish. You simply take it home and finish it on your outdoor grill. Serve with boiled new potatoes—it can grow on you very quickly.

Wrapping the black cod in Swiss chard adds flavor and contrasting texture to the soft flesh of the fish.

> *4 6-ounce blackcod fillets*
> *Salt and pepper*
> *4 tablespoons plus ¼ pound butter*
> *1 bunch Swiss chard, cleaned and stems removed*
> *Juice of ½ lemon*
> *¼ cup white wine*

Preheat the oven to 400°. Sprinkle fish with salt and pepper. Place a pat of butter (1 tablespoon) on top of each (reserve remaining butter for making the sauce.) Wrap the fillets individually each in a leaf of Swiss chard and then wrapped in foil, leaving them partially open on the top to let steam out. Bake in the oven for 10 minutes.

While the fish is cooking make the lemon butter sauce. Bring the lemon juice and wine to a simmer in a small saucepan and cook for several minutes. When the fish is cooked, quickly whisk the butter pieces into the lemon–wine mixture (off the heat) and spoon over each of the fish bundles.

Serves 4

Sesame–Ginger Ling Cod

Ling cod is fished from southern Oregon all the way up the coast to southeastern Alaska. Hook-and-line-caught ling cod gives you the best-quality fish.

The fillets should be white and have a good, clean, smooth surface and no separating or "gaping" in the flesh. A firm fish with a good texture, ling cod is typically used for fish and chips, but it is also delicious marinated and then grilled or baked.

> ½ *cup Japanese soy sauce*
> 2 *tablespoons sesame oil*
> ½ *cup brown sugar*
> ½ *cup water*
> ¼ *teaspoon hot red pepper flakes*
> 1 *teaspoon sesame seeds*
> 1 *tablespoon chopped green onion*
> 1 *clove garlic, minced*
> 4 *fillets of ling cod (6 to 8 ounces each)*

Mix all of the ingredients together, except the fish, to make marinade. Let the marinade sit for several hours to develop flavors. Transfer to a shallow dish. Marinate fish for 30 minutes on each side.

Broil the fish 8 inches from the source of heat for 8 to 10 minutes. Sprinkle with additional sesame seeds.

Note: Alternatively, the fillets can be steamed in a bamboo steamer for 6 to 8 minutes.

Serves 4

Sole Turbans with Salmon Mousse on a Bed of Sautéed Cucumber

This is an attractive dish that is always received as something special. It can be assembled ahead and then cooked and served.

1½ pounds fresh salmon, skin and bones removed
¾ cup heavy cream
1 teaspoon kosher salt
Dash of fresh nutmeg
8 thin fillets of sole (4–5 ounces each)
1 English cucumber, peeled

3 tablespoons butter	*¼ cup white wine*
3 tablespoons butter	*1 tablespoon lemon juice*
2 tablespoons flour	*Chopped green onion*
½ cup cream	*Salt and pepper*

Preheat the oven to 400°. Put salmon, cream, kosher salt and nutmeg in food processor and process until smooth.

Lay the fillets of sole on a work surface, skin side up. Place 3 ounces of salmon mixture (about ½ cup) in the center of each. Roll each fillet over to encircle the mousse mixture. Lay the rolls flat in a buttered glass baking dish. Cut a piece of wax paper the size of the baking pan and butter it on one side. Place the paper, buttered side down directly on top of fish. Bake in the oven for 25 to 30 minutes.

While the fish is cooking, cut the peeled cucumber in half. Remove seeds with a spoon. Slice the cucumber thinly. Sauté in butter for 3 to 5 minutes. Set aside.

To make the sauce, melt the butter, then stir in the flour until smooth. Add cream, wine and lemon juice. Keep warm, without boiling.

When the fish is ready, divide the sautéed cucumber among 6 plates, and place a turban on top of each, removing them carefully from the baking dish with a slotted spatula. Strain the juices left from cooking the fish into the sauce. Reheat gently, if necessary. Nap each turban with sauce and sprinkle on a little chopped green onion. Salt and pepper to taste.

Serves 6

SHELLFISH

D uane Fagergren and his eight-year-old daughter, Evie, stood in the kitchen at Ray's Boathouse in Seattle talking with the chef. It was the last delivery in a long day for Fagergren who makes his living, in part, digging clams and raising three kinds of oysters —the small, native Olympia, the European flat, and the ubiquitous Pacific—in the southern end of Puget Sound in Washington State. From October to May he distributes his shellfish every Thursday to restaurants from Olympia to Seattle.

Fagergren is responsible for the appearance in Pacific Northwest restaurants since the early 1980s of Olympia oysters served raw on the half shell. Throughout this century, the tiny oyster had been shucked, bottled in fresh water, and marketed from San Francisco to Seattle. In the Pacific Northwest, Olympias have been breaded and fried, simmered in stews, and served as oyster cocktails, the tastes of a past generation. By the mid-1950s, water pollution had so diminished the numbers of Olympias available for harvest that South Sound shellfish growers turned to other products, the Pacific oyster and hard-shell clam. Fagergren noticed a culinary tragedy in the making, but one that could be reversed given recently improved water conditions. He not only has focused his efforts on bringing Olympias back to commercially viable numbers, but he has convinced local chefs that they have available to them a regional delicacy of international standing, one that is best served raw and allowed to speak for itself.

Ostrea lurida, to give the Olympia its proper name, measures no more than the width of a silver dollar across its gray, shallow shell, but it has a distinct texture and flavor and lingering aftertaste that set it apart from any of the other oysters harvested in the Pacific Northwest, if not the world. Some say the Olympia is the best of all oysters, and no one who knows oysters would scoff at the possibility. More than one old boy has come up to Duane in a restaurant after being made aware of the grower's presence to exclaim, "I haven't had Olympias like that in twenty years. You made my meal."

Under the scrutiny of Evie, her nose just about level with the surface of the stainless steel worktable, Fagergren and the chef at Ray's Boathouse opened European flat oysters. Prep cooks scurried around the trio like fiddler crabs on a beach as the two men traded jokes and discussed the shellfish harvest and the merits of South Sound oysters over those from Willapa Bay out on the Washington coast. While they talked, Evie downed a half dozen flats as fast as her father could pop them open. She and her younger sister Anna, age five, have been raised on shellfish much the way their father was when he was a child. The Fagergren girls have no reservations about eating oysters, cooked or raw. They prefer their clams, they say, in a chowder or steamed and dipped one by one in melted butter redolent with crushed garlic.

As they left Ray's, Duane took his daughter's hand in his and they walked across the parking lot to the small blue Calm Cove Oyster Company pickup truck. It had started to rain, a classic Pacific Northwest soaking drizzle that locals hardly notice. Had it been accompanied by the kind of icy wind that drives rain down the back of the most protected neck, Fagergren would have called it oyster weather. "I'm still hungry for oysters," Evie told her father. Duane lowered the tailgate and fished in his pants pocket for the small Swiss Army knife he uses to open both flats and the little Olympias. He inserted the tip of the knife blade between the thin shell lips of a flat and, with the practiced skill of a jeweler working on a locket watch, carefully slipped the blade in and cut the adductor muscle. He flipped back the top shell to reveal a plump, crisp oyster awash in liquor, tinged with the flavor of the sea. Evie ate another half-dozen flats there in the rain at the back of the truck.

Father and daughter headed for the Greenlake Grill for dinner, finishing a series of pre-planned loops in Seattle. Karl Beckley, owner and chef at the Greenlake Grill, had opened his restaurant in 1978, quickly establishing a reputation as a culinary risk taker. For a time Beckley was something of a lone performance artist in a city of Norman Rockwell restaurants, a bellwether for the Pacific Northwest culinary revolution then evolving. His friend Wayne Ludvigsen, chef at Ray's, told Beckley about Fagergren's Olympia oysters after sampling them himself. The oysters have been on the menu at the Greenlake Grill ever since Beckley's first taste in 1981.

Duane Fagergren's stop at the Greenlake Grill put him only a few blocks from the highway he would take home. The truck tires hissed on a pavement growing ever more wet as the drizzle turned to a steady light rain likely to last all night. "I'm still hungry for oysters," Evie said. Duane suggested they wait until they reached the restaurant. "We can have them as hors d'oeuvres," he suggested. Evie gave her father a skeptical look and, in her most theatrical voice, stretching the words for maximum emphasis, said, "Those are going to be *our* oysters, aren't they? Because I don't think I could *handle* it if they were anyone else's."

Weeks later, Duane made the mistake of telling that story to a friend in front of Evie, savoring the word *handle* with the kind of delight common among proud parents. Evie got very upset. "That was private," she told her father. "That was between you and me."

It is unlikely that Evie Fagergren's palate is so well tuned at age eight that she can distinguish the difference between an oyster her father grows and one from across the bay. Her allegiance to the product probably comes from the inordinate amount of her father's time and attention the oysters consume. While she and Anna may not work at repairing dikes or culling Olympias or spreading seed or bagging restaurant orders, they are as aware of the demands and rewards of growing and marketing oysters as they are of the tides that rise and fall in Totten Inlet just beyond their front yard. The results are tangible on the table. They will discover the intangible results later when they realize how their father has struggled to revive the commercial viability of an important oyster simply because he believes in it, because he thinks it would be wrong to let it slide into oblivion. And when they understand the business of oysters as well as the physiology and gastronomy, they will see how their mother, Jonnel, currently underwrites the solvency of the company with her job as senior research analyst for a legislative caucus in the nearby state capital. When Duane says that Jonnel keeps him in oysters, he's only half kidding.

Starting at the Strait of Juan de Fuca in the north, Puget Sound stretches south for 100 miles, a long, deep trough of cold seawater that separates the majority of mainland Washington State along the eastern shore of the Sound from the Olympic Peninsula to the west. The Sound almost ends at Tacoma but instead surges south through the Narrows at five-and-a-half knots and opens on to a series of bays and inlets that hook back north and fan out into rural forest and farmland. Fagergren's home ground at Totten Inlet is about as far south as anyone can sail in the Sound. To the east, Hood Canal parallels the course of Puget Sound, with the Kitsap Peninsula separating the two bodies of water. The narrow, crooked finger of Hood Canal contains two bays near its northern end, where it feeds into Puget Sound. Some of the region's best Pacific oyster production takes place here, in Dabob and Quilcene bays, just around a tongue of land, the small Toandos Peninsula, from the Trident nuclear submarine base at Bangor.

Growing Olympias is a license to lose money. "They account for 30 percent of my business," Fagergren says, "but take the majority of my investment. In two or three years I'll have to look at it and see if I can make it in Olympias." Few other growers are trying quite as hard. The oyster money is in Pacifics, *Crassostrea gigas,* a Japanese cousin of *C. virginica,* the American oyster native to the eastern seaboard. *C. gigas* was brought into Washington State from Japan in the 1920s when Olympia oyster populations slipped into steep decline, the result of over-harvesting and rising levels of water pollution. Pacifics account for 20 percent of Fagergren's earnings. Another 25 percent of Calm Cove Oyster Company's revenues comes from a relative newcomer to the Pacific Northwest, *Ostrea edulis,* the European flat oyster commonly called Belon in France, or Piefleet, Colchester, or Whitstable in Great Britain. The final 25 percent of Fagergren's income comes from clams, both Manilas and native littleneck hardshells.

Duane Fagergren is pushing forty, young enough to muster the energy he needs to nudge a slow growing business along, and old enough to do that with considered wisdom and conviction. He has the look of a well-scrubbed altar boy grown to adult size, a strong-bodied, husky man with Nordic blue eyes, wind etched crow's-feet, the kind of white toothed smile usually seen in toothpaste ads, and big hands that show the wear of working constantly in inclement weather and salt water. Duane Fagergren has a patient and persuasive personality and the ability to listen closely, all of which sets him out on middle ground when opposing views break on the shores close to his home and business.

Water quality, Duane says, is the regulator of the oyster industry, so he makes a point of staying as involved as he can in the politics that directly affect his life. On the county level the debate is about property development, zoning, and construction ordinances, all with water quality in mind. The two rural counties that enclose the majority of the South Sound oyster grounds have a potential for rapid population growth, especially in areas with attractive views of the Sound. Developers want the water views, and oyster growers want clean water. When sewage from poorly built drain fields, or manure from cows and horses kept by weekend hobby farmers, seeps into the Sound, fecal coliform, a bacteria indicating the possible presence of human pathogens, shows up in the bay. When the count reaches a certain level in the water column, which it can after a heavy rain, the state shuts down shellfish harvesting until the condition clears, usually after a week. In areas where the fecal coliform background level remains too high, growers have to transport their shellfish to clean water to purge for a week, while the state attempts to identify and correct the problem on land. A number of major oyster producing bays have been decertified over the years. Shellfish grown there is not fit for human consumption, an indictment of the quality of pollution control procedures affecting the Sound.

Fagergren brings education and experience to the debate, both as an oyster grower and as a professional water quality and aquaculture specialist. After earning a degree in fishery science from the University of Washington, he worked three years as salt-water manager in charge of raising salmon for Domsea Farms, one of the country's biggest pen-raised salmon ventures, then owned by Union Carbide. From there he went to the forest products lab of a pulp company, researching water purity problems and industrial pollution. After seven years in a lab coat, Duane decided to revive the oyster company his father had started in the late 1940s. Rather than rebuild on the standard model of the oyster companies around him, growing and shucking Pacific oysters and selling to a distributor, Fagergren identified a need in the restaurant business in the Pacific Northwest for consistent, high-quality oysters for serving on the half shell, and aimed his production and marketing in that direction. He felt certain that careful management could revive his Olympia oyster beds. Then he convinced restaurant owners and chefs that the Olympia deserved special attention as a half-shell product, a tough sell considering its size.

Fagergren works with the Puget Sound Water Quality Authority; he also sits on the Washington State Department of Ecology's Shellfish Advisory Committee and the Department of Agriculture's Aquaculture Advisory Council. He is an associate of Fish Pro, Inc., an aquaculture consulting firm, a board member of the Pacific Coast Oyster Growers Association, and currently president of the Olympia Oyster Growers Association. Fagergren also regularly attends local school board meetings, and somewhere in all this he finds time to be with his wife and daughters, to ski in the winter, to fish in the summer, and to grow oysters: the Olympias in a style practiced since the turn of the century; the Pacifics and the European flat oysters in a way that takes maximum advantage of the most recent advances in oyster culture technology.

Until the turn of the century oyster production in the Pacific Northwest was a common ground fishery much like present-day oystering in Chesapeake Bay. The tidelands were owned by the state government (and even earlier by the territorial government). When the harvesters moved in they were anything but mindful of resource management. Many of the oyster bottoms were destroyed by over-harvesting, not an uncommon occurrence when Americans exploit a natural bounty that belongs to one and all, and to no one in particular. Early settlers had also cleaned out the oyster beds along the coasts of Maine and New Hampshire, ruining in a handful of years what had taken hundreds to grow.

In 1849, in Willapa Bay on the Washington coast, Olympias were being shoveled out of beds and shipped to San Francisco by the bushel. *Ostrea lurida* had already disappeared from much of its native ground on the West Coast. At one time the oyster could be found from Alaska to San Diego, though not always in the commercial quantities or quality that were obtained in Washington's waters. Schooners calling at Willapa Bay or Samish Bay at the north end of Puget Sound commonly took on tons of Olympias for ballast on their return voyages to San Francisco, dumping the dead bivalves overboard at the home port. When the state began keeping production records, the native oyster harvest in Willapa Bay was already doomed. In 1896, 90,000 bushels were taken, and 74,000 three years later. In 1914 production had slipped to 2,000 bushels, then dropped into the hundreds and dwindled to nothing.

The Olympia oysters in Puget Sound, particularly the South Sound where the last commercial vestiges of this American delicacy now exist, had it slightly better. Production figures reflect the rise of the style of cultivation still practiced by Fagergren; they also demonstrate the industry's subsequent pollution-caused decline. In 1896, 20,000 bushels of Olympias were taken from Puget Sound, primarily in the south end; in 1904 the harvest was 100,000 bushels. The peak year was 1914, with 225,706 bushels harvested. The next year the harvest dropped precipitously to 49,000 bushels, probably an indication of over-harvesting. Although production climbed back to 100,000 bushels by 1924, the opening in 1927 of a pulp mill that pumped effluent onto the prime South Sound oyster beds precluded any kind of recovery.

The pulp mill finally closed in 1958 after ruining the last of the Olympia oyster industry. South Sound oyster growers had given up on the Olympia and, like Willapa Bay and North Sound growers before them, had turned to the Pacific oyster which could withstand the ravages of pollution. Thirty years after the pulp mill closed, Duane Fagergren figures that 400 bushels of Olympia oysters might be harvested this season, and he's hoping to see an exponential growth in the overall Olympia oyster population from an ever-increasing brood stock. So there's still hope for one of the most delicious oysters in the world, and since clean water is the primary element of its current revival, there is hope too for a clean Puget Sound, which up until now has been showing all the signs of heading in the same discouraging direction as Chesapeake Bay.

Puget Sound is fed by nutrient-rich rivers like the Nooksak, Skagit, Stillaguamish, Snohomish, Puyallup, and Nisqually—all draining from the Cascade Mountains—and the Skokomish, Hamma Hamma, Duckabush, and Dosewalips—all draining from the Olympic Mountains into Hood Canal. The Sound's 1,500 miles of irregular shoreline and nearly 2,000 square miles of salt water have the potential to become the greatest center of marine aquaculture in the United States. Norwegian fin fish farming consortiums are already developing pen-raised Atlantic salmon ventures in the area. New shellfish production systems, such as long-line mussel growing in Penn Cove on Whidbey Island, demonstrate the feasibility of growing and marketing a food that has been largely ignored in the Pacific Northwest. The major hindrance to aquaculture development, aside from water pollution, comes from vacation and retirement homeowners who have sanctified their water views and organized into political blocks within small counties to prevent expansion of a multi-faceted industry. Fortunately for South Sound aquaculture, oyster growing can claim legitimate historic precedence over the more recently established leisure-time industry.

Oyster growers in Washington State have owned tidal lands since 1890. In the South Sound, in what is perhaps the oldest and most long-lived aquaculture tradition in the nation, Olympia oyster growers diked in acres of tidal lands in order to cultivate the threatened native oyster. With the passing of the native oyster in Willapa Bay (Willapa growers have never liked the term "Olympia" for *their* native oysters), oyster growing there and in bays in Puget Sound and Hood Canal changed from a wild fishery to something more like farming.

Specific growers planted specific oyster seed on specific ground they owned, then tended the crop until maturity when, like so much wheat, they reaped the harvest. When the adult Olympia oyster population declined to the point at which it couldn't reseed itself, growers first imported *Crassostrea virginica* seed from the East

Coast with disappointing results, then turned to Japan for *Crassostrea gigas* seed, which adapted. Hundreds of thousands of cases of oyster shell—sun-dried culch to which larval oysters had attached themselves—were shipped from Japan to Washington State between the mid-1920s and the mid-1950s. Manila clams, a Japanese hardshell littleneck, came in as well. And so too did the oyster drill, a devastating snail pest that attacks Olympia and Pacific oysters.

By the mid-1950s the *C. gigas* population in Dabob and Quilcene bays had reached the point of self-seeding. Willapa Bay also has developed a natural set. Importing seed from Japan gradually phased out as oyster growers began taking bags of culch to the bays to catch the set of what is now called the Pacific oyster. The growers spread the seed on their tidal ground and more or less watched it grow, moving it around and working different plots like so much crop rotation. The oysters matured in three or four years, characteristically growing in large clumps. Some of the Willapa Bay operations were big enough that the oysters were (and still are, for that matter) dredged up onto a scow, then taken to a processing plant to be shucked and bottled. That shucked product has always been and so remains the primary trade in oysters in the Pacific Northwest, even for the Olympia oyster.

Fagergren is part of the new generation of Pacific Northwest oyster growers who concentrate on supplying the ever-increasing restaurant and oyster bar half-shell trade. Randy Shuman grows Pacifics and flat oysters in Willapa Bay, calling his product Shoalwater Bay oysters. He employs a French rack-and-bag grow-out technique: single oysters grow on submerged nursery trays until they are big enough to place in open mesh bags made of heavy, stiff, rubberized material. The bags are placed on low-lying metal racks. Raised above the tidal flats in Willapa Bay, the oysters have never suffered from a muddy taste, and they grow at an accelerated rate. When the tide goes out, Shuman's tidelands look as if they are covered by acres of plump, black pillows.

Bill Webb at Westcott Bay on San Juan Island in the north end of Puget Sound has deep water to deal with, not shoreline tideland. He grows out his Westcott Bay oysters after the nursery stage in lantern nets as big around as basketball hoops that hang ten meters down in the water from buoys. Each net encloses ten grids upon which the oysters rest and feed twenty-four hours a day. They grow to maturity in a year but with shells as delicate and as beautiful as fluted bone china, which was a problem at first. The shells often cracked in transit to market, losing the liquor and killing the oysters. Now the oysters spend a couple of weeks of shell-toughening exposure to air like any oysters on the shore uncovered each day at the low tides. Webb hangs his Westcotts in trays beneath his dock before sending them to market in Seattle, California, or New York.

These growers all depend on a process called remote seeding to replenish their Pacific and flat oyster stock. Webb has the lab facilities to raise his own seed. Shuman and Fagergren send away for theirs. There are a couple of dozen suppliers on the West Coast. In the wild, oysters respond to an increasing abundance of food and rising water temperature to develop the unpleasant-tasting condition called "spawny." They become soft and milky, having converted all the sweet glycogen they stored up through winter into sperm and eggs. When conditions are just right, normally sometime in July, one oyster releases either its sperm or its eggs, and then every oyster releases what it has produced in a flurry of reproductive excess. Billions of resulting oyster embryos float in the sea, gradually growing into larval form. At what is called the eyed larvae stage, about a month after fertilization, the soon-to-be oysters look like microscopic clams and exhibit a dark, eye-like spot at their centers. Their fast-growing shell finally becomes too heavy for them to continue swimming, so they set, permanently attaching themselves to an anchor and getting on with the business of becoming mature oysters. At that point they are called spat.

Remote seeding follows the reproductive process in a lab: Eyed larvae are filtered out of breeding tanks and shipped to growers. A million larvae fit easily into a sock-sized container. The grower distributes the larvae in a tank containing warm salt water and bags of shell culch, and the larvae set on the shell in a day or two. Such remote seeding with the grower-controlled set has become a standard practice in the shucked oyster trade.

Oyster growers can now think of themselves as breeders and select those specimens from their beds they consider particularly attractive and fast growing, specimens that recover quickly from spawn, firming right up for the fall and winter oyster trade, an important factor for any grower hoping to extend his season. Bill Webb took advantage of the new technology and crossed two kinds of *Crassostrea gigas*—a delicious, small, slow-growing oyster the Japanese call Kumamoto, and a faster growing relative called Myagi—to create his Pacific oyster stock. The growers send their selected breeding stock to a remote seeding lab to be conditioned, as it is called, or they may simply use the seed produced at the lab in the first place.

The oysters in the laboratory lie in the bottom of plastic barrels enjoying a bath of fresh sea water, warmed sea water, and piped-in air. The trick is to gradually raise the water temperature while adding home-grown algae of a kind that suggests to the oysters, along with the water temperature, that it's time to reproduce. This can be accomplished at any time of the year. Once sexual maturity has been achieved it's a simple matter, though somehow barbaric, to open the oysters and check their gametes under a microscope, determining each oyster's sex. In a process called strip spawning, sperm is squeezed from the males, while the females are minced in a blender, the contents of which are dumped into a series of fine mesh screens that sieve away all but the eggs. Controlled ratios of sperm and eggs can then be stirred together, with the hoped-for result: a tank full of oyster larvae numbering in the multi-, multi-millions.

Until recently, the Pacific oyster has never had much of a culinary reputation, nothing like the splendid history of *Crassostrea virginica* or *Ostrea edulis*. In his authoritative *Encyclopedia of Fish Cookery* A. J. McLane states, "The Pacific oyster . . . is of no great moment to the gourmet; in flavor and appearance these imports are decidedly inferior to Eastern oysters, which are airlifted daily to West Coast markets." If left to their own whims and fancies, Pacific oysters tend to clump up when they set, finding some kind of comfort in shared anchorage. This has never made for an oyster ever likely to be accepted for the half-shell trade at an oyster bar because it is next to impossible to break clumps of oysters apart without damaging the goods. Besides that, growers concentrating on the shuck trade have always let their Pacifics grow larger than oysters served at bars. It is not uncommon to trip over a lone, old Pacific oyster on a Hood Canal beach that has grown to the size of a tennis shoe: a bowl of chowder on the half shell. These are the oysters sought out by Chinese restaurants in the region. *Crassostrea virginica* and *Ostrea edulis* are both inclined to set and grow as single oysters. Fortunately, a refinement on the remote seeding process— single setting—has changed the Pacific's clumping ways.

When the eyed larvae are about to set in their tank away from home, rather than giving them bags of oyster shell for anchorage, oyster shell ground so fine each speck only has room for one oyster larvae foot to cement itself in place, is scattered in the tank. This technique forces Pacific oysters for the half-shell trade to grow as singles. When these seed oysters are filtered out of the tank they look like so many grains of black sand against the fine mesh of the sieve. Once they are large enough, they leave the lab for grow-out nursery trays in their home waters, feeding for the first time on naturally occurring nutrients and not food grown for them in laboratory carboys.

Bill Webb and his lab crew have taken the process one step further, working with a procedure first demonstrated by Stanley Allen at the University of Maine, then perfected by Allen and fellow graduate student Sandra Downey at the University of Washington's Department of Fisheries. Webb grows neutered oysters. That means his oysters never get spawny and he can produce them for market all four seasons of the year.

Oysters of the kind that Webb now grows are new life forms. In the first hour of strip-spawned fertilization there is a twenty-minute window of opportunity when it is possible to interrupt the normal course of reproductive events with a massive dose of antibiotic that shocks the egg into retaining its two sets of maternal chromosomes while taking on the set of paternal chromosomes present in the sperm. The resulting triploid oyster will show signs of sexual maturity when the water temperature and the food is right, but because of the extra chromosomal baggage, will be too sexually constipated to ever get spawny. During the normal oyster marketing season, the triploid is indistinguishable from the diploid next to it. The value of the triploid becomes apparent in summer when it is palatable and the diploids are not. Sandra Downey is busy perfecting a tetraploid oyster in the Westcott Bay laboratories. With tetraploid brood stock, Bill Webb predicts, he will be able to naturally breed back to a triploid and eliminate the antibiotic shock, which somehow seems humane.

Duane Fagergren isn't convinced. He says the triploid in the summer has a better texture than a spawny oyster, but it has less texture than a normal diploid in prime condition. But then Fagergren doesn't grow triploids, and his marketing season is defined by the temperature of the water in Totten Inlet. Fagergren buys his seed for half-shell-quality Pacific and European flat oysters from Ted Kuiper in Bayside, California. It arrives in a styrofoam cooler, already grown to six to eight millimeters. Fagergren scatters the seed in fine mesh nursery trays that he keeps submerged in Totten Inlet. When the seed is too big for the trays, he moves it into larger mesh grow-out bags that rest on a long wooden frame anchored to his beach below the tide line, a cheaper version of Randy Shuman's racks. It takes a minimum of twenty-seven months for the flat oysters to reach market size, eighteen months for the Pacifics. Duane also spreads shell stock on his beach for shucking oysters, the common practice among Pacific oyster growers. The shell is covered with seed oysters that grow for twenty-seven months for the shuck trade, and in that time Fagergren tends his crop like a farmer, moving shell stock from one part of the beach to another as it grows, adding fresh shell stock at one end, removing oysters at the other.

The Olympias, though, consume the better part of his attention. They grow on four acres of diked tidelands on the opposite shore of Totten Inlet, fifteen minutes' travel from Fagergren's home by the big, open boat Duane uses like a marine pickup truck. He stands in the stern with a hand on the tiller extension of the motor, throttling up once he's clear of shallow water and any hidden mysteries. Vacation homes peek out through the madrona, cedar, fir, dogwood, and big leaf maple that grew in along the shore after the land was logged off. Flocks of black-feathered scoter ducks explode off the water with a sound like wet applause as the boat approaches, then land in a group a little ways away. Scoters eat young oysters and immature clams like popcorn. Now and then the Olympia Oyster Company, a big concern farther up the inlet, sends a man out with a gun in a boat to chase the ducks and shoot blanks, but it does little good. The same battle has gone on for all of the twentieth century.

Long sapling poles planted in the tidelands at low tide mark the boundary lines of various oyster grounds. The Fagergrens own thirty-four acres in mud ground that could conceivably be diked in for Olympia oyster production, but Duane figures it would cost $25,000 an acre to do the job. As it is, he borrowed that much for materials to repair four dikes built around the turn of the century. They hadn't held water in twenty years.

Anton Heilenberger is credited by some with first observing early in the century that ridges of gravel on the tideflats of Swindle Cove in Oakland Bay held water in place at low tide, and as a result Olympia oyster seed grew in abundance where it normally wasn't found at all. Heilenberger began re-creating the gravel ridge effect with sunken logs and boards staked in place, managing to hold back several inches of water at low tide. The difference in oyster population was impressive enough that other oystermen turned from the wild fishery-type harvest to dike cultivation. Improvements in the early 1900s included leveling the tidelands, a tedious process that could only be accomplished, like so much of the oyster work, between tides.

While Fagergren's Olympia oyster ground isn't considered the best around, it is typical for extending in a series of leveled, half-acre large dikes from the tide line near shore down to the plus three-foot tide level. Fagergren starts seed high in the Number One dike, then gradually moves it to the lower dikes where the nutrients are in greater abundance. He calls the lower dikes his fattening ground.

As the tide slips out of Totten Inlet, the tops of the dikes, first up near the shore, then soon enough farther out in the bay, begin to appear. Ragged-edged, creosote-soaked boards trace long, narrow rectangles on the tidelands. The lower the tide falls, the more obvious the action of the water becomes as it races out of the dikes and over the edge of the walls, until only a couple of inches of water remain trapped behind the boards. The water action is important. Olympia oysters easily smother beneath a layer of silt, and the water turbulence, both as the tide recedes and races back in, cleans the silt out of the dikes.

In summer the shallow layer of water protects the Olympia oysters from overheating and dying, and in winter it protects them from freezing and dying. Several winters ago, however, the temperature dropped so low that the water in the dike ponds froze, the majority of Fagergren's oyster stock stuck to the bottom of the ice, and at high tide the whole works floated away. Fagergren was able to send brood stock up to Bill Webb, on San Juan Island, who had his lab crew condition the oysters and produce seed. Webb sent 600,000 seed oysters back to Fagergren and kept 100,000 for himself which he now grows out in suspended tray culture, much like his lantern net system.

Olympias don't breed like Pacifics, which are considered broadcast spawners for the way male and female spew out eggs and sperm, and leave the rest to Providence. Olympia males spew their sperm into the water, but the females retain the eggs within their gill and mantle cavities, where they are fertilized by sperm brought in with the oyster's water pumping action. The growing embryos remain within the mother oyster for two weeks, leaving the brood chamber as free-swimming larvae. In another two weeks they set on culch and three years later, with considerable luck, they have grown to a marketable size.

Fagergren culches in two ways when the Olympia oyster set is on in mid-summer. He spreads shell culch—clam, mussel, and Pacific shell—on the seed beds. He also uses egg crates dipped in cement. The oyster larvae love the many rough surfaces, and set on egg crates with abandon. Fagergren ferries the crate culch to the dikes in his sink float, a half-submerged rectangular scow without benefit of top deck or closed ends. Fagergren normally uses the sink float to store market-ready clams which purge themselves of sand when totally submerged. But during the set he leaves the float and the culch for three months out where it can catch the Olympia larvae, then breaks the crate culch into two-inch pieces, scattering them among the shell culch on the seed beds. A year later, at low tide, he rakes the oysters in the seed beds into windrows, then pitchforks them onto the flat deck of his scow. At high tide he moves the scow to a lower dike, and scatters the growing oysters for another two years.

Harvesting is a similar process. But in winter, when the oysters are at their best, the lowest tides come at night. So Fagergren and an employee rake windrows of harvestable Olympia oysters by gas lantern light, then fork them up onto the scow for the trip back to the culling shed on the beach in front of Fagergren's house. During the day the oysters are run through the shed on a conveyer belt. The market-sized Olympias are culled from the pile; the rest go back to the dike. Other oyster companies in and around Totten Inlet do much the same, but with Pacific oyster stock. The Olympias go to the shucking table and end up in glass jars, packed in fresh water.

By mid-week the order book has filled, and the sink float moored in Totten Inlet out in front of Fagergren's house is riding low with plastic mesh bags of oysters and clams syphoning seawater to purge themselves of sand. Thursday morning before the sun shows any interest in the day Fagergren loads the blue pickup with the shellfish and heads north. Though the day will be long and the drive to Seattle and back wearying, Fagergren enjoys this final labor. It is a confirmation of the link between his efforts and the marketplace. He shares the day with his daughters when he can. And he always arranges his deliveries to have a meal at a favorite restaurant along the way. Without fail, he orders a plate of oysters still as cold as South Sound water.

If he were to sit down with his company's books laid out before him, Duane Fagergren would have a tough time explaining the enormous amount of time, energy, and cash he dumps into an oyster that year after year fails to show dramatic promise. It shows a little promise. Then a little more the next year. Two spawning seasons ago the set was the biggest any growers had seen in fifty years, and the winter kill of tender, young Olympias was minimal. But it still comes down to 400 bushels of oysters, not 4,000, or even 40,000—which makes the Olympia an exceedingly rare delicacy.

Had Duane Fagergren not taken the opportunity to revive a

family business and target the Olympia as a half-shell item that might eventually support a major part of his shellfish business, there's no telling how few of the oysters would be available in anything but shucked and bottled form. Perhaps that's what Evie Fagergren means about "our" oysters. Perhaps she understands on an instinctual level that the only reason the half-shell Olympia is on a menu at all is that her father believes in it—and that her father is the kind of man who does all he can to make his dreams tangible.

Shellfish of the Pacific Northwest

Oysters:

Olympia *(Ostrea lurida)*: the oyster native to the Pacific Northwest. The only commercial quantities grow in South Puget Sound. A tiny oyster, the Olympia has a mild flavor followed by a metallic aftertaste.

Pacific *(Crassostrea gigas)*: A native of Japan, the Pacific oyster was imported early in the century when the Olympia oyster population declined in the Pacific Northwest. By the 1950s natural reproduction was occurring in some Puget Sound bays, and today the Pacific oyster is as much a native as the Olympia. Quilcene, Hama Hama, Canterbury, Willapa Bay, Shoalwater—these are all names under which Pacific oysters are sold, and in most instances the names reflect flavor nuances as well as place of origin.

The **Kumamoto** oyster is a Pacific species. It is smaller, deeper cupped, and slower growing than the more common Pacific oyster, and has a rich, buttery flavor. The Pacific oysters sold by Bill Webb at Westcotts are a hybrid cross of Pacific and Kumamoto.

European flat oysters *(Ostrea edulis)* are grown in Pacific Northwest waters and like those grown in Maine are commonly marketed with the name Belon.

The oyster common to the Eastern Seaboard *(Crassostrea virginica)* won't grow and reproduce in the Pacific Northwest. Local oyster growers tried the Eastern oyster before importing Pacifics from Japan. Eastern oysters are commonly available in Pacific Northwest markets and restaurants.

Mussels: Oddly enough, mussels have only recently been discovered by a public in the Pacific Northwest wider than the eccentric beachcomber types who have always enjoyed harvesting these blue-black shelled mollusks off rocks and piers. French, Italian, Spanish and Asian mussel enthusiasts have had the Northwest mussel all to themselves. But in the last five years commercial mussel growing has started up, primarily in Penn Cove off Whidbey Island in the Puget Sound. With a consistent supply at hand, restaurants began serving mussels, and the appreciative public has grown. The sweet, delicate Penn Cove mussel is now available at fish markets throughout the Pacific Northwest. The bigger, coarser cousin brought in from Canada and Maine, where they are dredged and not grown on lines hanging in the water, are of course widely available.

Clams: There are two common hard-shell littleneck clams harvested and sold in the Pacific Northwest, the native littleneck and the Manila clam, a littleneck that was introduced to Pacific Northwest waters when oyster shell culch was imported from Japan. The Manila settled into an ecological niche and proved to be a rapid and hardy breeder. Today, Manila clams are the bulk of the Northwest clam industry. Where the native littleneck has a dull shell, the Manila sports a shell with beautiful black stripes, like *sumié* brushstrokes. Steaming is the most popular method of cooking either clam. The debate over which is better, sweeter, more clam-like is never ending.

Geoduck: pronounced "gooey-duck." This remarkably unattractive bivalve makes delicious chowder when ground. Sushi bars serve part of this clam as "giant clam," but geoduck it is. The clam commonly weighs several pounds, its long, flaccid siphon much too big for its shell. When you see them at a fish market, give the siphon a gentle poke. It should react, pulling in. If it doesn't, it's dead and should be avoided. The coarse skin that covers the geoduck is easily removed by plunging into boiling water, then into cold water to cool. The skin sloughs off. Like calamari, geoduck can either be cooked in an instant and served as a tender morsel, or cooked for hours to tenderize. Commercial harvesting is done by divers who uproot the geoduck from the sand with high-pressure hoses. They are next to impossible to dig at low tide because they can burrow deep into the sand at alarming rates.

Razor clam: another clam capable of burrowing at high speed. The shell—long, narrow and thin—is well named. The unsuspecting clam digger can split open a finger reaching too fast for a clam quickly disappearing into the sand. Razor clam sand digging has become something of a regional sport, attracting tens of thousands of people to beaches in the middle of winter in the middle of the night at low tide. Some commercial production makes these clams available in fish markets, most of them coming from Alaska. Ground razor clam makes magnificent chowder.

Shrimp: Coonstriped shrimp. Side stripe shrimp. Spotted prawns (actually a shrimp, not a prawn). The names accurately describe the markings on shrimp found in Hood Canal off Puget Sound, as well as in the waters off southeastern Alaska. Sweet, meaty morsels. Since they grow in cold water, there is no deveining necessary. When fresh Alaska spot prawns appear on the fishmonger's ice, it is time to get excited. These shrimp taste the way shrimp should taste, yet rarely do.

Crayfish: While they don't obtain the size of their Louisiana cousins, Pacific Northwest crayfish, trapped in lakes and streams, are becoming more and more available on the retail market. Scandinavians in particular are fond of boiled crayfish, chasing the meat of the fresh water crustaceans with a shot of ice-cold aquavit.

Crab: Dungeness crab is certainly what crab in the Pacific Northwest is all about. The industry has had some terrible years of late, though signs of a comeback are appearing. The same sad state is true of the Alaskan king crab, which all but disappeared but is now coming back strong. Popular with the Asian and Anglo communities alike, crab is boiled, steamed, even barbecued in the Pacific Northwest. The tradition in my family was to sit down to a plate of cold, cracked Dungeness crab that had been boiled, and then to pick out the meat and dip it in different sauces. There are pickers and pilers, and pickers and eaters, and it doesn't take long to find out which is which.

Scallops: **Pink** scallops have become popular in Pacific Northwest restaurants like Ray's Boathouse in Seattle. Small scallops with a lovely shell, they gape when steamed, giving them the appearance of open-mouthed singers, thus their popular name, "singing scallops."

Weathervane scallops are big and meaty and sweet. Shellfish enthusiasts who have given up on scallops for their bland flavor might give these a try. The scallop fishery is important both in Oregon and Alaska.

Alaska abalone: The meat is no bigger than a hockey puck and can be just as tough if overcooked (anything more than 10 seconds at high heat). While California abalone shells end up as soap dishes, the shell of the Alaska abalone is barely big enough to double as an ashtray.

Traditional Oyster Stew

Just oysters and milk—so simple, but an oyster lover's delight. I confess to liking lots of buttered saltines with oyster stew, but crusty French bread is another great accompaniment. Add a nice salad and you have a satisfying but easy dinner. Small bowls of oyster stew are also lovely as a first course at a more elegant dinner. I like our Quilcene (Pacific) oysters best for stew, but any fairly small, sweet oyster will do as well.

> *1 quart whole milk (or half-and-half if you like a richer*
> *mixture)*
> *4 tablespoons butter*
> *¼ cup thinly sliced yellow onion*
> *2 dozen small oysters with their liquid*
> *Salt and pepper*
> *Worcestershire sauce*
> *Additional butter*
> *Paprika*

Heat milk in a separate saucepan, just until steaming. Melt the butter in a 3-quart saucepan. Add the onion and cook until soft. Add the oysters and heat until the edges fan open. Pour in the hot milk. Bring to steaming, but not boiling point again. Remove from heat and season to taste with salt, pepper, and a dash of Worcestershire. Serve in large shallow bowls with a lump of butter and a dash of paprika. Oyster stew purists might say to leave out the onions, but I like the sweet flavor they add to the soup.

Yield: 4 main-course servings or 6 first-course servings

Baked Oysters with Peppered Bacon

Peppered bacon (p. 47) is a specialty of Oregon. When we go to Astoria for a visit, we bring several pounds home and freeze it.

2 cups spinach, cleaned, trimmed and roughly chopped
12 oysters
½ cup diced peppered (or thick-sliced) bacon, cooked
Freshly grated Parmesan cheese
2 tablespoons butter
French bread croutons
Soft butter

Preheat oven to 375°. Sauté spinach in butter. Carefully place 1 tablespoon spinach on each oyster in its shell. Sprinkle with bacon and cheese. Dot with butter and bake in the oven just until cheese melts. Serve with toasted, buttered French bread croutons.

Serves 4

Oyster Sausage

You have not lived until you have gone to the trouble of making, then eating, oyster sausages. The trouble isn't all that great; the sausages are absolutely remarkable. They are meant to be served the day they are prepared.

2 cups shucked oysters
2 cups fresh bread crumbs
2 eggs, beaten
2 tablespoons finely chopped parsley
Salt and pepper to taste
Dash of ground nutmeg
Hog casing
Sausage horn
Melted butter
Additional finely chopped parsley for garnish

Gently poach oysters in their own liquor until they plump up and their gills fan out. Drain off excess liquid and reserve in a bowl. Finely chop oysters with a chef's knife and add to bowl. Stir in bread crumbs, beaten eggs, parsley, salt, pepper, and nutmeg.

Hand-stuff into medium-sized hog casing, holding the sausage horn in one hand while stuffing the mixture with the fingers of the other hand. It is a soft, squishy endeavor that doesn't look too pleasing, but take care not to overstuff the casing because the egg, when cooked, will make these sausages expand. Make links, when finished, by squeezing the casing at the desired length, then flipping the sausage a couple of times to twist the casing. Refrigerate if not cooking immediately.

Thoroughly prick the sausage, place in pan with water coming halfway up the sausage. Bring the water to a simmer and put lid on pot. Don't let water boil. Poach gently for 6 to 8 minutes. If sausage shows signs of splitting, prick with fork. To serve, melt butter, add a good handful of finely chopped parsley, and pour over sausage.

Yield: 1 dozen

Oyster Loaf

For oyster lovers, this is a great sandwich, delicious for an informal supper to serve friends, along with your favorite beer on ice. (When buying oysters in a jar, be sure the liquid surrounding the oysters is clear. If the liquid is cloudy, the oysters are not fresh.)

> ½ head of iceberg lettuce
> 2 tomatoes
> ½ pound bacon strips, cut in half
> ½ cup milk
> 1 egg, beaten
> 1 cup flour
> ½ cup cornmeal
> 10-ounce jar of fresh oysters
> ¼ cup butter
> ¼ cup salad oil
> Salt and pepper to taste
> 1 long loaf French bread
> Tartar Sauce (p. 345)

Shred lettuce finely. Slice tomatoes. Cook bacon and drain well.

Mix milk and egg together. Dip the oysters in the egg mixture, then roll in the cornmeal–flour mixture.

Heat the butter and oil and then cook the oysters over medium heat until golden. Remove from pan and drain on paper towels. Season with salt and freshly ground black pepper.

Cut bread in half lengthwise, and with your fingers pull out some of the inside of the loaf, leaving a hollow. Spread each side with tartar sauce. Place the oysters on the bottom half of the loaf first, then layer the remaining ingredients over the oysters in the following order: bacon, tomatoes, and lettuce.

Serves 4

Heck's Oyster and Hazelnut Stuffing

Oregon hazelnuts and fresh oysters combine to make a moist, delicious dressing. This is enough to stuff a 20-pound turkey. I think it is the best part of the Thanksgiving dinner.

> *Turkey giblets*
> *1 cup water*
> *1¼ cups hazelnuts*
> *1 large yellow onion, finely chopped*
> *2 stalks celery, finely chopped*
> *4 tablespoons butter*
> *½ pound fresh mushrooms, sliced*
> *1 10-ounce jar fresh oysters, drained*
> *1 tablespoon poultry seasoning*
> *1 teaspoon thyme*
> *2 teaspoons sage*
> *6 tablespoons butter*
> *2 teaspoons kosher salt*
> *½ teaspoon freshly ground black pepper*
> *2½ quarts diced bread cubes (day-old white bread)*
> *Chicken stock*

Preheat the oven to 275°. Simmer giblets in water over low heat until tender, about 1 hour. Finely chop the giblets and reserve the cooking liquid.

Spread the shelled hazelnuts in a shallow pan and roast in the oven for 25 minutes. Remove and let cool. Remove skins by rubbing the hazelnuts with a cloth towel. Coarsely chop.

Sauté the onion and celery in the butter until soft, then add mushrooms, and continue cooking. Chop oysters.

Combine all the rest of the ingredients except the bread cubes and stock in a large bowl and mix well (be sure to include the butter left from sautéing the mushrooms, celery and onions). Mix in the bread cubes, and add enough chicken stock to make stuffing moist, but not soggy. Stuff dressing into turkey just before roasting. If you have any left over, put it in a buttered casserole, cover and bake for about 1 hour.

Yield: enough for a 20-pound turkey

Scalloped Oysters

This is an easy Friday night supper in the wintertime when fresh oysters that come in a jar are firm and flavorful. You may leave out the bacon, but it adds extra flavor; bacon and oysters seem to have a natural affinity.

> *6 tablespoons butter*
> *2 cups of coarsely crushed soda crackers (or a little more if needed to cover oysters)*
> *10-ounce jar of oysters, drained*
> *½ cup cooked diced bacon*
> *¾ cup half-and-half*
> *¼ cup melted butter*

Preheat the oven to 375°. Melt butter in a small pan. Spread half the crackers across the bottom of a 1½-quart casserole. Top with oysters. Sprinkle with bacon. Cover with remaining cracker crumbs. Add the half-and-half. Drizzle with melted butter.

Bake in the oven for 30 to 35 minutes.

Serves 2

Grilled Oysters in Herb-Butter Sauce

We enjoy gathering oysters and cooking them on an outdoor grill. They steam just a bit, the shells open and reveal a nice, plump cooked oyster.

4 ounces butter, melted
2 tablespoons lemon juice *½ teaspoon fresh dillweed*
½ teaspoon black pepper *Dash of Tabasco*
1 tablespoon chopped parsley *3 dozen fresh oysters in the shell*

Prepare your charcoal grill and let the coals reach a medium heat.

Mix together all of the ingredients, except the oysters, and keep warm.

Place oysters on the grill, 4 or 5 at a time. With a heavy oven mitt, remove the oysters to a serving platter as they open, being careful not to spill the nectar. Spoon a little of the herb-butter sauce over each oyster.

Yield: 6 appetizer servings

How to Catch and Cook Dungeness Crab

In the Northwest many people who go boating in the San Juan Islands have the opportunity to catch fresh Dungeness crab. Live crabs are also available in some of the fish markets. My friend Bill Karcher, who is a commercial crab fisherman in the Northwest, taught me how to catch and cook the live crabs.

Equipment for catching crab:
32-inch ring trap
Large ice chest
Damp burlap sacks
Bait—has to be fresh: chicken backs, fish heads and scraps or
horse clams work the best, but Dungeness crabs are fussy
eaters, so the fresher the bait, the better.

Put your baited trap 50 feet down. If you bring up all females, throw them back and move a little shallower or a little deeper. Crabs tend to cluster and the males are always close by. Be sure to throw back all females and any undersized males. The underbody of "keepers" must measure at least as wide as a dollar bill is long.

Place the crabs in the ice chest on a layer of ice and cover with a damp burlap sack. Don't keep the crabs in water. It is better to wait 8 hours to cook the freshly caught crabs, to allow the membranes joining the legs to the body to firm up; the crab will thus hold together when it is cooked. The crab can stay fresh refrigerated as described in the ice chest for several days.

> To cook the crab:
> *16-quart canning kettle*
> *Rock salt*

Fill the pot two-thirds full and add one *closed* handful of rock salt per crab to be cooked. Bring water to a boil. Put in crabs nose first and return the water to a boil for 15 minutes (turn heat down slightly, so that you have a gently rolling boil). When you remove the crabs from the water, cool them down immediately under slow-running cold tap water—this keeps the meat moist and easy to remove from the shell.

To clean the crab for eating: Pull off large back shell, and under running water, rinse crab clean. Pull off feather-like gills attached to body. Break in half and have on hand nutcrackers to crack the shells. The pointed tips of the small legs make good picks for removing meat from the other parts.

DEFINING THE PACIFIC NORTHWEST STYLE

Fresh Dungeness Crab Bisque

Chef Thierry Adam, owner of Rent-a-Chef Catering, came to our home and cooked live Dungeness crabs and then made this delicious soup.

2 medium leeks
1 Walla Walla sweet onion (outside the Northwest you
   can substitute Vidalia and Granex, depending on
   where you live)
2 medium carrots
3 cloves garlic
½ cup olive oil
2 medium (1½- to 2-pounds each) Dungeness crab,
   cooked and cleaned
1 tablespoon fresh tarragon, chopped
3 tablespoons fresh coriander, chopped
1 tablespoon fresh parsley, chopped
⅛ teaspoon thyme
2 bay leaves
1 teaspoon saffron threads
¼ teaspoon curry powder
⅛ teaspoon turmeric
2 tablespoons brandy
1 cup white wine
14 ounces tomato sauce
1½ quarts fish stock (or canned clam juice)
2 cups water
4 potatoes (medium-sized russets), peeled and diced
1 pint cream
1 cup sour cream
½ cup butter, softened
Chopped chives

Dice leeks, onion, carrots and garlic. In large stockpot heat olive oil and add diced vegetables. Let cook over medium heat for 6 minutes, stirring occasionally.

Cut legs off crabs and set aside. Chop body of each crab into 6 pieces and add body parts, including shell and juice, to diced vegetables in pot.

Add tarragon, coriander, parsley, thyme, bay leaves, saffron, curry powder, turmeric, and stir well.

Add brandy, white wine, tomato sauce and fish stock. Let simmer for one hour. Add water and diced potatoes and let simmer another hour.

Remove meat from crab legs and reserve. Remove crab pieces from soup mixture and remove meat from shells. Using blender, blend soup adding cream, sour cream and butter. Strain. Add crab-meat and legs to soup.

Serve hot with chopped chives sprinkled on top.

Serves 8

DEFINING THE PACIFIC NORTHWEST STYLE

This interpretation is from Marianne Zdobysz at Queen City Grill.

Crab Bisque

1 whole Dungeness crab
3 Dungeness crab shells (if using blue crab, then 3 whole
   crab and 9 shells)
¾ pound unsalted butter
2 carrots, chopped
1 onion, chopped
2 leeks, chopped
3 ribs celery, chopped
2 bay leaves
½ teaspoon black peppercorns
2 tablespoons tomato paste
½ cup flour
Water or fish stock to cover
1 tablespoon salt
½ teaspoon cayenne
1 tablespoon brandy

Preheat the oven to 500°. Sweat crab and crab shells in ¼ pound butter for 10 minutes. Add vegetables and roast in the oven for 30 minutes to 1 hour.

Melt ½ pound butter in a stockpot. Add roasted crab, shells, vegetables, bay leaves, peppercorns and tomato paste and sauté for 5 minutes. Add flour and stir while smashing crab to let out the flavor. Add enough water or fish stock to cover and simmer for 1 hour, skimming frequently.

Strain into a container, then strain again through a fine sieve. Season with salt, cayenne and brandy.

Serves 4

Kay Karcher's Crab, Cheese and Green Pepper Sandwich

Since her husband is a commercial crab fisherman, Kay always has a generous amount of crabmeat on hand. One of her favorite ways to serve it is in this delicious sandwich.

> *2 cups crabmeat*
> *2 cups grated cheddar cheese*
> *½ cup diced green pepper*
> *½ cup chopped green onion*
> *Mayonnaise*
> *Worcestershire sauce*
> *Lemon juice*
> *4 English muffins or French rolls, cut in half*

Preheat broiler. Mix together crabmeat, cheddar cheese, green pepper, green onion and just enough mayonnaise to bind the mixture. Season to taste with Worcestershire sauce and lemon juice. Spread generously on muffins or rolls and place on baking sheet. Place in broiler, 8 to 10 inches away from the source of heat and broil until bubbly and golden.

Note: Kay Karcher also recommends a method for freezing crabmeat: pack it into a plastic container, add cold water to fill any air spaces and seal with a tight-fitting lid. Once thawed, she claims, the crabmeat tastes just as fresh as when you caught it.

Yield: 8 sandwiches

Dungeness Crab Cakes with Tarragon Mayonnaise

These are crunchy on the outside and smooth and creamy on the inside. The sweet flavor of the Dungeness crab is complemented by the tangy mustard. Although this is not a traditional dish in the Northwest, in the past two years it has become very popular, possibly due to the influence of Cajun and Creole cooking. This is a delicious way to use Dungeness or any other sweet, fresh crabmeat for a simple but elegant dinner. Serve with shoestring fries and a tangy coleslaw.

> *¼ cup butter*
> *½ cup finely diced yellow onion*
> *¼ cup finely chopped red pepper*
> *1 tablespoon Dijon mustard*
> *¼ cup chopped parsley*
> *½ cup mayonnaise*
> *1 pound Dungeness (or local) crabmeat*
> *1 tablespoon lemon juice*
> *¼ teaspoon Tabasco*
> *½ cup bread crumbs*
> *2 cups toasted fine bread crumbs*
> *Butter and salad oil for frying*
> *Tarragon Mayonnaise (recipe follows)*

Melt butter. Add onion and red pepper and cook over low heat for 5 minutes. Remove from heat and let cool. Add mustard, parsley, and stir in mayonnaise. Add crabmeat, lemon juice, Tabasco and bread crumbs. Chill the mixture for at least 2 hours.

After chilling, shape the crab mixture into 12 small round cakes, 3 inches in diameter, ½-inch thick. Lightly coat with the toasted bread crumbs.

Over medium heat, let the skillet warm to moderate heat. Add butter and oil as needed. (An electric griddle works very well.) Cook the cakes for 2–3 minutes on each side—until golden brown. If necessary, place on paper towel-lined baking sheet and keep warm in a low oven until ready to serve.

Serve with tarragon mayonnaise.

Yield: 12 cakes

> Tarragon Mayonnaise:
> *1 egg*
> *¼ teaspoon dry mustard*
> *2 tablespoons tarragon vinegar*
> *1 tablespoon fresh tarragon*
> *1 cup salad oil*
> *Salt and pepper to taste*

Put egg, mustard, vinegar and tarragon in food processor or blender and process briefly. Then with machine running on low speed, add oil in a slow, steady stream until mixture thickens. Season to taste with salt and pepper.

Grilled Crab and Cheddar Cheese Sandwich

Crab and cheddar cheese—a classic combination. Larry Brown, a good friend and an excellent cook, developed this version of a Northwest favorite.

> ½ *cup mayonnaise*
> ½ *cup Chili Sauce*
> 1 *cup Dungeness crabmeat*
> 4 *cups grated medium cheddar cheese*
> ¼ *cup chopped green olives*
> ¼ *cup chopped green onion*
> ¼ *cup chopped green bell pepper*
> ¼ *cup chopped celery*
> 12 *slices sourdough bread (p. 334)*
> ½ *cup butter, melted*

In a medium bowl, stir together the mayonnaise, chili sauce and crabmeat. Add the cheese, olives, onion, pepper and celery and mix thoroughly.

Divide the filling between 6 slices of the bread and top with the remaining slices. Brush the top side with melted butter. Grill, buttered side down in a skillet, until cheese melts (cook over low heat so the bread doesn't brown too quickly). Brush remaining side with melted butter, turn and continue cooking until both sides are golden.

Yield: 6 sandwiches

Avocados Stuffed with Crab Salad

A favorite first course or a simple lunch. The combination, which is by now classic, really developed farther south along the Pacific Coast. Eventually, universal availability of avocados brought the dish "home," where the Dungeness reigns.

½ pound Dungeness or other fresh, sweet crabmeat
Juice of ½ lemon
½ cup mayonnaise
1 tablespoon ketchup
4 drops Tabasco
½ cup finely diced celery
½ cup finely chopped green onion
4 large ripe avocado halves
Lemon wedges and fresh parsley

Mix the first seven ingredients together. Mound into the avocado halves. Garnish with lemon wedges and fresh parsley.

Serves 4

Marinated Prawns

Chilled marinated prawns, deviled eggs, and chicken sandwiches make a great picnic. This is also a good dish for a first course, served with sliced avocados.

2 pounds medium-sized prawns
¼ cup pickling spices
1 cup salad oil
¾ cup white vinegar
½ cup sugar
1 teaspoon salt
1 large white onion, cut in half and sliced

Place prawns in saucepan. Cover with water. Add pickling spices. Cover and simmer very gently for 5 minutes. (If you keep the water just below the boiling point, the prawns won't toughen.) Remove from water and cool to room temperature. Peel and devein shrimp.

Mix together salad oil, vinegar, sugar and salt. Layer shrimp and onion in a bowl. Pour in the vinegar mixture and refrigerate for 4 to 6 hours.

Serves 8–10

Alaska Spot Prawns with Roe

There is a 3-week season when these delicious, sweet prawns are available from Hood Canal, near Seattle. You can also find them at the fish markets, when they are brought down from Alaska. These are a great delicacy. They are soft, not rubbery, and sweet. The larger size usually all have roe, which is attached to the body and is considered a delicacy. You first eat the roe and then peel and eat the prawn. If you purchase them in the market, they should always have the head off. If any black spots appear on the shell, don't buy them.

> 12 fresh Alaska spot prawns, with roe, unpeeled
> 2 cups water
> 1 teaspoon salt
> 2 thin slices of fresh ginger

Place prawns in a 2-quart saucepan. Add water, salt and ginger. Bring water to a slow rolling boil and cook 4–5 minutes. Remove and place in a serving dish. Serve while still warm.

Yield: 4 appetizer servings

Crayfish

Whether you gather your own crayfish, or buy them (they are being farmed in the South and are becoming available in fish stores all over the country) the best and simplest method of cooking is to drop them into a large pot of boiling water with a generous amount of salt added. Cook them just until they turn a nice orange color and then remove them from the cooking liquid. Serve with home-made mayonnaise as a dipping sauce. For a variation we like the flavor when they are cooked the following way:

> ¼ cup salt
> 2 cups red wine
> 1 white onion, sliced
> 2 oranges, sliced

1 lemon, sliced
2 tablespoons pickling spices
3 quarts water
Crayfish

Bring this mixture to a boil. Let boil hard for several minutes. Plunge as many live crayfish as you can into the pot and cook until color changes to orange. Remove from liquid, cool to room temperature, and serve.

Serves 12

How to Clean Littleneck Clams

Dean Pugh is a Northwest fisherman whose family has been in the fishing business for several generations. Following is his method for purging the sand from clams that you dig yourself on the beaches while camping. (The clams you buy in a fish market have already been purged.)

1. Rinse well with salt water to remove outside sand.

2. Place clams in a 5-gallon container and fill with clean *salt* water. Let them relax for an hour, then sneak up on them and bang the bucket. Repeat 3 times, changing the water each time.

3. Cook them over the fire in a large clam cooker, or take them home on a bed of ice in an ice chest covered with damp burlap sacks.

Steamer Clam Soup

This makes a light broth-based first-course soup, very easy and very good, or can be served with steamed rice and a cucumber salad for a light lunch.

> *1¼ pounds small clams*
> *1 quart cold water*
> Hon-Dashi *to taste (available at Japanese and specialty food stores)*
> *4 small strips of lime peel*
> *Fresh coriander*

Scrub and rinse clams well. Place in saucepan. Add water. Bring to a boil. Skim off foam. Add a little *Hon-Dashi* to taste. Put clams and a strip of lime peel in each bowl. Pour in hot broth. Garnish with fresh coriander.

Serves 4

Hap's Clam Chowder

Happy Braden is a good friend who loves to cook. This is her recipe for a traditional Northwest clam chowder. The soda crackers thicken the soup to a nice consistency. Fresh clams are best, but good-quality canned clams can be substituted. Small steamer clams, steamed open, also can be used. If you are using a larger clam, such as a razor or geoduck, remove the stomach and then grind the rest of the raw clam. (The large neck of the geoduck must also have the heavy outside skin removed.)

> *½ cup finely diced bacon*
> *¼ cup butter*
> *½ cup diced yellow onion*
> *½ cup diced celery*
> *1 cup diced potatoes (I like the texture of the boiling potatoes)*
> *1 bay leaf*
> *3 cups bottled clam juice   1 cup half-and-half*
> *½ cup to 1 cup crushed unsalted soda crackers (do this in a food processor)*

2 cups chopped fresh clams, or small whole (see above)
¼ cup minced parsley
Freshly cracked pepper

Sauté the bacon, drain on paper towels and set aside.

In a large enamel soup pot, melt the butter. Add the vegetables and bay leaf and cook for several minutes. Add the clam juice and continue to simmer until the potatoes are tender. Add the half-and-half. Thicken the broth to the desired consistency by stirring in the crushed soda crackers, a little at a time. Add the clams, sprinkle with the cooked bacon, parsley, and freshly cracked pepper. Cook just to heat—do not boil—and serve immediately.

Serves 6

Pinot Gris Steamed Clams with Garden Herbs

Oregon pinot gris and fresh herbs add a delicious flavor to the small steamer clams.

2 tablespoons butter
4 tablespoons chopped fresh garden herbs (thyme, oregano, tarragon, parsley, rosemary, etc.)
2 tablespoons minced garlic
¼ tablespoon crushed red chili pepper
2 cups pinot gris
Juice of one lemon
4 pounds small steamer clams   *1 lemon, cut into wedges*
Salt and pepper to taste   *Herbs for garnish*

In a large saucepan with a tight-fitting lid place the butter, herbs, garlic and chili pepper. Simmer over medium heat for 2 to 3 minutes. Add the pinot gris, lemon juice and clams. Cover. Bring to a boil and boil for 3 to 5 minutes until all clams have opened. (Discard any which have not opened in 5 minutes.) Adjust the seasoning with salt and pepper to taste.

Serve in shallow bowls with lemon wedges and herb garnishes.

Serves 4

Steamed Clams with Parsley Butter

The parsley butter drizzled over the clams makes them look shiny and gives them a delicious taste. The butter mixes in with the juices and is delectable. The most important thing is to serve the clams *steaming hot* (and sand-free).

> *2 pounds fresh steamer clams*
> *1 cup water*
> *⅓ cup butter*
> *¼ cup minced fresh parsley*

Place steamer clams in a colander and rinse under cold, running water.

Place clams in a 2- to 3-quart saucepan. Pour in water. Cover. Bring to a boil and cook for several minutes (until clams open).

Transfer clams and juice to a 2-quart shallow serving bowl. Melt butter immediately. As soon as the butter foams, add the parsley and pour instantly over the clams, drizzling the butter over all of the clams as you pour.

Yield: 4 first-course servings

Spaghettini with Fresh Steamed Clams, Parsley and Parmesan Cheese

When we go to our cabin at the beach I always take pasta, olive oil, garlic, fresh parsley and Parmesan cheese, and cook this dish with freshly dug clams. This recipe varies from the traditional, but the result is just right.

> *2 pounds steamer clams*
> *1 cup water*
> *2 cloves garlic, minced*
> *3 tablespoons butter*
> *3 tablespoons plus 2 tablespoons olive oil*

¼ teaspoon red pepper flakes
¼ cup white wine
1 cup reserved clam juice
½ pound spaghettini
Kosher salt and freshly ground black pepper to taste
2 tablespoons minced parsley
Freshly grated Parmesan cheese

Place the clams in a 4- to 5-quart pot. Pour the cup of water over them. Bring to a boil. Cover and steam for 3 to 4 minutes, until clams open. Drain off liquid and reserve. Remove clams from their shells.

In a large frying pan, sauté the garlic in the butter and 3 table-spoons of olive oil. Add the pepper flakes, white wine and clam juice. Bring to a boil and simmer for 2 to 3 minutes.

Cook pasta just until tender in a large pot of boiling water. Drain well and add cooked noodles to sauce. Add the clams. Simmer until the dish is nice and hot. Drizzle over it the remaining 2 table-spoons olive oil. Transfer to warm serving dish. Season with salt and pepper. Sprinkle with parsley and cheese and serve.

Serves 2

Razor Clam Fritters

This is a good way to use chopped razor clams for a nice appetizer.

1½ cups flour
2 teaspoons baking powder
1 teaspoon salt
½ cup clam juice
2 eggs, beaten
1 cup chopped clams
1 tablespoon melted butter
2 tablespoons grated white onion

Mix all of the ingredients together. Drop by spoonfuls into hot deep fat and cook until golden. It's important not to make the spoonfuls too large or the fritter won't cook all the way through.

Serve with Tartar Sauce (p. 347) for dipping.

Yield: 4–6 appetizer servings

DEFINING THE PACIFIC NORTHWEST STYLE

> ## *Stir-fried Geoduck with Vegetables*

Judy Lew teaches this recipe for geoduck at her cooking school at Uwajimaya—a combination grocery and department store that sells everything from woks to sashimi. This is a good way to cook geoduck so that it stays tender. The geoduck is also used to make chowder, and is a favorite for sashimi.

1 medium geoduck clam
2 tablespoons white wine
½ teaspoon salt
¼ teaspoon pepper
1 teaspoon sesame oil
2 teaspoons cornstarch
3 tablespoons salad oil
2 cloves garlic, minced

½ pound pea pods (stringed, rinsed and drained)
1 small onion, cut in wedges
1 tablespoon slivered ginger root
2 teaspoons soy sauce
2 tablespoons water
Slivered green onion for garnish

Pour boiling water over the neck of the clam until the skin separates from the neck. Run a knife around the inside of the shell to open the clam. Discard stomach and pull off neck. Cut off the tip of the neck and slice open what's left lengthwise. Rinse carefully. Cut into thin ⅛-inch slices. Combine with 1 tablespoon of the wine, salt, pepper, sesame oil, and cornstarch.

Heat wok or heavy frying pan and add 1 tablespoon oil. Add half the garlic and all the vegetables. Stir-fry for 1 minute. Remove to platter. Clean wok. Heat again and add remaining 2 tablespoons oil. Add the rest of the garlic, ginger and clam slices. Stir-fry for 30 seconds. Add soy sauce, water and the other tablespoon of wine. Serve over vegetables. Sprinkle with green onion. (Don't overcook the geoduck, or it becomes tough and rubbery.)

Yield: 4 appetizer servings

Fried Razor Clams

A true delicacy. Razor clams are fun to gather, because they dig to escape as you are digging after them. Traditionally, in late spring, many people head to the Washington and Oregon coasts to dig for razor clams and then enjoy a great feast afterwards. Razors have a very thin lightweight shell with sharp edges which give them their name. And they are time-consuming to clean.

To clean the clams: extract the clam from its shell, and with a pair of kitchen scissors cut away anything that's dark, the tip of the neck, the gut muscle, and any sand residue. Cut each digger in half so that it will lie flat for frying. The soft, puffy meat inside the digger is the best part, so be careful not to scrape it away. *Dry* the clams well with paper towels.

To prepare the clams: Heat ½ inch of oil in a heavy frying pan—the fat must be quite hot so that the clams will brown quickly—*30 seconds on each side* is the rule. Dip each clam in dry pancake mix, then drop into the hot fat. Remove the clams from the pan with a slotted spoon, sprinkle with salt and pepper, and eat them right away. It's important not to overcook the clams or they will be tough.

Steamed Mussels

Ten years ago in the Northwest, mussels were gathered by only a few people. Today mussel gathering is much more common. I like to make a light dipping sauce to serve with steamed mussels, something that will "stick to the ribs" a little more than just melted butter.

> *2 pounds mussels*
> *½ cup white wine*
> *1½ cups water*
> *½ cup chopped white onion*
> *4 tablespoons soft butter mixed thoroughly with*
> *　3 tablespoons flour*
> *Fresh lemon juice*
> *¼ cup chopped fresh parsley*

Remove the beard from the mussels and scrub them. Put the wine, water and onion in a 3-quart saucepan. Bring to a boil for 1 minute to cook off the alcohol in the wine. Add the mussels. Cover and cook (turning heat down a little so the pot won't boil over) just until the mussels open—don't overcook, or they will be tough. Transfer the mussels to a serving bowl.

Strain the broth through a double thickness of cheesecloth back into the saucepan and thicken slightly with the butter–flour mixture. Add a little lemon juice to taste and stir in the parsley. Serve in a small bowl as a dipping sauce for the mussels.

Yield: 4 first-course servings

DEFINING THE PACIFIC NORTHWEST STYLE

> *Captain Whidbey's*
> *Citrus-Steamed Mussels*

The Captain Whidbey Inn is a unique log inn built in 1907. Located on beautiful Whidbey Island, it overlooks Penn Cove, one of the world's best mussel-growing areas. Chef Lorren W. Garlichs and his staff have created the Penn Cove Mussel Festival held every January at the Inn, to honor this tender and tasty seafood. These are two recipes created especially for this event.

> 1 cup water
> ¼ cup sugar
> ½ cup Johannisberg Riesling
> 1 tablespoon calvados
> Grated rind of 1 orange
> Grated rind of ½ lemon
> ½ cup orange juice
> ½ cup grapefruit juice
> ¼ cup lemon juice
> 3 pounds Penn Cove mussels

Combine the water and sugar in a saucepan, and bring to a boil over medium heat, washing down any crystals clinging to the sides of the pan with a brush dipped in cold water. Simmer for 5 minutes. Add wine, calvados, citrus rinds and juices. (This much may be done in advance.)

In a large pot, combine the above poaching liquid and the mussels and steam over high heat until the mussels are open and opaque.

Serves 6–8

DEFINING THE PACIFIC NORTHWEST STYLE

Captain Whidbey's Mussels and Saffron Purses

This is another mussel recipe from Chef Lorren Garlichs at the Captain Whidbey Inn.

½ cup white wine
1 ounce clarified butter
½ teaspoon basil
1 pound mussels, scrubbed and debearded
Pinch of saffron threads
1 tablespoon minced shallots
½ cup cream
Salt and pepper to taste
12 5-inch crepes
12 whole scallions, blanched and cut into thin strips

Preheat the oven to 350°. Bring wine, butter and basil to a boil. Add mussels. Cook until just done. Remove mussels from liquid. Reduce liquid by half. Add saffron threads, shallots and cream. Boil until thick, remove mussels from shell and add. Salt and pepper to taste.

Lay out crepes and put 1–2 tablespoons of mussel–saffron mix in the center of each crepe. Tie up with scallion string. Place on cookie sheet. Heat in the oven for 5 minutes and serve.

Yield: 12 "purses"

Marinated Scallops with Salsa

I like the small Oregon scallops marinated and served chilled. Mixed with fresh salsa, it makes a favorite summer dish.

1 pound small Oregon scallops, or other bay scallops
¼ cup fresh lime juice
¼ cup fresh lemon juice
1–1½ cups fresh Salsa (p. 346)
¼ cup olive oil
2 avocados, cut into bite-sized pieces
Salt and pepper to taste

Place the scallops in a glass bowl. Pour in the lime and lemon juices. Mix well. Cover with plastic wrap and refrigerate for 2 hours. Remove from refrigerator and drain off excess liquid.

Mix scallops gently with salsa, olive oil and avocados. Season to taste with salt and pepper. Serve chilled in small glass dishes as a first course.

Yield: 6 first-course servings

Gingered Oregon Scallops with Lemon Zest and Coriander

Oregon scallops are very small and thus can easily be overcooked. They are best prepared sautéed quickly in butter.

1 small knob of fresh ginger
4 tablespoons butter
1 teaspoon lemon zest
½ pound fresh scallops
2 tablespoons fresh coriander, chopped

Peel the ginger and cut into thin strips. Melt the butter in a 10 inch skillet over low heat. Add the ginger and lemon zest. Pat scallops dry, add to ginger butter. Sauté quickly, turning up the heat as the scallops cook. Transfer to warm serving dish and sprinkle with fresh coriander (or parsley).

Serves 2

DEFINING THE PACIFIC NORTHWEST STYLE

Caprial Pence has quickly established her own style in one of Seattle's more visible restaurants, Fullers, in the Sheraton Hotel.

Singing Scallops Poached in Citrus

> 3 pounds singing scallops, washed (sea scallops may be substituted)
> ¼ cup each lime, orange, and grapefruit juice
> ½ cup white wine
> 3 shallots, chopped
> 4 cloves garlic, chopped
> 1 cup crème fraîche
> 1 teaspoon freshly cracked black pepper
> Citrus segments and watercress for garnish

Place scallops in a large, heavy saucepan with the citrus juices, wine, shallots and garlic. Bring to a boil over high heat and continue to cook until scallop shells have opened and the meat has loosened or, in the case of the sea scallops, until the meat is translucent. Remove scallops with a slotted spoon onto individual plates. Cover and keep warm. Reduce cooking liquid by half, stir in crème fraîche. Season with pepper. Pour sauce over scallops. Garnish with citrus segments and watercress.

Serves 6

DEFINING THE PACIFIC NORTHWEST STYLE

Rockers Iko

The name suggests a Creole mood, and such was the case for H. Stuart ("Rip") Ripley, sous chef at the Greenlake Grill, who invented this spicy dish. On a cold, wet winter day in Seattle, there is nothing quite like it.

Sauce:
1 medium red onion, diced
1 medium red pepper, diced
1 tablespoon olive oil
2½ teaspoons cumin
2 teaspoons coriander
1 teaspoon thyme
2½ teaspoons fresh ginger, diced
1 bay leaf
1 teaspoon chopped garlic
1 tablespoon fresh chili pepper, chopped
1 tablespoon lemon juice
½ cup white wine
1 28-ounce can diced tomatoes in puree, or 3 pounds
   peeled and chopped fresh tomatoes

Sauté onion and pepper in oil in a saucepan until soft. Add spices, garlic and chili pepper, and sauté 30 seconds more. Add lemon juice, wine and tomatoes. Simmer 15 to 20 minutes, until flavors are well blended.

Seafood:
½ red pepper, julienned
1 carrot, julienned
2 stalks celery, julienned
1 leek, julienned
2 tablespoons olive oil
3 pounds seafood (a variety is best and should include
   clams, mussels and crawfish; fish cut in 1-inch squares
   that could include rockfish, cod and salmon; and
   scallops, prawns and shucked oysters)

Sauté pepper, carrot, celery and leek in olive oil. Add sauce (above) and bring to a simmer. Add seafood, starting with clams, mussels and crawfish. Then add the fish chunks when the clams start to open. Finally, after 3 or 4 minutes, add the scallops, prawns and oysters. Let simmer for another 3 or 4 minutes, or until done.

Serves 4–6

Cioppino

This is a traditional San Francisco dish that migrated north about 20 years ago after it was celebrated in the popular West Coast magazine *Sunset*. It adapted extraordinarily well to our local seafood and is now found on many Northwest restaurant menus.

4 cloves garlic, finely minced
½ cup fresh basil, chopped
1 bunch Swiss chard, coarsely chopped—leaves and stems
¼ cup combined fresh oregano and thyme, chopped
½ cup chopped parsley
1 or 2 small hot red peppers, finely chopped (to taste)
2 teaspoons freshly ground black pepper
1 tablespoon kosher salt
2 pounds clams, in their shells, scrubbed
2 Dungeness crabs, or 3 pounds other hard-shell crabs, cleaned and cracked
1 dozen fresh crayfish (or 1 pound medium-sized prawns or large shrimp, shelled and cleaned)
2 pounds firm fleshed white fish (ling cod, halibut or rockfish), cut into 2-inch pieces
2 cups dry white wine
1 6-ounce can tomato paste
2 28-ounce cans diced tomatoes, with juice (or whole canned tomatoes chopped in food processor)
¾ cup olive oil

Combine the first 8 ingredients to make an herb, chard and seasoning mixture.

Layer clams in the bottom of a 10- to 12-quart stockpot. Add the cracked crab and the crayfish, (or prawns or shrimp) to the pot. Sprinkle with half of the herb, chard and seasoning mixture. Add the white fish.

Mix together the wine, tomato paste, tomatoes and olive oil, and pour over the fish. Sprinkle with remaining herb, chard and seasoning mixture.

Cover and cook on medium heat for 25–35 minutes, until mixture comes to a gentle boil. Remove and serve in large bowls with toasted garlic bread.

Serves 6

Loaves and Fishes Stew

Summertime in the Northwest signals a trip by boat to the San Juan Islands. If you take a large pot for cooking freshly caught Dungeness crab, clams and mussels, and a few planned extra ingredients, you can serve a delicious fish soup from the day's catch.

> *½ cup olive oil*
> *1 cup chopped yellow onion*
> *2 cloves garlic, minced*
> *1½ cups white wine*
> *1 28-ounce can chopped tomatoes, and juice*
> *1 teaspoon fennel seed*
> *Dash of red pepper flakes*
> *Salt and pepper to taste*
> *1 Dungeness crab, cleaned and cracked*
> *1 pound cleaned mussels*
> *1 pound fresh shrimp*
> *1 pound fresh white-fleshed fish, cut into 2-inch strips*
> *1 teaspoon grated orange zest*

In a large enamel pan, pour in the olive oil and onion. Cook gently for 5 minutes, until the onion is soft, but not browned. Add the garlic and then the wine. Cook for 5 minutes. Add tomatoes and their juice, fennel seed, red pepper flakes, and simmer for 10 minutes. Season to taste with salt and pepper.

Add seafood all at once and turn up heat to medium. Cover and cook for 5–7 minutes, until the fish is cooked. Sprinkle with the orange zest and serve in large bowls.

Serves 4

MEAT, POULTRY AND GAME

G wen and Theo Caldwell's sheep all had names when Gwen started their breeding flock twelve years ago with twenty-one ewes and a stud buck named Tim. Gwen's four children—the Davises of Caldwell/Davis Farm—and Theo's youngest son used to attend to the naming; Rhoda, Llwanee, Dr. J, Celeste, and Arthur were among the more memorable. But the children's enthusiasm and imagination were overwhelmed by a flock that doubled, then nearly doubled again before Gwen and Theo trimmed the number of ewes back from eighty-five to an intensively managed fifty. A Caldwell/Davis sheep today might be called 28 Pink Tag, for the number on the plastic tag in the ewe's ear, or C/D 929, a mother of triplets, which look as much alike as matched pearls on a string. With or without names, Gwen Caldwell can tell all her sheep apart, and she is rightfully proud of their well-bred looks. Stylish ladies, Theo often called the ewes.

Gwen Caldwell is an open-faced woman in her early 50s with prominent, padded cheekbones and eyes that can go so wide with wonder and amusement that the whites completely circle their brown centers. Her movements are fast and strong, and she speaks in bursts that more often than not begin in the middle of a thought before she backs up. Her New England upbringing and Ivy League education share a box seat in her cultured voice. She may have come late to farming—after a career in the Seattle restaurant business—but she is a very serious breeder of Columbia sheep.

Commercial growers rely on sheep breeders like Gwen Caldwell to produce pure-bred stock that will enhance the quality and vigor of their own bands of sheep. The labor involved in breeding is so complex they'd rather not do it themselves in order to concentrate on growing good meat and wool animals. While the judges in the show ring are looking for extremes—for a longer, taller, leaner animal that will change the breed—the commercial growers look for animals that can survive and breed and put on weight with what they find to eat on the open range before being sent off to the abattoir. Sheep have a tough life on the range, and it is to Gwen

Caldwell's credit that her pure-bred Columbia rams trail with the best of them when they leave her flock and join a band of sheep 1,200 strong.

Caldwell/Davis sheep have been consistent winners in West Coast livestock shows. There have been two champion rams in five years at the Cow Palace in San Francisco, the most prestigious livestock show in this part of the country. In 1986 a Caldwell/Davis ram was supreme champion at the Idaho State Fair, where the Columbia was the featured breed. And the same year, at the Portland International, a Caldwell/Davis ewe took Supreme Ewe, earning a $250 prize from the Pendleton Woolen Mills. They will all be going to California to compete in the Columbia Nationals. Gwen Caldwell has never had a national champion, and it could be the big year for Caldwell/Davis Columbias after twelve years of building the flock. But it may be her last national as a Columbia breeder. She has some decisions to make, now that Theo's gone.

It was one thing to move with husband, family, and sheep from a small, part-time farm outside Seattle to the relative isolation of Goldendale, Washington, a farming community tucked in among the rolling Columbia Hills on the east side of the Cascade Mountains, about four hours' drive from the city. But it's wholly different to live there alone, a new widow with only a hired hand for company. Sam Davis, the youngest of Gwen's children, started college this year.

Theo Caldwell's passing was as sudden and as unexpected as a rock slide. He was five months shy of his sixty-fourth birthday. He lived at an easy pace with endless vitality and seemed so completely involved in the world around him—the land, the animals, the plants, the people—that those who knew him were shocked to find themselves driving to Goldendale one September weekend to attend a memorial service for him. There were lawyers and doctors and contractors from Seattle, old friends of Theo's who had worked with him building houses, or who had traveled by pack horse with him into the most remote corners of Washington's wilderness to thrive for a time in the mountains. And there were farmers from nearby communities, and mill workers and sheep breeders and young cowboys who fidgeted during the memorial in ill-fitting corduroy jackets and ties too tight at the neck, young men of few words who had come to tell Gwen and her children and Theo's five boys, all grown men, how sorry they were. Theo had touched a remarkably wide range of people.

Theo was a calm man, for the most part, sure of himself and

what he could do, a man with firm convictions and a devilish humor he often directed his own way. He weathered the years like storm-whipped mountain stone, and no one who knew him ever thought he would simply vanish over the hill without a wave from the top, least of all Gwen. The two of them walking along the crest line of the Columbia Hills, the land dropping away into the Columbia River, Oregon rising in the distance, the heat of the high desert launching white clouds high into a sky too pale to be called blue: Most people look small against so wide and open a view. Gwen and Theo Caldwell looked like they fit right in. They looked like they would go on forever.

They had found the property after deciding that sheep breeding on the west side of the Cascades, the wet side, meant too much mud. The Goldendale winters are mild and brief, the summers long and warm and dry. They could grow two alfalfa crops a year, then turn the sheep out into the cut fields to graze. Goldendale seemed like an open, friendly community with a new, attractive school, home of the Timberwolves. Theo's youngest son, Sam Caldwell, and Gwen's children—Megan, Piper, Ben, and Sam Davis—would all be making the move.

It took two-and-a-half years of weekends and vacations to clean up the 240-acre mess of cast-off farm machinery, rusting car hulks, fields gone to hell, bitter brush range land, and clustered stands of pine and white oak. To be an effective sheep breeding operation, Caldwell/Davis Farm demanded five-and-a-half miles of electrified fence, a machine shed, separate hay storage and feeding facilities for the ewes and the rams, a barn, and a house. Theo and his son Ben built the barn in seven weeks, then started on the house. The family and the sheep moved down from Seattle that last winter before the house was finished and shared the barn.

The sheep had been Gwen's idea, right from the beginning. Her father and his father before him had been gentlemen farmers. Gwen grew up in Sudbury, Massachusetts, with black-faced Hampshires, a British mutton breed built to browse the gently rolling hills of Dorset. The Columbia sheep that Gwen and Theo decided to breed, however, are part of the West. Up through the early part of the century the great bands of sheep that trailed through the western states were raised mostly for their wool. As the economic importance of lamb as a meat animal became more apparent, some growers began crossing their fine wool ewes with coarse wool rams to produce good wool and a heavier lamb. It would be far more ideal to have one breed of sheep producing both wool and good lambs for the meat market than to constantly be breeding back and forth, so the Animal Husbandry Division of the Bureau of Animal Industry began breeding experiments at the King Brothers Ranch in Laramie, Wyoming, in the fall of 1912. What started as a cross between Rambouillet ewes and a Lincoln ram resulted in a new sheep built to handle the rugged country of the West. The breed was named Columbia in 1919.

The Caldwell's first Columbia ewes came from Montana in 1975, and Gwen found the buck named Tim at the annual Washington ram sale. She bought him because the sheep expert standing next to her kept bidding on Tim with ill-concealed enthusiasm. The buck hung his head out the station wagon window all the way back home, where the flock of ewes awaited his advances. Sheep breeding proceeded apace until 1979, when the Caldwells faced something of a sheep breeder's crisis.

By then they had a flock of good but not great ewes. The season before they had paid $1,500 for a fancy buck that proved to be wormy with genetic material gone awry, a stud that produced offspring fit for a freak show. So Gwen and Theo went to the Columbia Nationals, held that year in Minot, North Dakota, in search of a new buck. They argued and fussed over every likely-looking candidate on display, watching sheep after sheep sell at inordinately high prices they couldn't afford. More out of desperation than any kind of studied fondness, they bought the eighteenth place buck at the show's ram sale. They paid $2,600 for him, worried all the way back to Goldendale, turned him out in the field with the ewes, and sweated through the 145 days of gestation. "He was an incredible buck," Theo had said with a laugh. "He put us on the map. We bought a buck we didn't want, and he did a hell of a job for us. That's how smart we are."

One of the results that lambing season was C/D 81-034 "Wilson" HH4834, a buck that took the yearling ram championship at the Portland International stock show in Portland, Oregon, then again at the Cow Palace stock show in San Francisco. The buck went on to sell fourth highest that year at the Columbia Nationals. A big-time commercial operation bought him for $2,700. "He weighed 275 pounds at seven months," Gwen recalls, still proud. "His only great fault, he was a little too open-faced, not as typey in the head as he might be." Since the sheep market today is for meat animals, not wool, growers look for stock like the Caldwell's winner that put weight on fast. The genetic trait for rapid weight gain has a 30 percent inheritance factor, which means that the lambs of the winner are likely to grow just as rapidly.

Before the turn of the century and up until synthetic textiles arrived with World War II, sheep were raised primarily for their wool. During shearing, millions of dollars would change hands in a matter of days in Shaniko, a high desert town in eastern Oregon once dubbed the "wool capital of the world." Shaniko is a ghost town today, and the center of the Oregon lamb industry, now a meat industry, has moved west to Roseburg. Today Oregon is the eighth-largest lamb producer in the nation.

Like other Columbia breeders, Gwen Caldwell selects for size, for sheep that can put on weight fast where the expensive cuts are found: long, square legs; flat, straight backs. "If you look at photos of a Columbia champion from twenty-five years ago," Gwen says, "you might not recognize it as the same sheep down in the barn." The old Columbia looks like a dwarf in comparison. "As a breeder," Gwen says, "I have to move toward an efficient lamb that .will make money for a butcher. That means greater muscle-to-bone ratio, less waste on the floor. We call that cutability, and a carcass is graded accordingly."

Butchers used to hang lamb in their cold lockers, but those days are gone. Like beef, most lamb is portion-controlled and neatly trimmed at the processing plant, and specific cuts are sold by the box. Lamb was once bred for a thick layer of fat on the back to keep the meat from drying when whole carcasses were shipped around the country. Now lamb hardly has any fat at all, only the thinnest covering.

Lamb today is lean, and lean meat is the direction the meat industry is headed in response to consumer demand. This isn't to say that lamb has achieved sudden popularity with American meat eaters. As a nation we eat about one-and-a-half pounds of lamb per capita a year. By contrast, we eat sixty to seventy pounds of pork and 120 pounds of beef.

Beef has the power of identity riding with it. We identify beef as the meat that made America. The mythology of the cowboy and the great cattle drives holds much greater power in the American unconscious than the image of a lonely sheepherder trailing thousands of sheep from summer pasture to winter grazing land. Beef cattle have come to stand for the independent spirit. It's hard to respect an animal like the sheep that doesn't need rounding up, but flocks from the day it is born. That's foreign to the American way, so lamb remains a coastal meat, a thing for ethnic enclaves in New York or Boston, San Francisco or Los Angeles, meat for Greeks and Jews and Lebanese and French, but not for Americans in Kansas City. In Wyoming and Montana, where so much of it is produced, lamb rarely appears on the family dinner table.

Fifty percent of the lamb eaten in America comes out of the high mountain West. Typically, the sheep go directly to market from mountain pastures, making for some of the most natural, flavorful meat available in America. By contrast, most beef cattle spend six months standing in their own manure in cramped feedlots, eating antibiotic-laced food to stay disease-free, to put on weight and to put marble fat into their muscle tissue. While beef today is far more lean than it was ten years ago, lamb still has less fat. Pound for pound the cholesterol levels in beef and lamb are the same. The difference is in the age of the butchered animal. Lamb is butchered young, well before marbling can occur. As American consumers look more for fat-free, hence lower cholesterol, flavorful red meat not likely to be tainted with drugs, they are sure to turn to lamb. The sheep industry today is growing the meat of America's future.

On his last day, Theo Caldwell drove a truckload of rams from Goldendale to the lamb processing plant in Ellensburg. Theo didn't linger. He unloaded his rams, then drove back to the Caldwell/Davis Farm, stopping only in Goldendale to vote in the state primary election. He found Gwen in the barn, and they chatted for a bit about the sheep and the prospects of the latest buck. It was getting close to breeding time. The ewes had been on an enhanced diet and would soon be spending a couple of weeks in the field with a teaser ram, a castrated buck who, in Gwen's words, "does all the love talk" to get the ewes interested in mating once the fully equipped buck is released in their midst to do his job.

Theo didn't complain of any discomfort. He just dropped like a sack of feed and was gone, leaving everyone who knew him to snatch at memories. He had lived a full life with a flawed heart. As it turned out, no examination would ever have spotted the problem. Had he been in an operating room, no surgeon could have saved him.

After the memorial, after everyone had returned home to Seattle or Portland, or their farms in the outlying countryside, Gwen Caldwell had to consider her flock and her future. She and Theo had been preparing for the San Francisco Cow Palace livestock show, but it was coming too soon, so in the end she let it pass. But she did make arrangements with a young woman in Goldendale to take the best ewes and yearling ram and lamb flock to the Portland International. The animals deserved a showing.

Meanwhile, Gwen got a man out from town to show her how to run the crawler, the small bulldozer Theo used instead of a tractor. She had never bothered to learn before; there had been no point. Now, she'd need a hired hand. There had always been too much work for one person. Her son Ben helped with the breeding that fall, and by late January the lambs were beginning to come, filling the barn with their bleating. One ewe died, leaving big twin orphans to bottle-feed. Another ewe had somehow managed to end up in the field with her brother, breeding a single lamb that was half the size it should have been. "We're lucky it didn't have two heads," Gwen said.

Louis Alcana, a Basque sheep breeder, visited Gwen as the nationals approached. They would be held in California, in Orland, and Columbia breeders from all over the country would bring their best animals to compete in the judging ring. Theo had always been the one to shear the chosen sheep prior to a show. It's a painstaking job called "cutting out," which creates a fleece silhouette that with just the right amount of time will grow out to show-ring perfection. This time Louis Alcana helped cut out the rams and the ewes. He particularly liked the ewe that had won so big at the Portland International. He thought she might have the national championship in her. In Louis Alcana's honor, they began calling C/D 85-127 "Louise."

As the months pass, so do Gwen's plans. Should she stay at the farm? Should she stay in sheep breeding? She considered the Peace Corps, where her knowledge of breeding techniques to improve livestock would be invaluable. And she has thought about building a small house on the land for a caretaker couple, and dealing with sheep breeding from a distance, from Seattle perhaps. She has also thought about disbanding her flock, selling off the stylish ladies and their young men, and turning the Caldwell/Davis Farm into a family country retreat. It is a big family and growing, though there don't seem to be any farmers in the ranks.

So she waits and she watches the land change from winter to spring. The chickens lay their eggs each morning. The horses need feed and love. The dogs will lay down their lives if only to be taken on the daily walk. The ewes watch with quizzical looks for the oat bucket to appear. And the young bucks, with their white fleecy muttonchop sideburns, huddle close together, looking for all the world like Gay Nineties freshman senators milling about in caucus. There is little time to ponder the future, and the Columbia Nationals are approaching. This could be the big year for the Caldwell/Davis Columbias. For Gwen Caldwell, too. She has some decisions to make. This time they are hers alone.

Note: C/D 85-127, also known as "Louise," was selected as the champion ewe at the 1987 Columbia National Show and Sale at

Orland, California. Eighty ewes from all over the country were shown, and seventy-two of them sold, Louise second highest at $1,500. She now lives and breeds somewhere in Ohio. A Caldwell/Davis yearling ram sold highest at the same show for $4,700 (he placed sixth in competition) and has moved to New York State. A ewe and ram were both champions at the Cow Palace show in San Francisco later in the year. It was the best season ever for Caldwell/Davis Columbias.

With winter coming on in 1987, Gwenyth Caldwell watched a cement crew pour the foundation of what will be the caretaker's house at the farm. A young couple, both local school teachers with kids, will be moving in.

Meat Temperature Guide

Today, we are eating meat rarer than we did twenty years ago; however, the meat thermometers have not changed their readings, so many roasts, sadly, are overcooked. Here is a current chart for easy reference.

Meat	Temperature
Poultry (chicken, turkey)	160°–170°
Lamb	130°–135° (medium rare)
	145°–150° (well done)
Pork	160°–170°
Beef	120°–125° (rare)
	125°–130° (medium rare)
	135°–140° (medium)
	140°–150° (well done)

Remember that the temperature will rise 5–7° after you remove the roast or the fowl from the oven.

Gwen Caldwell's Lamb Meat Loaf

Gwen Caldwell says, "I tend to make meat loaf the way I make bread: with whatever is on hand. The end result is good, fresh sandwich meat." Have the butcher use boned shoulder for the ground lamb. Packaged lamb patties available in many markets have too high a fat content and won't taste good. (Lamb is so much more tender than beef that a meat loaf made of ground lamb alone would crumble, which is why the ground beef is added.)

> *1 pound lean ground lamb*
> *1 pound lean ground beef*
> *1 cup fresh bread crumbs*
> *½ cup finely chopped onion*
> *1 egg, beaten*
> *½ cup ketchup*
> *1 teaspoon salt (seasoned salt if available)*
> *½ teaspoon freshly ground pepper*
> *Thyme (optional)*

Preheat the oven to 325°. Mix together all the ingredients, being careful not to overmix. If the bread crumbs are exceptionally dry, moisten them first with a little milk. Otherwise, adjust the moistness of the meat loaf with ketchup. Seasoned salt is nice to use. So is a little thyme.

Press meat loaf into a large oven-proof glass loaf pan, 8 x 3 x 4 inches. Bake in the oven for 1 hour. Remove from oven and let drain immediately. For the best results, let cool, remove from pan, wrap and refrigerate overnight.

Serves 6

DEFINING THE PACIFIC NORTHWEST STYLE

Medallions of Lamb with Pinot Noir and Hazelnut Sauce

Here, Greg Higgins, an inspired Northwest chef, uses the region's products to great advantage.

> *2½ pounds boneless lamb loins*
> *Flour for dredging*
> *Salt and pepper to taste*
> *2 ounces oil*
> *2 tablespoons minced shallots*
> *1 tablespoon minced garlic*
> *1 pint pinot noir*
> *2 tablespoons red wine vinegar*
> *¼ cup ground toasted hazelnuts (filberts)*
> *1 tablespoon coarse grained mustard*
> *3 ounces butter*
> *1 bunch spinach, cut* chiffonade *(see Note)*

Preheat the oven to 400°. Dredge the lamb loins in the flour and season with salt and pepper. Heat the oil in a medium sauté pan. When the pan is quite hot add the lamb loins and brown well on all sides. Remove the lamb and place in the oven. Sauté the shallots and garlic in the pan. Just as they begin to brown, add the pinot noir and vinegar, and reduce the heat to medium. Whisk in the nuts and mustard, and continue to reduce the liquid until it coats a spoon. Remove from the heat and add three ounces of butter.

Slice the lamb loins at a 45° angle to form 1-inch slices. Arrange over the spinach *chiffonade*. Whisk the butter into the pan, and glaze until smooth and glossy. Pour over the medallions.

NOTE: *Chiffonade* means finely shredded.

Serves 6

DEFINING THE PACIFIC NORTHWEST STYLE

Carré d'Agneau à la Provençale

What could be better than a restaurant in the center of Seattle's Pike Place Market that celebrates the spirit of French country cuisine? Susan Vanderbeek makes that spirit manifest in one delicious creation after another in the kitchen at Campagne.

> 2 "frenched" lamb racks to serve 4
> 4 tablespoons olive oil
> White wine
> 4 tablespoons compound butter (recipe below)
> 8 tablespoons veal glace (or twice that amount in stock,
>   or 4 tablespoons Madeira)
> Parsley, chopped

Preheat the oven to 500°. Sauté racks in olive oil in a pan on top of the stove. Brown on meaty side; turn. Place in the hot oven. Roast for 6 minutes, turn meat over in pan, and roast for 6 minutes more. Remove lamb from oven and keep warm.

Deglaze pan with a little white wine. Add compound butter, the veal glace (or stock or Madeira), and a little chopped parsley. Carve meat and place on warm plate. Pour sauce over top and serve.

Serves 4

Compound Butter for Lamb

> ¼ pound unsalted butter, softened
> 1 clove garlic, peeled and sliced
> ¼ cup Niçoise olives, pitted
> ½ small bunch basil (about 2 tablespoons julienned)
> 2 ounces sun-dried tomatoes, in oil
> Squeeze of lemon juice
> Salt and pepper

Process all ingredients in a food processor. Roll into a log and wrap in plastic. Refrigerate until ready to use.

Butterflied Leg of Lamb

The addition of coriander and ginger to the marinade gives the lamb a delicious middle-Eastern flavor. Serve with Couscous Salad, p. 219.

> *3 cloves garlic*
> *1½ teaspoons kosher salt*
> *1 teaspoon pepper*
> *1 teaspoon ground coriander*
> *½ teaspoon ground ginger*
> *2 teaspoons fresh rosemary, chopped*
> *2 teaspoons fresh thyme, chopped*
> *¼ cup olive oil*
> *2 tablespoons dry sherry*
> *4–5 pound boned and butterflied leg of lamb*

Crush garlic. Mix together with salt, pepper, coriander and ginger. Crumble rosemary in the palm of your hand and add to garlic mixture. Crush the thyme leaves between the palms of your hands and blend with the rest of the herbs. Add the olive oil and sherry.

Carefully trim as much fat and silver connective tissue as you can from the outside of the leg of lamb. Spread half of the marinade on one side of the meat and half on the other. Marinate for 4–6 hours (or overnight).

To cook, prepare your grill ahead of time so that you have a nice evenly-heated bed of coals. Grill the lamb 15–20 minutes on each side and serve immediately on a heated platter.

Serves 6–8

Roast Rack of Lamb

There couldn't be an easier or better dinner for two. The rack cooks perfectly every time. This method is for stoves that have a broiler inside the oven.

1 rack of standard domestic lamb (7 bones)—well trimmed of
  excess fat
Kosher salt and freshly ground pepper
1 teaspoon crushed rosemary

For broiling in the oven: Place the rack of lamb on your broiler pan. Sprinkle with salt, pepper and rosemary. Place the pan in the oven with the tops of the rack of lamb 8 inches from the source of heat. Close the oven door. Broil 8 to 10 minutes, until fat begins to burn slightly. Turn heat down to 325°, leaving oven door closed and cook 20 minutes longer.

If you don't have a broiler in your oven, here is a high-heat method for rack of lamb in gas ovens.

1 rack of lamb
Kosher salt and pepper
1 teaspoon crushed rosemary
4 tablespoons soft butter
1 teaspoon chopped parsley
2 teaspoons Dijon-style mustard

Preheat the oven to 425°. Sprinkle the rack with salt, pepper and rosemary. Roast in the oven for 25 minutes.

Mix butter, parsley and mustard together and brush over the lamb after removing from the oven.

Serve with oven-roasted potatoes and fresh spring asparagus.

Serves 2

Herbed Lamb Shanks

The shank part of the leg of lamb is delicious when cooked slowly with herbs, onion, garlic and orange peel. Ellensburg lamb is available throughout the Northwest and is my favorite.

> *4 lamb shanks*
> *4 cloves garlic, cut into slivers*
> *Kosher salt and freshly ground pepper*
> *Fresh rosemary*
> *½ yellow onion, cut into thin rings*
> *8 strips of orange peel, 1½- to 2-inches long, ½-inch wide*
> *(orange part only)*

Preheat the oven to 375°. Lay each lamb shank on a 12-inch square piece of brown paper or parchment. Make small incisions with the tip of a sharp knife and insert garlic slivers. Sprinkle with salt and pepper. Sprinkle with fresh rosemary to taste.

   Place a few rings of onion and two strips of peel on each shank. Fold the paper to seal tightly and place on a baking sheet. Bake in the oven for 1 hour. Unwrap and serve with new potatoes, fresh asparagus and mint sauce.

Serves 4

Perfect Leg of Lamb

This method of cooking a leg of lamb works on any standard sized leg of lamb, whether it's 5, 6 or 7 pounds, and it's delicious time after time. You don't even need to use a meat thermometer.

> *1 leg of lamb*
> *1 lemon, cut*
> *2 cloves garlic, cut into slivers*
> *Salt and pepper*
> *1 teaspoon each rosemary, thyme, marjoram*
> *2 tablespoons butter*
> *Flour–water mixture for gravy (4 tablespoons flour mixed with*
> *1 cup water)*

Preheat the oven to 425°. Always wash the leg of lamb. Pat dry. Trim away fat and silver. Rub the leg all over with the cut lemon. With the tip of a sharp knife, poke small slits and insert the garlic slivers. Place leg in roasting pan. Sprinkle with salt, pepper and herbs. Dot top of leg with butter.

Start roast in the oven at 425° for 15–20 minutes. Drop temperature to 325° and bake for 2 hours. Remove from oven and transfer to serving platter.

Pour off excess fat and on top of stove make the gravy, by stirring the flour–water mixture into the roasting pan until desired consistency is reached. Add the juices that have accumulated from the resting roast. Then carve the roast and serve. Fresh mint sauce goes well with this.

Serves 6–8

1, 2, 3 Irish Stew

The true flavor of an Irish stew is lost if carrots or turnips are added, or if it has too much liquid. There are really only three ingredients, plus liquid and seasonings.

> 1 pound yellow onion
> 2 pounds potatoes
> 3 pounds lamb stew meat
> 1 tablespoon chopped parsley
> 1 teaspoon thyme
> 2 teaspoons kosher salt
> 1 teaspoon freshly cracked pepper
> 2 cups water

Preheat the oven to 350°. Peel and slice the onion and potatoes. Trim any fat off the meat. Put a layer of potatoes in a pan, then herbs, then meat and finally the onion. Season each layer well and repeat this once more, finishing with a layer of potatoes. Pour in the water, cover with foil, and bake in the oven for 2 hours. Check after 1½ hours and add a little more liquid if the stew seems to be getting dry.

Season to taste with additional salt and pepper. Serve with soft white bread to dip in the gravy and hot tea with lemon.

Serves 6

Grilled Lamb Sirloin Steaks with Fresh Herb Crust

Ask your butcher to cut these steaks from the top of the leg. The crusty topping adds texture. These can be broiled entirely indoors but if first grilled over charcoal, they are superb. This is a specialty of Cutter's Bay House in Seattle.

> *1 tablespoon lemon juice*
> *½ cup olive oil*
> *2 cloves garlic, mashed*
> *2 teaspoons Dijon mustard*
> *6 8-ounce lamb sirloin steaks*
> *Kosher salt and freshly ground black pepper*
> *2 cups fresh bread crumbs*
> *¼ cup chopped parsley*
> *2 cloves garlic, minced*
> *1½ teaspoons fresh rosemary, chopped*
> *2 ounces melted butter*

Prepare a charcoal fire.

Mix together the lemon juice, olive oil, garlic and mustard. Marinate the lamb steaks in this mixture for ½ hour. Remove the steaks from the marinade and place on your grill. Sprinkle with salt and pepper. Brush with marinade while grilling.

Mix together bread crumbs, parsley, garlic, rosemary, and melted butter.

When lamb steaks are cooked just to medium, about 4–5 minutes on each side, remove from grill. Place on baking sheet. Top generously with bread crumb mixture and place under broiler for 1–2 minutes, until crumbs are crisp and golden.

Serves 6

Grilled Flank Steak

In the summertime in the Northwest, on nice sunny days, everyone moves outside. Barbecuing is a way of life through the season, and grilled flank steak is a favorite.

> *2-pound flank steak*
> *¼ cup salad oil*
> *¼ cup soy sauce*
> *3 tablespoons red wine vinegar*
> *2 tablespoons brown sugar*
> *1-inch piece of fresh ginger, sliced*
> *2 cloves garlic, sliced*
> *1 teaspoon sesame oil*
> *½ teaspoon red pepper flakes*
> *1 teaspoon toasted sesame seeds*
> *¼ cup chopped green onion*

Combine ingredients and marinate flank steak for 1–2 hours. Broil in the oven or grill, 5–10 minutes on each side. Slice across the grain. I like to serve the Peanut Sauce from the Bon-Bon Chicken recipe (p. 148).

Serves 4

Calves' Liver with Sautéed Walla Walla Sweet Onions and Peppered Bacon

Calves' liver is delicious cut in strips, floured and quickly sautéed. The peppery bacon and soft, sweet onions complement the liver. Wonderful served with crisp matchstick fries and steamed rhubarb chard, sprinkled with red wine vinegar.

> *1 pound Walla Walla sweet onions (substitute similar onions,*
> *   or, in winter, use yellow onions)*
> *4 tablespoons butter*
> *½ pound thick-sliced peppered bacon*
> *1½ pounds calves' liver*

Flour seasoned with salt and pepper
2 tablespoons oil
2 tablespoons red wine vinegar

Cut the onions in quarters and then slice thinly. Sauté in 2 table-spoons of butter until soft. Reserve. Cut bacon into ½-inch pieces and cook until crisp. Drain and save.

Cut the liver into 1½-inch strips. Pat gently with a paper towel. Shake in a paper bag with the seasoned flour to coat, then transfer to a wire strainer and toss gently to remove excess flour.

Heat the remaining 2 tablespoons of butter and oil in a large Teflon-coated frying pan over moderate heat and add floured strips of liver. Turn up heat and cook quickly, adding more oil and butter if necessary, to brown the meat all over. Add vinegar. Transfer to a warm serving platter. I like to grind a little freshly ground pepper over the liver just before topping with the onions and bacon.

Serves 4

Stuffed Flank Steak

I like flank steak stuffed or marinated and grilled. It's a good value, even though it's more expensive than it used to be.

¾ pound mild Italian sausage
½ cup chopped yellow onion
½ cup diced carrot
1 Granny Smith apple, peeled and chopped
2 cups seasoned bread stuffing
1 egg, lightly beaten
¼ cup chopped parsley
1 cup beef broth
2-pound flank steak (ask the butcher to butterfly it for you)
1 cup beef broth

Preheat the oven to 350°. Break sausage into small pieces and sauté in frying pan over medium heat. Transfer to bowl. Add onion and carrot to frying pan and sauté in drippings until soft. Stir in apple and cook for 1 minute longer. Add to sausage. Stir in bread stuff-ing, egg, parsley and beef broth.

Lay steak open and spread with sausage mixture, leaving ¼-inch border on all sides. Loosely roll steak lengthwise and secure at intervals with string. Place in roasting pan, seam side down. Pour in the beef broth and bake, covered, for 1½ hours. Let cool 10 minutes before slicing. Serve with Herb Sauce (p. 348).

Serves 6

DEFINING THE PACIFIC NORTHWEST STYLE

Venison Medallions with Gin and Thyme

This original preparation comes from Karl Beckley, the chef at Greenlake Grill, one of the outstanding restaurants where the regional style is evident.

> *18 2½-ounce venison medallions, cut from either the loin*
>   *or from a boned saddle of venison*
> *Olive oil*
> *18 whole shallot cloves*
> *½ cup Beefeater gin*
> *2½ cups rich brown veal stock*
> *8 stems of fresh thyme (use only the leaves)*
> *½ cup sour cream*
> *6 tablespoons butter*
> *Salt and pepper*

Brown the venison in olive oil over high heat and set aside. Add whole shallot cloves, reduce heat, and brown. Deglaze pan with gin, averting your face to avoid fumes. Add stock and thyme leaves, and reduce to ½–¾ cup liquid. Whip in sour cream. Over low heat, whip in butter, 1 tablespoon at a time. Add salt and pepper to taste.

Arrange 3 medallions and 3 shallots on each plate. Spoon on the sauce and serve.

Serves 6

DEFINING THE PACIFIC NORTHWEST STYLE

*Peppered Beef Tenderloin
with Apple–Onion Purée*

This is another presentation characteristic of Caprial Pence's cooking style at Fullers, in the Sheraton Hotel.

> Apple–Onion Purée:
> *4 red onions, chopped*
> *2 yellow onions, chopped*
> *3 tart apples (Granny Smith), chopped*
> *4 shallots, chopped*
> *2 garlic cloves, chopped*
> *¾ cup white wine*
> *½ cup brandy*
> *½ pound butter*
> *Salt and pepper to taste*
>
> *6 5-ounce tenderloin fillets*
> *Freshly cracked black pepper*
> *2 tablespoons vegetable oil*
> *Red apple slices and diced red onion for garnish*

Place the first 7 ingredients in a heavy saucepan. Simmer onions and apples for about 1 hour or until soft. Purée in blender or food processor. Return to saucepan on low heat and whisk in butter. Season with salt and pepper.

Roll tenderloins in cracked black pepper. Add oil to pan and heat. Add steaks and sauté to desired doneness. Place sauce on plates, then steaks on sauce. Garnish with red apple slices and diced red onion arranged around the steaks.

Serves 6

DEFINING THE PACIFIC NORTHWEST STYLE

Elk Stew with Cranberries and Horseradish

H. Stuart "Rip" Ripley is the talented sous chef at Greenlake Grill in Seattle. This is another of his creations.

3 pounds elk meat
1 cup red wine
1 thumb-sized piece fresh
 ginger, peeled and sliced thin
4 whole cloves
2 bay leaves
6–8 black peppercorns
1 healthy pinch of thyme
1 cup each celery, onion,
 and carrot, roughly diced

¼–⅓ cup balsamic or
 sherry vinegar
½ cup flour seasoned with
 salt and pepper
½ cup vegetable oil
1 cup veal or game stock
½ cup orange juice
1 pound (1 bag) cranberries
Freshly grated horseradish

Cut the elk meat into ¾-inch cubes. In a glass or stainless steel bowl, mix the red wine, ginger, cloves, bay leaves, peppercorns, thyme, celery, onion, carrot and vinegar. Add meat to a bowl and marinate overnight in refrigerator.

Remove meat from marinade (pat to remove excess moisture) and dust with flour seasoned with salt and pepper. Pour enough oil into a large skillet to coat the bottom and heat over high heat. Brown the meat in the oil; do not crowd the pan—it may be necessary to do this in batches. Add oil as needed. Remove the meat and set aside. Strain marinade, reserving liquid. Add the herbs and vegetables to the pan. Brown the vegetables, then add marinade with veal stock and orange juice to deglaze the pan. Reduce to about 2 cups liquid and strain to remove vegetables and herbs.

Return liquid to pan, add meat and cranberries, and simmer until cranberries pop and meat is tender. Add water as desired to adjust the thickness of the sauce.

Serve with grated fresh horseradish on the side.

Note: Venison, moose or caribou may be substituted for the elk.

Serves 6

DEFINING THE PACIFIC NORTHWEST STYLE

Tenderloin of Beef with Red Wine,
Walnuts and Oregon
Blue Cheese Butter

Karl Beckley, chef and owner of the Greenlake Grill in Seattle, was one of the first young chefs to create culinary excitement in the Pacific Northwest. He continues to set a pace and a standard few can match, mixing a grab bag of ethnic culinary tradition with his own farm–kitchen grounding.

> *2 cups red wine*
> *1½ cups veal stock*
> *4 small tomatoes, chopped*
> *2 bay leaves*
> *½ tablespoon thyme*
> *1 tablespoon peppercorns*
> *2 tablespoons shallots*
> *1 pound softened, unsalted butter, cut in pieces*
> *⅓ cup blue cheese*
> *½ cup walnuts, broken in pieces*
> *4 tenderloin of beef steaks*

Place wine, stock, tomatoes, herbs, peppercorns and shallots in a saucepan and bring to a boil. Reduce by half and strain into another saucepan. Return to a boil and reduce to ¼ cup. Cool.

Place butter, blue cheese and walnuts in a mixing bowl and begin to whip at low speed. Slowly add the reduced liquid to the butter while whipping. When the ingredients are incorporated, roll the mixture into a log in waxed paper, and refrigerate until serving.

Cook the steaks. Top each one with a slice of the compound butter and serve.

Serves 4

DEFINING THE PACIFIC NORTHWEST STYLE

Sautéed Medallions of Venison with Deep-Fried Garlic–Mushroom Cream

Though a relatively recent arrival to the Pacific Northwest by way of some of New York's finest restaurants and Spago in Los Angeles, Barbara Figueroa, chef at the Hunt Club in the small, elegant Sorrento Hotel in Seattle, matches the region's considerable array of produce and other foods with boundless skill and imagination.

1 2½-pound boneless
  saddle of venison
20 medium-sized fresh
  shiitake mushrooms
2 tablespoons butter

5 large cloves elephant garlic
⅓ cup half-and-half
3 eggs
Salt and pepper

Sauce:
1 cup black muscat wine
  (Quady's Elysium)
2 tablespoons balsamic
  vinegar
1 bay leaf
1 small sprig fresh thyme
2 shallots, peeled and
  chopped
1 juniper berry, crushed
3½ cups brown venison
  or veal stock, or ⅔ cup
  veal stock and ⅓ cup
  lamb stock

¼ cup sweet butter
Peanut oil
2 tablespoons butter
¼ cup venison or chicken stock
1 cup flour seasoned with salt
  and pepper
2 whole eggs, beaten
1 cup fine, dry bread crumbs
2 tablespoons pink peppercorns,
  coarsely ground

Preheat the oven to 325°. Cut venison into 12 medallions of equal size. Separate shiitake caps from stems. Wipe caps clean with a dry cloth. Cut 8 caps into thin strips, reserving the remaining 12. Sauté the strips in butter over moderate heat until the liquid has evaporated and the mushrooms are lightly browned. Set aside to cool.

Cut each clove of garlic into 4 pieces. Put in small saucepan and cover with cold water. Bring to a boil over moderate heat, then drain. Repeat this process until the garlic is soft. Puree garlic in a blender with the half-and-half and eggs.

Butter the inside of a loaf pan (about 8- x 4-inches). Scatter the sautéed mushrooms evenly over the bottom. Add the garlic puree. Cover pan with foil. Set in a larger pan and add hot water to a level 1 inch up the sides of the loaf pan. Cook in the oven until the mixture sets and a knife blade inserted near the center comes out clean. Allow to chill for several hours until thoroughly cooled.

In a small saucepan, make the sauce by combining black muscat wine, balsamic vinegar, bay leaf, thyme, shallots and juniper berry. Reduce liquid to about ¼ cup. Add venison stock and reduce again by about ⅔. Remove pan from heat and whisk in butter, a tablespoon at a time. Strain through a fine sieve and keep warm.

In a skillet over high heat, sauté venison medallions in enough butter and oil to cover pan, until rare. Remove from pan and keep warm. Deglaze pan with stock. Add reserved shiitake caps, cover, and braise over low heat, turning caps once, until cooked through (about 10 minutes).

Meanwhile, cut garlic–mushroom cream into 6 squares, carefully removing them from the loaf pan with a spatula. Dip each square in seasoned flour, then beaten eggs, then bread crumbs. Add oil to the level of 1 inch in a skillet; the oil should be quite hot. Fry the garlic–mushroom cream squares over medium-high flame until crisp. Drain on paper towels.

To serve, place a garlic–mushroom cream square on each of 6 plates, resting the two medallions against it. Arrange two shiitake caps on plate. Nap with sauce, sprinkle on pink peppercorns.

Serves 6

Beef Brisket with Chili–Beer Sauce

Brisket has always been my favorite cut of beef. This is an easy, flavorful way to cook it.

1 4- to 5-pound beef brisket
Flour
2 tablespoons salad oil
½ teaspoon salt and pepper
1 cup Chili Sauce
1 12-ounce can of beer
1 medium yellow onion, sliced into thin rings

Preheat the oven to 350°. Flour the meat lightly. Heat the oil in a heavy frying pan. Brown the meat on all sides. Sprinkle with salt and pepper. Transfer to an oven-proof baking dish.

Mix the chili sauce with the beer and pour over the brisket. Scatter onion rings over the top. Place a piece of waxed paper on top of meat. Cover and bake in the oven for 3 hours, or until meat is tender. Uncover and let rest for 10 minutes before serving.

Serves 6–8

Anita's Swedish Meatballs

Anita Myrfors is the best Swedish cook I know. She loves to cook and her kitchen is always filled with good things to eat. (Washington and Oregon have large communities of Scandinavian fishermen.)

¾ pound lean ground beef
¼ pound ground pork
1 slice white bread
1 cup heavy cream
1 egg
½ medium yellow onion, finely chopped and sautéed
1 teaspoon salt   ½ teaspoon allspice
¼ teaspoon white pepper   Butter for frying

Mix the beef and pork together. Soak the bread in the cream. Mix bread and cream with the ground meat. Stir in the egg, onion and seasonings.

Roll the meat mixture into small walnut-sized balls. Dip your hands into cold water now and then while rolling, so the meat won't stick to your fingers. Put the formed meatballs on a platter that you've rinsed with cold water.

Brown the butter until golden brown and nutty smelling. Fry the meatballs a few at a time, shaking the frying pan to make them roll around in the butter, browning evenly. After the meatballs are all browned, return them to the pan and cover them. Cook over low heat until finished cooking (about 5–10 minutes). (Another easy way is to bake them on a baking sheet at 350° for 10–15 minutes. Then sauté in a little butter to add flavor, and make drippings for gravy.) Transfer to a warm serving dish and make the gravy.

Gravy:	1 cup water
¼ cup flour	½- to ¾-cup cream

Sprinkle the flour into the frying pan. Stir in the water. Let cook, stirring with a whisk, until you have a nice velvety sauce. Mix in cream.

Serve with boiled new potatoes, lingonberry or cranberry preserves and pickles. *Väl bekomme!*

Serves 4

Bernie Manofsky's Cabbage Rolls

Stuffed cabbage leaves can be made any size. The smaller size is nice for a buffet or as an accompaniment to roast chicken; larger, they are substantial enough for a main course.

2 heads green cabbage
1 pound lean ground beef
½ pound lean ground pork
½ cup uncooked long-grain rice
½ onion, grated
1 clove garlic, minced
2 teaspoons salt
1 teaspoon pepper
1 large can tomato juice (46 ounces)
16 ounces of sauerkraut, homemade or fresh store-bought
1 to 2 pounds kielbasa (Polish sausage)

To prepare cabbage leaves: Cut deeply around core of cabbage. Steam or parboil cabbage until leaves are soft enough to be removed. Separate the leaves and cool on paper towels.

Combine beef, pork, rice, onion, garlic, salt, pepper and ½ cup of tomato juice. Mix well.

Place 3 tablespoons of meat mixture on stem end of cabbage leaf. Roll until leaf is wrapped around meat mixture. Tuck sides in by pushing excess leaf into mixture with index finger. Repeat until all meat mixture is used.

To cook: Preheat the oven to 350°. Place a layer of sauerkraut on bottom of roasting pan, next place a layer of cabbage rolls, placing them side by side with leaf end down. Continue layering. Pour in enough tomato juice to barely cover. Place kielbasa on top. Cover and bake in the oven for 1½ hours.

Serves 6–8

Roast Veal with Morels

A good choice for a spring dinner, when the morels are showing up in the woods and the markets. They are heavenly prepared this way. Serve this with fresh asparagus and oven-roasted potatoes.

> 1 3-pound veal shoulder roast, well-trimmed and tied
> 2 tablespoons butter
> 1½ cups chicken stock
> ½ pound fresh morels, brushed clean with a mushroom brush
> 1½ cups heavy cream
> Salt and pepper to taste
> Dash of nutmeg

Preheat the oven to 350°. Brown the roast slowly in a Dutch oven in the butter. Add the chicken stock. Remove from the heat. Lay a piece of waxed paper directly on top of the meat and then cover the pot. Bake in the oven for 2½ hours, or until the meat is tender.

Slice the morels and place in a sauté pan. Pour in the cream and simmer for 20 minutes, or until the cream has been absorbed by the mushrooms. Season with salt, pepper and nutmeg.

Remove roast from pan. Place on serving dish. Add ½ to 1 cup of the pan juices to the mushrooms, and heat and serve with the roast.

Serves 6

DEFINING THE PACIFIC NORTHWEST STYLE

The following two recipes are creations of Susan Vanderbeck.

> ### Rôti de Porc
> ### au Poivre
> ### Vert

2 1–1¼-pound pork tenderloins, exterior fat and silver
  removed
Salt and pepper
4 tablespoons olive oil
¼ cup water
2 tart cooking apples, peeled and thinly sliced
Sugar
Pinch of salt
White wine
3 tablespoons green peppercorns, in brine
1½ tablespoons chopped fresh sage
6 tablespoons veal glace (or 8 tablespoons chicken stock
  or light, fruity red wine)
6 tablespoons butter
Lemon juice

Preheat the oven to 500°. Salt and pepper the meat and brown in a sauté pan in the olive oil. Place in the oven, uncovered, for 6–10 minutes or just until done.

Remove meat from pan and keep warm. Place the pan on top of the stove; add water to pan. Add the slices of cooking apple, dust with sugar and a pinch of salt. Brown apple slices on both sides, caramelizing slightly. Deglaze the pan with a few tablespoonfuls of white wine. Add green peppercorns and chopped fresh sage. Add veal glace (or stock or red wine) and butter, some lemon juice, and additional salt and pepper if desired.

Carve meat, place on warm plate and pour sauce around it.

Serves 4

Rôti de Veau à L'Ail

2-pound piece of veal top sirloin, cleaned and cut into
    1½- x 4-inch chunks
6 tablespoons olive oil
1 head garlic, each clove peeled and halved
4 tablespoons white wine
⅓ cup veal glace (or 1 cup chicken stock, or 1 cup light,
    fruity red wine)
½ cup water
2 tablespoons julienned fresh basil
4 tablespoons butter
1 tablespoon lemon juice
Salt and pepper

Preheat the oven to 500°. Brown veal in olive oil in a sauté pan. When all pieces are browned, add garlic, white wine, veal glace (or stock or wine), and water. Cover pan and place in the oven. Braise for 6 to 10 minutes, depending on the thickness of the meat.

Pull the pan from the oven and keep warm. Add to the juices in the pan the basil, butter, lemon juice, and salt and pepper. Carve the 4-inch pieces into thin slices across the grain and arrange on warm plate while heating the sauce. Pour the sauce over and serve.

Serves 4

Baked Methow Valley Ham

Oregon and Washington produce some delicious bone-in smoked hams that need no soaking or precooking and require a shorter roasting period than the old-style cured hams. I like baked ham for Sunday dinner with old-fashioned baked beans, creamy coleslaw and pumpernickel bread.

1 6-pound half ham
1 teaspoon dry mustard
¼ teaspoon powdered cloves
1 cup brown sugar
4 tablespoons apple cider vinegar

Preheat the oven to 300°. Place ham, skin side up, on a rack in a shallow roasting pan. Do not add water. Do not cover. Bake for 20 minutes per pound at 300° (or until internal temperature reaches 155° to 160°). Remove ham from oven three-quarters of the way through baking, peel off rind, and with a sharp knife, score the surface of the fat.

Mix together the mustard, cloves, brown sugar and vinegar. Spread over ham. Return ham to oven for about ¾ hour until nicely browned and glazed.

Serves 8–10

Pork Loin Roast with Sautéed Apple Slices and Fresh Sauerkraut

---

Cooking a pork roast on a bed of sauerkraut keeps it moist; the garlic permeates the meat and gives it a wonderful flavor.

4-pound double pork loin roast, rolled and tied (2 loins tied
   together)
3–4 cloves fresh garlic
2 tablespoons salad oil
2 cups fresh sauerkraut, rinsed and drained
Kosher salt and freshly cracked pepper
1 cup apple cider
2–3 Granny Smith apples
3 tablespoons butter
2 tablespoons sugar

Preheat the oven to 350°. Poke holes 1-inch deep into the pork roast with the tip of a paring knife. Peel the garlic and cut into slivers. Insert the garlic slivers into the holes in the pork. Heat the oil in a large skillet over medium-high heat. Brown the roast on all sides. Spread sauerkraut in the bottom of a roasting pan, then place the browned roast on top. Insert meat thermometer. Sprinkle with salt and pepper. Bake in the oven for 1 hour. Add the cider. Continue cooking for 1 hour longer, or until roast reaches 165° internal temperature.

Toward the end of the roasting time, peel and slice the apples. Sauté in butter in a skillet. Sprinkle with sugar and just before serving put under the broiler to glaze. Remove the roast from the oven and let rest 10 minutes before slicing. Serve the apples as a side dish.

Serves 6–8

DEFINING THE PACIFIC NORTHWEST STYLE

There is no better French chef working in the Pacific Northwest than Dominique Place, chef and owner of Dominique's Place in Seattle. He is a master saucier and is at ease in the rarefied atmosphere of truly international cuisine. In winter, when local ingredients are few, he marries a delicate sauce of local quince with veal sweetbreads and kidneys. The recipe is elaborate and a challenge to any cook's skills, but demonstrates the lengths to which Place is willing to go for the perfect dish.

Le Petit Sauté de Ris et de Rognon de Veau à la Puree de Coing (Sautéed Veal Sweetbreads and Kidneys with a Quince Sauce)

3–4 sweetbreads from milk-fed veal calf only (no substitute—they must be white and round)
2–3 small kidneys from milk-fed veal calf

Braising Liquid:
1 small onion   *1 small carrot*

2 cloves garlic   1 ounce butter
1 cup white wine
Fresh thyme, rosemary, bay leaf—a little of each
1 cup veal or light beef bouillon
4 teaspoons whipping cream
Freshly cracked black pepper

Sauce:
2 quinces
4 tablespoons excellent red wine vinegar
1 cup dry white wine

Cooking oil   1½ cups whipping cream
                               1–2 ounces butter

Vinegar
White wine   Fresh herbs for garnish

Put sweetbreads in cold running water for 1 hour or so to eliminate all blood particles. With fingers, remove skin from kidneys.

To make *fond de braisage* (braising liquid): Peel and slice onion and carrot, and chop garlic. Simmer slowly in a deep skillet with butter. Add wine, herbs, bouillon, whipping cream, and pepper, and raise to a boil.

Immerse the sweetbreads and simmer for 7–8 minutes. Set the whole skillet to the side to cool. When sweetbreads are lukewarm, remove from the cooking liquid to a plate and cover with a towel or plastic wrap to keep them moist. Reserve the liquid.

To make the sauce: Cook sweetbread stock for a few minutes at high heat, then pass through a fine strainer. Return stock to skillet and reduce by half. Set aside.

Cut quinces in half, remove the center and pits, then slice thin. Put in a deep saucepan with the vinegar and reduce. Add wine and reduce a bit. Add the stock. Cook slowly until the quince are tender. Puree in a food processor, then pass through a fine strainer and set aside.

To sauté the meat: Peel skin from sweetbreads. Slice the sweetbreads and kidneys in nice round slices about ⅜-inch thick. The kidneys should have some fat in the center, which will melt when they are sautéed.

In a flat skillet heat cooking oil until smoking hot and sauté the kidneys first. Caramelize them on both sides, making sure they don't boil (they will if the pan is not hot enough). If they appear to be boiling, quickly remove to a plate and start over. Boiled kidneys become very tough and chewy. In another flat skillet, sauté sweetbreads in additional oil. When golden and crisp on both sides, remove and place on plate with kidneys.

To finish the sauce: Degrease both skillets and deglaze with a bit of vinegar, then white wine. Reduce and add cream. Then, scraping with a spatula, pour into a saucepan. Add quince base. Stirring with a whip, cook sauce slowly. Correct seasoning, skim, balance acidity and sweeteners. Turn fire off and whisk in butter. Make certain sauce is thick enough to coat the back of a spoon: not watery, but not as thick as gravy. It should shine. Pass through a fine sieve.

To assemble: Have 6 dinner plates ready. Place sauce in the middle of each plate, leaving at least ½-inch empty space—the frame—around it. Display kidneys and sweetbreads artistically. Place each plate in a very hot oven for 30 seconds. Remove, decorate with fresh herbs and serve.

Serves 6

Barbecued Pork Tenderloin

Another example of the way the Chinese community has added to the Northwest's food-style. This is a great appetizer.

> ¼ cup brown sugar
> ½ teaspoon salt
> 2 tablespoons hoisin sauce
> ¾ teaspoon Chinese 5-spice powder
> 1 clove garlic, minced
> 1 teaspoon grated fresh ginger
> ¼ cup white wine

2 tablespoons soy sauce
2½ pounds boneless pork tenderloin
Hot mustard
Toasted sesame seeds

Mix together the first 8 ingredients to make a marinade.

Cut the pork lengthwise into 2½- x 2- x 7-inch strips. Marinate the pork strips for at least 2 hours, or overnight in the refrigerator.

When ready to cook, make a charcoal fire and let it burn for 20 minutes. Separate coals, pushing half to the left and half to the right. Place pork strips on grill rack, exactly in the center. Close hood of barbecue and cook slowly with the coals always off to the side, not directly underneath.

Allow to cool. Cut into ¼-inch slices. Serve with hot mustard and toasted sesame seeds.

Yield: 8 appetizer servings

Homemade Italian Sausage

Donnie Vey has been in the meat business for 30 years. Every year he, his family and friends make fresh Italian sausage, which they then freeze.

If you are interested in making your own sausage, I would recommend looking into an electric stuffing machine. They are not too expensive and they make sausage-making fun, not a chore.

10 pounds pork butt (ask the butcher to grind twice as for chili
—be sure thyroid gland is removed)
5½ ounces salt
½ ounce crushed red pepper
1 ounce ground black pepper
¼ ounce granulated, dehydrated garlic
¾ ounce fennel seed
8 ounces red wine
Hog casing (soak in cold water—changing several times)

Mix the ground pork with the spices and wine. Cover with plastic wrap and refrigerate overnight.

Rinse hog casing well. Squeeze off excess water. Bunch a strip of casing all the way up on the stuffing nozzle. Tie a knot in the end and slowly start the machine stuffing. Don't overfill—leave a little slack, so you can twist or tie the links every 4 inches.

Lay sausages on baking sheet lined with a cotton dish towel. Let rest, uncovered, in the refrigerator overnight to allow the skin to dry out before freezing. Then put in freezer bags, wrap in foil and freeze.

Yield: Approximately 10 pounds of plump sausage links

Roast Turkey

This is the way James Beard taught us to roast a turkey without stuffing at Gearhart, Oregon, during one of his summer-session classes. The turkey is golden and moist. This is a great way to cook a turkey for sandwich meat.

> 1 11- to 13-pound turkey
> 1 lemon, cut
> ¼ pound butter, melted
> Salt and freshly ground black pepper

Preheat the oven to 400°. Wipe the interior of the turkey with paper towels to absorb excess juices. Rub the inside with the cut lemon, squeezing out the juice as you rub.

Place the bird on a rack in a shallow roasting pan. Brush completely with melted butter. Sprinkle with salt and lots of pepper. Turn the bird on its side and roast in the oven for ½ hour. Turn it onto the other side and roast for ½ hour more. Turn it breast side up and baste with the pan juices. Roast for another hour. Test for doneness by inserting a meat thermometer into the thigh joint. At 160° it's done. Take care not to overcook the turkey.

Serves 6

Boppo's Turkey Dressing

If you want to stuff the turkey, here is a wonderful dressing recipe that is 100 years old and was passed down by a grandfather to his granddaughters, with love. As he said, "After about 30 to 45 years, making dressing will come easy. Hope everything turns out 'A-OK' and you have a fine dinner. Will drink a toast to your success!"

> *1 large loaf white bread, about 3 days old*
> *Giblets and meat from turkey neck*
> *3–4 slices of bacon*
> *Onion*
> *Butter*
> *1 cup celery*
> *2 apples, peeled and cored*
> *Salt and pepper to taste*
> *20 or more almond nut meats, ground*
> *2 eggs, beaten*

Tear loaf of bread into small cubes the night before you make your dressing. Place the cubes in a large pan and leave uncovered to dry overnight. That same night cook the neck, gizzard, heart and liver. When cool enough to handle, remove neck meat from bone and remove gristle and inside lining from gizzard. Save the cooking juices for dressing.

Dice bacon into small squares and fry until slightly crisp.

Run neck meat and giblets through meat grinder and add to bacon; stir until well mixed with bacon. Set aside on a plate to cool.

The next step is somewhat messy. Finely chop or grind the onion. Then fry it slowly in enough butter to avoid burning until it starts to brown. Grind the celery and add to onion. Grind apples and add to onion–celery mixture. Cook on low heat for 2 to 3 minutes. Remove from pan and set aside to cool.

While ingredients are cooling, sprinkle the bread cubes with salt and pepper and mix with hands. Mix in ground nuts, and then the ground meat.

Add the onion, celery and apple mixture to the bread mixture, a little at a time. Taste for seasoning.

If dressing seems dry, add sparingly some of the reserved cooking juices from the meats by dipping fingers into liquid and stirring into dressing. Add the eggs the same way, being careful not to let the dressing get too soggy.

Rub a little salt into the rib cage and breast of the bird.

Spoon the dressing into the cavity, but do not pack it in too firmly.

Yield: Dressing for an 11- to 13-pound turkey

DEFINING THE PACIFIC NORTHWEST STYLE

Karl's Boar

This is from Greenlake Grill's talented chef, Karl Beckley, who likes the assertive flavorings to bring out the rich boar flavor.

1 boar hindquarter, boned and cut into ¾-inch cubes
Flour
Chili powder
Olive oil
16 whole boiling onions
24 green French olives
3 cups red wine
3 cups veal stock
4 bay leaves
Cumin
Salt and pepper to taste

Dust the cubes of the boar hindquarter with flour and chili powder, then sauté in olive oil, in a large pan over high heat, until browned. Add the boiling onions and continue to sauté until they take on some color, then add the olives. Deglaze the pan with red wine. Add veal stock and bring to a full, rolling boil. Add bay leaves. Then reduce to a simmer.

Let boar simmer for a couple of hours or more until tender. Add a sprinkling of cumin, and salt and pepper to taste. The liquid will reduce to a thick, glossy sauce.

Serves 8

Grilled Elk Chops
Thanks-to-Jim

Mark Manley is known for the boldly flavored dishes he turns out of his kitchen at the Union Bay Café, an unpretentious neighborhood restaurant in Seattle. Hunter/naturalist Jim Erickson was kind enough to provide the elk chops, which are about the size of an average individual steak. The meat has a flavor closer to beef than venison, so this sauce will work just as well with grilled steak.

4 elk chops

Marinade:
1 shallot, sliced
1 clove garlic, peeled and slightly crushed
6 juniper berries, slightly crushed
1 teaspoon black peppercorns, crushed and chopped

1 tablespoon German mustard
⅓ cup balsamic vinegar
½ cup port
¼ cup raisins
1 teaspoon green peppercorns, crushed

Sauce:
1 teaspoon chopped shallot
1 tablespoon butter
½ pound morels, washed (they can be sandy) and halved

⅓ cup port
1 cup veal stock
½ teaspoon fresh sage, coarsely chopped

Mix together marinade ingredients in a shallow glass or stainless steel bowl, or in a deep dish. Add the elk chops and place in the refrigerator for several hours. Turn chops several times.

To prepare the sauce, sauté the chopped shallot in butter. Add morels and sauté for a moment, then add the port and veal stock and slowly reduce liquid to a thick consistency, making sure the morels have cooked through. Add the sage.

Meanwhile, remove the chops from the marinade and lightly season them with salt and pepper. Either grill them over charcoal or broil them. Keep in mind that elk is lean, three minutes on each side will probably ensure rare meat.

Serve chops on warm plates, with sauce spooned over.

Serves 4

Lynn's Baked Chicken Dijon

This is an easy dish to prepare ahead of time and serve for a dinner party.

> *4 ounces butter*
> *3 tablespoons Dijon mustard*
> *1 clove garlic, minced*
> *⅓ cup minced parsley*
> *1 cup freshly grated Parmesan cheese*
> *2 cups fresh soft bread crumbs*
> *6 half chicken breasts, skinned and boned, lightly pounded to*
> * flatten slightly*

Preheat the oven to 350°. Melt butter in small saucepan. Blend in mustard and garlic, remove from heat, and stir until mustard binds with butter and starts to thicken. Hold away from the heat.

Mix parsley, Parmesan cheese and crumbs, blending well.

Dip chicken breasts in butter mixture, coating all surfaces, then in crumb mixture, patting crumbs into the chicken to coat well. Place in shallow baking dish.

Chicken may be refrigerated at this point for several hours, covered with plastic wrap and aluminum foil. Remove chicken from refrigerator ½ hour before preparing.

Bake in the oven for 25 to 30 minutes, until golden brown.

Serves 6

Bon-Bon Chicken

Grilled chicken breasts served with spicy peanut sauce for dipping are a favorite at our house. I serve a basket of fresh vegetables for dipping in the sauce along with the chicken. It seems that today, everyone is enjoying finger food. This fits right in.

> *6 half chicken breasts, boned and skinned and lightly flattened*
> *so that they are the same thickness all the way across*

Marinade:
4 tablespoons soy sauce
1 tablespoon sugar
1 teaspoon sesame oil
1 clove garlic, minced
1 small piece of fresh ginger, sliced

Peanut Sauce:
3 tablespoons peanut butter
¼ cup hot chicken stock
2 tablespoons soy sauce
1 teaspoon sugar
1 teaspoon sesame oil
1 teaspoon chili oil
2 teaspoons rice vinegar
2 cloves garlic, minced
1 teaspoon grated ginger root
¼ cup chopped green onion

Mix together marinade ingredients. Marinate chicken at room temperature for 30 minutes. Prepare dipping sauce. Place chicken on charcoal grill and cook, turning once, for 5–6 minutes. Remove and serve with dipping sauce.

Serves 6

Gretchen's Roast Chicken with Walla Walla Sweet Onions

Walla Walla Sweet Onions are exceptionally sweet, large onions that have too short of a summer season. The Walla Walla Sweet Onions are practically legendary in the Pacific Northwest. "You can eat them like an apple," many claim. My father always made onion sandwiches with them. I slice them, sauté them in a little butter and keep them in freezer bags, so we can enjoy them year-round.

3 Walla Walla Sweet Onions, about 1½ pounds (can
substitute Vidalia)
2 chickens, 2½- to 3 pounds each
¼ cup melted butter
¾ cup white wine
Salt and pepper to taste

Preheat the oven to 400°. Cut onions in quarters, then slice thinly. Stuff the inside of each chicken with some of the sliced onions. Sprinkle the remaining onions in an 11- x 13-inch baking pan, forming a bed for the chickens. Place the chickens on the onions and brush with melted butter. Bake in the oven for 50 minutes.

Remove the chickens to a warm serving dish. Pour juices and the browned onions into a saucepan. Add wine and cook quickly over high heat for 5 minutes. Season to taste with salt and pepper. Cut the chicken into serving pieces and pour the sauce over them.

In the summertime, I like to roast a chicken the Italian way: Slice a lemon and place it inside the cavity of the chicken, brush with melted butter and roast at 400° for 50 minutes. Serve with two or three summer salads, crusty bread, and fresh berries and cream for dessert.

Serves 6

DEFINING THE PACIFIC NORTHWEST STYLE

Honey and Chili Roasted Duck

2 cups pinot gris or other dry white wine
1 cup honey
Juice of 2 lemons
2 tablespoons Dijon mustard
1 tablespoon Chinese chili paste (available at Oriental grocers)
1 4½- to 5-pound duck
Salt and pepper
1 large onion, diced
3 stalks celery, diced
1 carrot, diced
1 tablespoon cornstarch mixed with 2 tablespoons orange juice

Preheat the oven to 450°. In a mixing bowl combine the pinot gris, honey, lemon juice, mustard, and chili paste. Season the cavity of the duck with salt and pepper. Place atop the mixed

chopped vegetables and giblets in a roasting pan. Roast at 450°
for the first 20 minutes. Baste frequently (every 7–10 minutes). After 20 minutes, lower the oven temperature to 400°
and continue to baste the duck every 10 minutes. After half an
hour, prick the duck at the thigh to test for doneness. The
juices should run from pink to clear. Remove from the oven.
Place the duck on a serving platter and keep in a warm place.
Strain the pan juices into a saucepan. Bring to a simmer and
thicken with the cornstarch and orange juice mixture. Season
to taste with salt and pepper. Serve the sauce on the side with
the duck.

Serves 4–6

Dan Block's Braised Rabbit

This is such a pleasant way to serve rabbit, because the meat is
removed from the bone. It is delicious served with broiled polenta
or wide egg noodles.

Serves 6

> 2 ounces salt pork, diced
> ½ cup olive oil
> 1 cup sliced onion
> 3 carrots, peeled and sliced
> 1 tablespoon parsley, chopped
> 2 cloves garlic, chopped
> 1 teaspoon thyme
> 1 teaspoon marjoram
> 1 tablespoon fresh chervil or 1 teaspoon dried
> 1 bay leaf
> 1 teaspoon kosher salt
> 1 bottle red wine
> 5 pounds rabbit, cut into pieces
> 5 cups chicken stock
> 1 28-ounce can peeled and chopped tomatoes
> ½ pound mushrooms, sliced
> 2 tablespoons butter

Preheat the oven to 375°. Simmer the pork in boiling water for 10 minutes. Drain and refresh under cold water. Pat dry.

Heat olive oil in large heavy skillet, add salt pork and cook for a few minutes over medium heat. Add vegetables and sauté for 10 minutes. Add parsley, herbs and salt, and continue cooking for 5 minutes. Add wine and bring to a boil. Boil for several minutes. (This prevents any noticeable alcohol flavor.)

Place rabbit in Dutch oven or roasting pan. Pour in the wine mixture, chicken stock and tomatoes. Place waxed paper directly on top of rabbit, cover and bake for 1½ hours. Remove from oven and let it cool so that it can be handled. Remove meat from bones and reserve. Return bones to roasting pan and simmer on top of stove for 30 minutes to reduce stock. Strain the stock, pressing the liquid from the vegetables with the back of a wooden spoon. De-grease the stock. Lightly thicken the stock with a cooked roux and simmer over low heat for 10 minutes. Add rabbit meat. Sauté mushrooms in butter and add to rabbit.

Serves 6

DEFINING THE PACIFIC NORTHWEST STYLE

Roast Rabbit with Garlic and Roasted Peppers

The recipe for this pungent dish also comes from Karl Beckley.

> *2 young rabbits*
> *2 tablespoons olive oil*
> *1 head of garlic, peeled, the cloves left whole*
> *1 cup dry vermouth*
> *1½ cups rabbit or veal stock*
> *2 red peppers, roasted, peeled and sliced in ½-inch strips*
> *¼ pound unsalted butter, cut into pieces*

Preheat oven to 350°. Remove hind legs from rabbit carcasses and bone as you would a chicken leg with thigh attached. To remove loins, first cut away side flaps from back to front. Place rabbit on its back, then inside each body cavity run the tip of a knife down either side of spine from rib cage to hind legs. Turn rabbit over and cut loins away from spine by working the tip of a knife from back to front up either side of the spine. The loins should come away in one piece. If the kidneys are still attached, then they too will come away with the loins and should be left as is for this recipe. Use the carcasses and the bones from the hind legs for a rabbit stock.

In a large sauté pan brown the rabbit on both sides in the olive oil. Remove rabbit to a small roasting pan. Quickly brown garlic cloves in sauté pan, then deglaze pan with vermouth, bringing it to a boil. Add stock and return to a boil. Reduce liquid to ⅓ cup. Add peppers.

While sauce is reducing, place rabbit in oven for no longer than 8 minutes. When the sauce has reduced sufficiently, whisk in butter, 1 piece at a time. Arrange rabbit on plates, with 1 loin and 1 leg for each person, and pour the sauce over.

Serves 4

DEFINING THE PACIFIC NORTHWEST STYLE

Jeune Lapereau Sauté aux Myrtilles (Sautéed Young Rabbit with a Blueberry Sauce)

This is another specialty by Dominique Place.

> 2 young rabbits, about 2 pounds each
> Cooking oil
> 2 onions, coarsely diced
> 1 carrot, chopped
> 4 cloves garlic, chopped
> 1 plus ½ cups excellent wine vinegar
> 3 cups dry white wine
> 2 cups blueberries, fresh or frozen
> 1 cup raspberries, fresh or frozen
> 1 teaspoon Dijon mustard
> A pinch each of fresh rosemary, bay leaf and thyme
> Freshly cracked or ground black pepper
> 4 cups beef or veal bouillon
> Salt and pepper

To make the stock: Bone each rabbit by cutting hind legs from carcass at the joints, and cutting forelegs from carcass right under the shoulder blade. Leave forelegs intact. Bone out hip and thigh of rear legs, leaving shank intact. Carefully remove loins from backbone by running tip of sharp knife in parallel lines down either side of backbone, then follow vertebrae and ribs with knife tip, working the meat away from the bones. Refrigerate meat. Chop all bones into small pieces.

Heat a little cooking oil in a large, deep skillet and sauté rabbit bones until they turn a caramel brown. Add onions, carrot and garlic, and sauté until they have taken on color, too —but don't burn. Remove excess grease from the skillet.

Deglaze skillet with 1 cup of wine vinegar and reduce while stirring to a thick syrup. Add 2 cups of wine, 1 cup of blueberries, raspberries, mustard, herbs, and pepper, and cook down for a few minutes. Then add beef or veal bouillon. Cook stock slowly for 1½ hours, being sure to skim surface as often as necessary. Pass the stock through a fine strainer, being sure to push the blueberries through. You should have 3 cups of stock. Set aside.

To cook the rabbit: Preheat the oven to 425°. Heat cooking oil in a large, flat skillet and sauté rabbit pieces until they develop a nice rich golden color. Season with salt and pepper. Place pan in the oven for 7 to 8 minutes, then remove loins to a plate. Finish cooking legs and shoulders for 12 to 15 minutes, being careful not to overcook. Keep the meat moist, almost pink. Remove to plate with loins and keep hot.

To make the sauce: Deglaze rabbit skillet with ½ cup vinegar, reduce, then add 1 cup of wine and reduce a bit. Transfer to a saucepan. Add second cup of blueberries and the stock, and slowly cook for 5 to 10 minutes, skimming frequently.

To assemble: Have 6 dinner plates ready. Correct seasoning, balancing sweetness and acidity. Pile rabbit meat like a dome in the center of each plate and coat with the sauce. Place in a very hot oven for 30 seconds before serving.

Serves 6

DEFINING THE PACIFIC NORTHWEST STYLE

Charbroiled Curried Quail with Spicy Noodles

Chef Tom Douglas at Café Sport, in the Pike Place Market, works much fresh game into his menu. Quail are available in many markets in Seattle. They are moist and tender cooked this way, and the spicy noodles make a good accompaniment.

8 quail
6 ounces canned unsweetened coconut milk (available at specialty food stores)
2 tablespoons Thai curry paste (hot yellow variety)
10 grinds coarse black pepper
4 cloves garlic, mashed

Split the quail in half and remove the backbone. Mix together the rest of the ingredients and marinate overnight in the refrigerator.

Spicy Noodles:
3 tablespoons peanut butter
2 tablespoons water
2 tablespoons soy sauce
3 tablespoons well-stirred tahini
1½ tablespoons soy oil
1½ tablespoons Oriental sesame oil
1½ tablespoons dry sherry
1½ tablespoons rice vinegar
2 tablespoons honey
¾ teaspoon minced garlic
¾ teaspoon crushed red pepper flakes
¾ teaspoon grated ginger root
8 ounces Chinese egg noodles
¼ cup chopped green onion

In a bowl stir together the peanut butter and water. Add the soy sauce, tahini, soy oil, sesame oil, sherry, rice vinegar, honey, garlic, red pepper flakes and ginger root, whisking the mixture well after each addition. Chill covered.

Cook the egg noodles according to instructions on the package, then rinse under cold water. Drain well and chill, covered.

Mix noodles and sauce together and sprinkle with green onion just before you are ready to grill quail. Grill the quail over medium-hot coals for 3 minutes, turn it over and grill for 2 minutes more.

Serve the quail with the spicy cold noodles—a great contrast.

Note: You can use 4 chicken breasts if you can't get quail.

Serves 4

The rise of Marianne Zdobysz, chef at the Queen City Grill in Seattle, has been steady and strong. She cooks in a way that cuts right through to the essential flavor of the dish, the truth of which can be found in her recipes for grilled quail, crab bisque, and salad of sweetbreads.

Grilled Quail on Seasonal Greens with a Calamata Olive Vinaigrette

1 cup olive oil
¼ cup white wine
1 tablespoon fresh rosemary, chopped
1 tablespoon shallots, chopped
4 quail (have your butcher bone them)

Combine the olive oil, wine, rosemary, and shallots. Place the quail, skin side down, in a shallow baking dish and pour in the marinade. Set aside at room temperature to marinate for 2 hours.

Calamata Olive Vinaigrette:
¼ cup Calamata olives
⅛ cup sherry vinegar
Salt and pepper
¾ cup olive oil

Seasonal greens: Bibb lettuce, radicchio, watercress, endive
¼ red pepper, julienned

Pit and coarsely chop olives in a bowl. Combine vinegar and salt and pepper to taste. Whisk in oil and add olives.

Remove quail from marinade. Grill, skin side down, for 4 minutes. Turn and grill for 4 minutes longer. Quail could also be quickly sautéed over high heat in a heavy-duty pan with two tablespoons oil, but the grilled quality will be lost.

Toss greens in vinaigrette and place on plate. Place quail on greens and garnish with julienne of red pepper.

Serves 2–4

Slow-baked Pheasant with Sweet Onions and Chanterelles

In the fall in the Pacific Northwest many a young man's fancy turns to bird hunting: pheasant, quail, ducks, geese. If you are fortunate to have a hunter in your family, you can enjoy the bounty of a successful hunt.

In this recipe, the slow cooking makes the pheasant fall off the bone, and the sweet flavor of the onions gives a rich savor to the dish.

> 2 tablespoons olive oil
> 1¾ bars butter
> 3 pheasants, cut into pieces and lightly floured
> 1 quart red wine
> 4 tablespoons flour
> 1 tablespoon sugar
> 2 cups sliced yellow onion
> ½ pound sliced chanterelles

Preheat the oven to 350°. Heat olive oil and 2 tablespoons of the butter together and sauté pheasant pieces until browned all over. Transfer to a baking dish.

Pour the red wine into a saucepan and bring to a boil. Boil for several minutes to remove any harsh alcohol flavor.

Mix 4 tablespoons butter and flour together until well blended. Stir into boiling wine in bits, turn heat down and stir to thicken. Pour over pheasant and place a piece of waxed paper directly on top. Bake in the oven for 2 hours.

Right before the pheasant has been baking for an hour, melt 4 tablespoons butter, and add sugar and onion. Cook onion over low heat until soft. Add to the pheasant. Cover with waxed paper and continue baking.

Melt the remaining 4 tablespoons butter in a 10-inch skillet and add sliced chanterelles. Turn up heat and cook very quickly. Pour over baked pheasant and serve.

Note: It's important to cook chanterelles in a large, open frying pan as quickly as possible; otherwise they "stew" in their own juices.

Serves 6

DEFINING THE PACIFIC NORTHWEST STYLE

> ## *Breast of Pheasant and Braised Lemons with Walla Walla Sweet Onions in Lemon Thyme Cream Sauce*

This is another specialty of Caprial Pence's, of Fullers in the Sheraton Hotel.

> *6 whole pheasants, 3–4 pounds each (have your butcher*
> *remove the breasts, which will be sautéed later, and*
> *leave them whole; reserve carcasses for stock)*
> *6 carrots, coarsely chopped*
> *6 stalks celery, coarsely chopped*
> *4 onions, coarsely chopped*
> *3 shallots, chopped*
> *2 cloves garlic, chopped*
> *1 bay leaf*
> *Any fresh herb sprigs to taste*

Preheat the oven to 450°–500°. Brown the pheasant carcasses in the oven for 45 minutes or until golden brown. Place with all the other ingredients in a heavy stockpot, cover with water, and simmer 4 to 6 hours, or until stock has good flavor. Strain and reserve.

> Lemon Thyme Cream Sauce:
> *½ cup white wine*
> *½ cup sherry*
> *1 cup pheasant stock (freeze the rest)*
> *2 shallots, chopped*
> *1 clove garlic*
> *2 cups cream*
> *2 tablespoons chopped lemon thyme (substitute with*
> *regular thyme and the juice of ½ lemon)*
> *Salt and pepper to taste*

In a heavy saucepan reduce white wine and sherry to about ½ cup. Add stock, shallots, garlic, and reduce again to about ½ cup, then add cream and simmer. When cream starts to thicken, add half the lemon thyme and cook for 10 to 15 minutes. Strain, season with salt and pepper, and add remaining lemon thyme.

> Braised Lemons with Walla Walla Onions:
> *2 lemons*
> *4 Walla Walla sweet onions*
> *¼ cup butter*
> *¾ cup white wine*
> *1 teaspoon freshly cracked black pepper*

Preheat the oven to 350°. Slice lemons and onions very thin. Place in heavy saucepan with butter, wine, and pepper. Braise in the oven for 20 minutes. Set aside.

To assemble: Have 6 dinner plates ready. Quickly sauté whole pheasant breasts in a heavy-duty pan over high heat with 2 tablespoons of oil until done (you can also broil them). Pour a pool of the cream sauce into the center of each plate. Then spoon some lemon–onion mixture over the sauce. Slice the pheasant breasts and arrange around the mixture. Garnish with fresh currants, if desired, and thyme.

Serves 6

VEGETABLES

I suspect Peter Chan plants two vegetable gardens each year, the one in his backyard that attracts a thousand visitors each summer, and one in his mind. The one in his backyard takes full advantage of the maritime climate of Gresham, Oregon, a bedroom suburb of Portland. There the visitor finds several kinds of lettuce, Blue Lake beans, sugar snap peas, head cabbage, carrots, spinach, Swiss chard, scallions, garlic, onions, leeks, zucchini, rhubarb, cucumbers, tomatoes, peppers, and kohlrabi, all growing as though they anticipate the arrival of a professional photographer. There too the visitor might notice bok choy, edible chrysanthemum, Chinese broccoli, winter melon, and pungent greens from the Chinese mustard family. This is where the garden in the backyard and the garden in Peter Chan's mind overlap. If he could have his way, Peter Chan would love to grow and eat any number of vegetables from the land around his native Canton. But he is the first to realize this is not possible.

"It's semi-tropical there, like the South Pacific," Chan says, his hands making waves break on the table and run up on sandy beaches. "In Canton you never see snow in all your life. In fact, there is only one word for both snow and ice." Peter Chan left Canton in the early 1960s and joined his wife Sylvia and three sons in Hong Kong. In 1967 the family moved to Oregon.

In China, Chan had been a plant pathologist, first working with farmers in the provinces like a county agent, then teaching at the university in Canton where the agriculture department maintained a small experimental farm. "You bring a student to the field," Chan says, turning his kitchen table into cropland with a sweep or two of his hands, "they will ask you a hundred questions. And you have to know. The Chinese teacher is not allowed to say he doesn't know, not like here where they have other students answer. You say, 'I'm not sure, but I will answer exactly tomorrow.' So even as a teacher I had to study hard." In Portland, Chan works at Portland State University supervising the greenhouses and the biology labs.

He does some lecuturing each term, but his real audience is made up of gardeners and landscapers. He has changed from the county agent advising entire Chinese communes on pest control to the suburban neighbor demonstrating just what can be done in an average American backyard.

Peter Chan is a short, balding man whose cheerful enthusiasm makes him appear much younger than his fifty-seven years. When he stands in his yard he seems to be bouncing gently on his toes, even though both feet are flat on the lawn. His smile is an easy thing that erupts across his face, and his laugh can be surprisingly deep and thorough. He involves his entire body in the act of communicating, almost miming his message. His hands are in constant motion while he speaks, but so too are his arms and his shoulders. Peter Chan literally leans in to a conversation.

There is no concentrated Chinese community in Portland, like the ones in Seattle or Vancouver, British Columbia, where the Chinese enclaves are almost as old as the cities. Peter Chan says his is the only Chinese family he knows of for miles around. His neighborhood is made up of tract homes all built on cleared land at the same time. It is the kind of neighborhood where families move in and out and rarely settle. Unlike most of his neighbors, Peter Chan has lived in the same house for seventeen years.

When he and Sylvia and the boys broke ground for a garden in the backyard in 1970 the land was high with weeds and cheat grass, and the soil was as rocky as a creek bottom. Five years later Peter Chan won *Sunset* magazine's gardening contest. Of 1,400 gardeners in thirteen western states, Peter Chan's garden was selected as the best. "In five years the garden was established and normal," Chan says, "and I thought I should extend this technique and show more people. That's why we entered the contest." One admirer was Garden Way Publishing, and Chan was soon busy writing what would become *Better Vegetable Gardens the Chinese Way; Peter Chan's Raised-Bed System*. The first 20,000 copies sold out in five weeks. The next 30,000 copies sold shortly thereafter. Since its initial publication in 1977, Chan's book has sold 70,000 copies and has recently been translated into German. And the visitors come to visit, a thousand a summer since 1975, sometimes as many as 200 on a single Saturday.

Peter Chan lays no claims to his gardening system. He simply observed what his American neighbors were doing around him, realized it didn't work, and fell back on a Chinese system of raised-bed vegetable gardening that produces the maximum yield in minimum space, an important issue in the Chan family when three growing boys lived at home. The system had been perfected over a couple of thousand years in China, where every scrap of arable land is under some kind of cultivation to feed the enormous population. "Other Chinese gardeners look at what I'm doing," Chan explains, "and they recognize it from growing up in the same place I did." Chan's success has been his ability to reduce the lessons of the Chinese farmer to the scale of the backyard garden. His teaching instincts have led him to spread his gospel.

When Chan arrived in Portland he realized that if he was going to eat Chinese vegetables he was going to have to grow them. There were canned items and dried items and some leaf vegetables available in a few stores, but not out in Gresham, and really not to any extent in Portland. The big change in the last fifteen years has been the wide availability of good, fresh Asian vegetables. Bok choy is a normal sight in Pacific Northwest markets, and bean sprouts are as common as potatoes. Crops that once grew only in southern China are now being produced in and shipped out of Hawaii and California and Mexico. "We can get flat pea pods almost all year now," Chan says. But in the early years, Chan and his family had to face up to new conditions. "We had to change ourselves to meet the new circumstances. Our style had to change."

The Chans found themselves exploring the many possibilities of lettuce, a green they cook more often than eat raw. "Once in a while we grill a steak," Chan says, breaking into a rolling laugh as though he's telling a joke on himself, "so we eat salad to make ourselves more like Western people." The Chans developed a taste for head cabbage, like Golden Acre, and continue to plant it even though seeds for some Chinese cabbage varieties are now readily available. In China, Chan points out, there are hundreds of kinds of cabbage and bok choy. "There are so many people you need big producing vegetables like the *brassicas*. Big quantities fast. It's not like asparagus, you know, waiting a whole year for a few pieces." Members of the *brassica* genus, such as cabbage, cauliflower, broccoli, brussels sprouts, the kales and turnips, grow well in the Pacific Northwest climate, almost year-round, particularly when raised beds are employed.

Chan's beds are twenty-five feet long and four feet wide. There are ten of them, five on either side of a wide path made of the rock removed from the soil. Narrow paths separate the beds, so access to the crops is possible from either side. In late fall Chan turns the beds, adding compost. Any weeds that may have started in fall are thus uprooted and, come spring, the garden is virtually weed-free. The first peas are planted in February, so by January Chan has raked a bed into its characteristic shape with sides slanting up from a four-foot base to a top that is three feet wide. A natural ditch occurs between the hard paths and the base of the beds, so any water runoff is always caught and filtered back to growing plants. Convenience is one reason for the raised bed system: Once established, the beds are never walked on or otherwise disturbed, demanding additional labor each year. But their greatest value comes from their ability to heat much faster than the surrounding soil, and to retain the heat. As a result, Chan gets his vegetable starts in the ground weeks before most gardeners are even looking at seed catalogs.

Once the vegetable garden is established it becomes a part of the overall landscape in Peter Chan's backyard. It is neat and orderly, attractive for its geometry of green. "A vegetable garden should be pretty," says Peter Chan. "It should be part of your landscape. If it ruins your landscape, that's not right." It is also not right, Chan continues, if the gardener finds himself harried by what he has planted. "I try to maintain the yard with as little work as it can be," Chan says. "If it gives you too much pressure, gardening is not fun. I'm just a weekend gardener."

The Chan boys have all left home. The eldest is finishing a Ph.D. in electrical engineering. The youngest just finished a B.S. in the same field. The middle boy went to medical school and will soon start his residency. But their father still plants all ten raised beds with vegetables. "Two people can't use all those vegetables," Chan says. "We give them away. But people keep coming and want to see the garden, so I have to maintain it for them." With a flip of his hands Peter Chan diminishes whatever burden this might appear to be.

Asian Vegetables

While the primary commercial farming of Asian vegetables is Californian, there are many truck farmers in the Pacific Northwest growing specialty Asian produce on a small, seasonal scale. Many of them sell their produce at Seattle's Pike Place Market, or from the backs of their trucks in Asian business neighborhoods. Some of their produce includes:

Gai Lan: Chinese broccoli. The flowerettes grow in tight, clustered sprigs rather than in broad bunches. Leaves, stems and flowers are eaten.

Bok Choy: Large, spoon-shaped leaves with thick white stems. In the *brassica* family along with cabbage, kale, broccoli and the mustards. Bok choy is a mainstay with many varieties.

Yu Choy: Very tender. Cooks as soon as it hits heat. Usually stir-fried with a little oil and soup stock.

Baby Bok Choy: A miniature version that has become popular in the Pacific Northwest. It is difficult to get the leaves and the stems to cook at the same rate. Best to settle for tender leaves with slightly crunchy stems.

Choy Sum: The heart—the most tender part—of bok choy.

Gai Choy: A mustard green similar to turnip greens.

Mizuna: A mustard green with a peppery flavor.

Daikon: A long, hot, white radish.

Lobak Daikon: A sweeter and crunchier version of daikon. Grows to about half the size of a football.

Shingiku: An edible chrysanthemum. Used in sukiyaki and soups. Spicy flavor.

Nira: Korean chives, or garlic chives. Large, flat-bladed chive with distinct garlic taste.

Mitsuba: Japanese parsley. Big-leaf parsley.

No Kabu: A small, round turnip with delicious greens.

Kabocha: Japanese pumpkin. Small and squat with smooth textured flesh.

Greens, Herbs, Roots, Tubers, Mushrooms, Nuts, Month-by-Month

This list shows what is available during the year to customers at Seattle's Pike Place Market, the oldest farmer's retail market still doing business in America. There are high stalls in the market, tended by vendors of commercial fruits and vegetables shipped in from all over, and there are low tables where local farmers sell their wares on Friday and Saturday. This list is taken from the weekly "fresh sheet" published by the Pike Place Market. Only the produce of local farmers is listed, to give a sense of what is fresh and local by season. For the most part, items are listed only when they first appear at the Market—not throughout their entire season. So, all of this is in addition to what is normally available in major supermarkets.

February: Russian red kale, Scotch curled kale, overwintered cabbage (January King), overwintered cauliflower (Inca), chives, leeks.

March: Radishes, baby carrots, last of the broccoli di rappa, Nappa cabbage, Swiss chard, spinach; leeks, shallots; collard greens, arugula, chicory, endive, dandelion greens, radicchio, French sorrel, wild nettle stalks, mache; watercress; French tarragon, Italian parsley, horseradish root, garlic chives, rosemary, sage, thyme; false morels; turnips, rutabaga.

April: Kale, green chard, asparagus, Skagit Valley cauliflower, red and green lettuce (Red Sail, green leaf, romaine); green onions; field-grown rhubarb; mint, oregano; black morels.

May: Chinese mustard greens, ya choy, baby bok choy, pea vine (the top six inches of the pea vine, used in salads or cooked—a big product for the Indochinese Farming Project), Chinese broccoli, butter lettuce; pepper cress, lamb's-quarter, fennel, dill; calendula and viola (edible flowers); boletus mushrooms (porcini, cepes).

June: Sugar snap peas, daikon radish, sea asparagus (a wild succulent harvested in marine estuaries, also called sea bean—the green is vaguely bean-shaped; it has an intense, salty flavor and is used as a pickle), English shelling peas, Chinese snow peas, haricots verts, zucchini, red kohlrabi; mustard greens, shingiku; fennel, savory, marjoram.

July: Golden beets, vine-ripened tomatoes, sweet slicing cucumbers, kohlrabi, sweet corn, beans (Kentucky Wonder, Blue Lake, fava, Romano, Royal Purple), squash blossoms, Skagit Valley broccoli, baby scaloppine squash; red and white Swiss chard, Chinese spinach (calunay), chrysanthemum leaves; nasturtium (edible flower, peppery); basil, anise hyssop; Walla Walla sweet onions, baby red onions; German purple potatoes.

August: Pickling cucumbers, purple cauliflower, lemon cucumbers, peppers (jalapeño, yellow wax, green bell, red pimiento, peperoncini), eggplant (purple and white, Japanese miniature), haricots verts, baby yellow zucchini, patty-pan squash, yellow wax beans, red and white shell beans; endive; cinnamon basil, fresh dill; chanterelles.

September: Yellow pear tomatoes, peppers (Hot Portugal, Hungarian Hot Wax, Crooked Green Bell, Sweet Chocolate); squash (golden acorn, Sweet Dumpling, Green Hokkaido winter squash, buttercup), Jack-Be-Little miniature pumpkins, green tomatoes, fall asparagus, Savoy cabbage, red cabbage, spinach, sauce tomatoes, Yellow Taxi tomatoes, okra, Romanesque broccoli, Russian red kale, French sorrel; oregano, thyme, watercress, caraway, lovage, rosemary, epazote (peppery flavored herb from Mexico); shiitake mushrooms; chestnuts, walnuts.

October: Siberian tomatoes, orange bell peppers, flowering kale, fall radicchio, brussels sprouts; leeks; hazelnuts.

November: Jerusalem artichokes, Savoy cabbage, kale, chard, golden and red beets, Siberian kale, acorn squash; radicchio, escarole; turnips, parsnips; bulb fennel, Roja garlic (very spicy); chestnuts, walnuts.

December: turnips, parsnips, salsify.

How to Select and Store Vegetables

Always buy *firm,* unblemished produce. Store in your refrigerator and use right away. Growing your own is the best. In Seattle we have the Farmer's Market, which is a wonderful source for fresh vegetables. Some retail grocery stores have also begun to provide fresh local produce.

Buy tomatoes only in the late summer, when they are the real thing and are very sweet. Fresh corn should be picked and eaten as soon as possible—as should sweet fresh peas.

Fiddlehead Ferns

The small unopened frond of the fern is gathered in the spring. Remove the papery brown wrapping. Wash the fern carefully in cold water. Cover with water, add a few drops of salad oil and boil for a few minutes. Drain in strainer. Sprinkle lightly with a little sugar. Place in shallow serving dish and pour a small amount of light soy sauce over the fronds. Serve at room temperature. These have a "wild" taste and an interesting texture, a flavor of wild asparagus.

Italian Sausage-Stuffed Mushrooms

Sometimes the market will have huge mushrooms, perfect for stuffing. This is the way my family likes them. I serve them with warm marinara sauce on the side.

4 ounces Italian sausage
1 clove garlic
1 cup fresh bread crumbs
½ cup Parmesan cheese
2 tablespoons fresh parsley
1 teaspoon fresh marjoram
¼ cup butter
12 jumbo fresh mushrooms
¼ cup white wine

Preheat the oven to 375°. Sauté sausage, remove skin and break into small pieces. Drain off excess grease. Add garlic. Remove from heat and stir in bread crumbs, Parmesan cheese, parsley and marjoram. Melt butter and pour over bread crumb mixture.

Remove stems from mushrooms. Fill with bread crumb mixture, mounding the filling in each cap. Place in a buttered shallow baking dish. Pour in the wine. Bake in the oven for 15 minutes.

Yield: 4 appetizer servings

Baked Morels with Herb Crust

In the springtime in the Northwest we are able to hunt fresh morels. This is the beginning of our Northwest bounty which runs well into September.

1 pound fresh morels (you can substitute fresh cultivated
mushrooms)
4 tablespoons butter
½ cup heavy cream
2 cups fresh bread crumbs
1 tablespoon fresh thyme
1 tablespoon chopped chives
4 tablespoons butter, melted

Preheat the oven to 375°. Slice mushrooms and sauté in 4 tablespoons of butter. Place in a 9-inch glass quiche pan or pie dish. Pour in the cream. Mix together bread crumbs, thyme, chives, and melted butter. Spread crumbs over mushrooms and bake in the oven for 25 minutes until crisp and golden.

This dish is a nice complement to roast chicken or meat.

Serves 6

DEFINING THE PACIFIC NORTHWEST STYLE

> # *Sautéed Chanterelle Mushrooms with Port and Plum Cream Sauce*

This recipe is from Chef Cheri Walker at The Shoalwater Restaurant in Seaview, Washington, which is run by restaurateurs Tony and Ann Kischner. The dining room is part of the charming Shelburne Inn on the coast.

> *1½ pounds sweet plums (about 4 cups whole)*
> *2 cups chicken stock*
> *½ cup port*
> *1 ounce Kirschwasser*
> *1 ounce raspberry wine vinegar*
> *¼ cup cream*
> *2 ounces butter*
> *6 tablespoons butter*
> *3 pounds chanterelle mushrooms*

Put whole plums and chicken stock in saucepan, bring to boil and simmer until skins pop. Strain into another saucepan, pushing fruit through strainer to purée.

Add port, Kirschwasser and vinegar to purée and simmer until reduced by half.

Add the cream and let simmer until sauce begins to thicken and clear. Add butter, a little at a time, whisking continuously, until thickened. Keep warm over hot water until ready to use.

Melt butter in saucepan, sauté mushrooms until butter is absorbed. Pour sauce into pan to coat mushrooms. Serve immediately.

Serves 8

Green Beans and Tomatoes

A dish for July and August when the green beans are crisp and sweet, and tomatoes are at their peak. In winter, you can substitute canned tomatoes, but it won't be quite the same.

> 1 pound fresh green beans
> 2 cloves garlic, sliced
> ⅓ cup olive oil
> 4 large fresh tomatoes, seeded and chopped (or 1 large can chopped tomatoes)

Wash and trim green beans. Snap in half. Warm garlic in olive oil. Add beans, coating well with olive oil, and sauté for 5 minutes. Add tomatoes. Cover partially and simmer over low heat for 30 minutes, adding a little water if necessary.

   Leave the lid slightly ajar, to prevent condensation from forming inside the lid, which can spoil the dish.

Serves 4

Buttered Peas with Fresh Mint

The peas grown at Seaside, Oregon, are considered some of the best. Peas are like corn, once they are picked, the sugar turns to starch and the flavor fades. In an ideal world, you can pick, shell, and eat your peas all in one summer evening.

> 4 cups shelled fresh peas
> 1 cup water
> ½ teaspoon sugar
> 4 tablespoons soft butter
> 1 tablespoon fresh mint

Put peas, water and sugar in a saucepan. Cover and cook for 5 minutes over high heat. Remove from heat, drain, and stir in butter and mint.

Serves 4

Skagit Valley Yellow Pea Soup

Skagit Valley is a fertile farmland valley one hour north of Seattle. One of its main crops is peas. You can buy bags of dried Skagit Valley peas and make a delicious soup. In Swedish homes in the Northwest, yellow pea soup is a traditional dish. Serve with grilled ham and cheese sandwiches.

2 cups dried yellow split peas
6 cups cold water
1 large onion, chopped
1 ham hock, cut into 1-inch slices
6 whole allspice
Freshly ground pepper

Wash peas. Place in a 4-quart stockpot. Add water and bring to a boil. Boil for 5 minutes, turn off heat and let peas soak for 1 hour. Add remaining ingredients and simmer for 1½ hours.

Season to taste with salt and freshly ground pepper.

Note: You'll need to have your butcher cut through the ham hock with a meat saw, unless you are willing and able to wield a hacksaw at home.

Serves 4–6

Stir-Fried Baby Bok Choy, Shiitake Mushrooms, Pea Pods and Yellow Peppers

This is a good-looking, stylish combination that takes full advantage of some of the produce we now routinely enjoy in the Pacific Northwest. The shiitake are part of the region's great mushroom bounty; yellow peppers and pea pods thrive in season here and are widely cultivated to meet market demand. The method of cooking is part of a long tradition of the Chinese immigrants who settled here.

High heat is the essential ingredient of effective stir-fry technique. With a small amount of oil, all that remains is quickly tossing and sautéing the ingredients. The key to success is adding the ingredients in the right order, beginning with those that will take the longest time to cook.

Always do your stir-fried dish just before serving, and remember, the whole procedure should take only 3–5 minutes.

> *1½ pounds baby bok choy*
> *2 large fresh shiitake mushrooms*
> *½ pound pea pods*
> *½ red bell pepper*
> *½ yellow bell pepper*
> *1 tablespoon salad oil*
> *1 clove garlic*
> *1 small piece fresh ginger, peeled*
> *1–2 tablespoons light soy sauce*
> *1–2 teaspoons sesame oil*
> *½ teaspoon black sesame seeds*

Cut bok choy into diagonal slices ½-inch thick. Slice mushrooms into thin strips. String, rinse and drain pea pods. Seed peppers and slice into thin julienned strips.

Heat heavy skillet or wok, add oil, and fry garlic and ginger for a few seconds and remove. Add pepper strips and cook for 1 minute. Then add pea pods and cook 1 minute longer, always stirring and tossing the vegetables as they cook. Add the mushrooms and finally the bok choy. Transfer to a warm serving dish and sprinkle with soy sauce, sesame oil, and sesame seeds. Serve immediately.

Serves 6

Murphy's French-fried Onion Rings

Serve these as an appetizer to your friends while they are visiting and waiting for dinner.

> 2 large Walla Walla sweet onions, or another type of sweet
>   onion
> 1 egg, separated
> 1 cup milk
> 1 tablespoon salad oil
> ¾ cup plus 2 tablespoons all-purpose flour
> 2 teaspoons salt
> 1½ teaspoons baking powder
> Vegetable oil for deep fat frying

Peel onions and cut slices about ⅜-inch thick. Separate rings. Cover with cold water for 30 minutes. Drain on paper towels.

Beat together egg yolk, milk, and salad oil. Mix together flour, salt and baking powder and add to liquid mixture, blending to a smooth batter. Heat vegetable oil to 360°. Beat egg white until stiff and fold into batter. Dip onion rings in batter and fry in hot oil until golden, turning once. Serve in a napkin-lined basket. Sprinkle lightly with salt.

Yield: 4 appetizer servings

Onion Marmalade

The sweet and sour taste of the onions complements roasts, cold meats and game.

> 2 large Walla Walla sweet onions
> ¼ cup butter
> ¼ cup water
> ¼ cup sugar
> 1 teaspoon salt
> ¼ cup white wine vinegar

Preheat the oven to 275°. Slice onions crosswise, ½-inch thick. Heat butter and water in 10-inch black iron skillet. Stir in sugar and salt, then add vinegar and onions. Bake in the oven, uncovered, for 1 hour. The onions cook down and become lightly glazed.

Serves 4

Diane's Harvest Onion Soup

A fast, easy and lighter version of the classic French onion soup. Serve with toasted slices of French bread—baguette size—to eat with the soup, rather than in it. I like to serve it in mugs while everyone is still standing as a signal that dinner's ready.

It's a good soup for a thermos, too.

> *⅓ cup butter*
> *3 cups thinly sliced Walla Walla sweet onions*
> *¼ cup chopped celery leaves*
> *2 sprigs parsley*
> *4 cups chicken broth*
> *Salt and pepper to taste*
> *Parmesan cheese*

Melt butter and add onions, celery leaves and parsley. Partially cover and cook over low heat until onions are tender, about 20–25 minutes.

Put onion mixture and broth in blender and salt and pepper to taste; *process quickly*. Reheat and serve sprinkled with Parmesan cheese.

Serves 8

Ellie's Dilly Green Beans

I give a jar of these beans and a quart jar of my homemade Bloody Mary mix to my friends for Christmas presents.

> *4 pounds whole green beans*
> *7 hot, sterilized pint canning jars*
> *Hot red pepper flakes*
> *Whole mustard seed*
> *Fresh dill*
> *7 cloves garlic, peeled*
> *5 cups vinegar*
> *5 cups water*
> *½ cup pickling salt*

Wash beans, pack into the jars. Add ¼ teaspoon hot red pepper flakes, mustard seed, sprig of fresh dill and garlic clove to each jar.

Boil together vinegar, water and salt. Pour into jars to within ½-inch of the top. Screw on and process in boiling water for 5 minutes to seal properly.

Yield: enough for 7 pint jars

Irene's Pickled Walla Walla Sweet Onions

This onion is so good it should be renamed the Washington State Flower. The sad part is that the season is over much too quickly. This is a way to stretch it through the winter.

> *2 pounds Walla Walla sweet onions, each onion cut into eighths*
> *4 cups water*
> *7 tablespoons kosher salt*
> *4 cups distilled white vinegar*
> *1 cup sugar*
> *1 whole chili pepper per jar*
>
> *8 hot, sterilized pint canning jars*

Put onion sections into a large bowl. Combine the water and 6 tablespoons salt and pour over the onions. Cover and refrigerate overnight. Drain onions; rinse with cold running water.

Bring vinegar, sugar, the remaining 1 tablespoon salt and chili pepper to a boil, and then add onions and simmer for 3 minutes. Pack in the jars (boil lids) and seal. Cool to room temperature. Refrigerate until cold. Will store up to 3 months unrefrigerated.

Yield: enough for 8 pint jars

Walla Walla Sweet Onion and Cheddar Cheese Strata

A wonderful side dish with baked ham or leg of lamb.

> *6 eggs*
> *2½ cups half-and-half*
> *1 teaspoon Dijon mustard*
> *1 teaspoon Worcestershire sauce*
> *1 teaspoon kosher salt*
> *5 cups firm-textured white bread cut in ½-inch cubes (crust can be left on)*
> *3 cups Walla Walla sweet onions cut into quarters and thinly sliced*
> *2 cups cheddar cheese, grated*

Preheat the oven to 350°. Beat together the eggs, half-and-half, mustard, Worcestershire sauce and salt. Place half the bread in a 2-quart soufflé dish. Layer half the onions, then the cheese, and repeat. Slowly pour egg mixture over the top. Let set in refrigerator for at least 2 hours, or as long as overnight. Bake in the oven until golden brown on top, 50 to 60 minutes.

Serves 6

Golden Marinated Carrots

These are a good accompaniment to smoked meats, or are fine packed along on a picnic.

> *2 pounds carrots*
> *1 green pepper*
> *1 white onion*
> *½ cup salad oil*
> *¾ cup cider vinegar*
> *1 10¾-ounce can tomato soup*
> *¾ cup sugar*
> *1 teaspoon prepared Dijon mustard*

Peel carrots and slice diagonally into ½-inch slices. Cook in simmering water until just tender. Drain and cool. Seed green pepper and cut into thin strips. Cut onion into slices ½-inch thick. Mix vegetables together. Thoroughly blend oil, vinegar, soup, sugar, and mustard. Pour over mixed vegetables and refrigerate overnight.

Serve as a condiment, like pickles.

Labor Day Corn on the Cob

Every Labor Day we visit close friends in Ellensburg, Washington, and feast on fresh corn. James Beard thought that fresh corn was the perfect first course. We put the pot on to boil, and our boys go out and get the corn. We drop it in and eat it within a half hour of its being picked, an annual treat.

> *Ears of corn, freshly picked*
> *Large pot one-third full of boiling water*
> *Butter*
> *Salt and pepper*

Husk the corn. Drop into boiling water and cover. Cook for 3 minutes. Remove ears with tongs and serve immediately with lots of butter, salt and pepper.

Cauliflower with Tillamook Cheddar Cheese

Cauliflower is a major crop in the Northwest, especially in the Skagit Valley in northwest Washington. Tillamook is a regional cheddar from Oregon and a great favorite. You will find that the cheddar cheese alone is much lighter and of course much easier to prepare than the more traditional cheese.

> *1 small head cauliflower*
> *4 tablespoons soft butter*
> *1 cup grated Tillamook cheddar cheese*
> *Pepper*

Trim cauliflower but leave head whole. Plunge into boiling water, cover, and cook for 10 to 12 minutes, until a knife inserts easily into the center of the head. Drain well. Break head into pieces over a warm serving bowl. Spread with soft butter and add a few grinds of coarse pepper. Sprinkle with cheddar cheese.

Serves 6

One-Minute Asparagus

I like to have everyone seated before cooking the asparagus. To me, asparagus in the spring is a star and deserves full attention at the right moment.

> *1 pound asparagus*
> *4 tablespoons butter*
> *1 lemon, cut into wedges*

Trim or break white ends off asparagus. Wash well. If you have early spring asparagus, you won't need to peel it; otherwise, give each spear several strokes of a vegetable peeler, rotating the spear on a cutting board as you go. Place asparagus in a shallow frying pan and cover with lukewarm water. Bring to a boil, uncovered, and count 1 minute. Immediately drain and place on a cloth napkin to absorb excess moisture, then transfer to a warm serving dish.

Meanwhile, quickly melt the butter in the same pan and just when it begins to bubble and turn a golden brown, pour it over the asparagus. Serve immediately with lemon wedges.

Yield: 4 first-course servings

Baked Spaghetti Squash with Parmesan Cheese

If I have it, I like to add a cup of grated raw zucchini to the cooked spaghetti squash. It adds a sweet flavor and a nice green color.

> *2 pounds spaghetti squash*
> *6 tablespoons butter*
> *1 cup grated raw zucchini (optional)*
> *Salt and pepper*
> *Dash of nutmeg*
> *½ cup grated Parmesan cheese*

Preheat the oven to 375°. Place the whole spaghetti squash in a baking pan and bake in the oven for 1 hour, or until soft to the touch.

Remove from oven and let it cool so that it can be handled. Cut in half, lengthwise. Remove seeds. Scrape out spaghetti-like strands of squash into shallow baking dish. Toss with the butter. (Add the zucchini at this point if desired.) Add salt, pepper, and a dash of nutmeg to taste. Sprinkle with freshly grated Parmesan and serve.

Serves 6

Baked Acorn Squash

If your squash is too hard to cut, bake it first.

> *1 acorn squash*
> *4 tablespoons butter*
> *½ cup brown sugar*

Preheat the oven to 400°. Bake squash whole until soft, about 50 minutes. Remove and let it cool enough to be handled. Cut in half, remove seeds and strings, then fill each center with 2 tablespoons butter and ¼ cup brown sugar. Return to oven for 10 minutes, then serve.

Serves 2

Odessa's Squash Casserole

If you have a garden in the Northwest, you usually have an abundance of summer squash. This method of cooking seals in the moisture so that you don't end up with a watery concoction.

1 small red bell pepper
1½ pounds summer squash
1 small yellow onion
3 tablespoons butter
Kosher salt and pepper to taste
½ teaspoon sugar
2 eggs, well beaten
1 cup light cream
½ cup grated cheddar cheese

Preheat the oven to 325°. Dice the pepper into small pieces. Cut the squash in half lengthwise, then cut crosswise into ½-inch slices. Dice the onion. Sauté pepper, squash and onion briefly in butter. Season to taste with salt and pepper. Transfer to a buttered shallow baking dish.

Mix together sugar, eggs, cream and cheese, and pour over the vegetables in the dish.

Bake in the oven for 45 minutes, or until set and golden brown on top.

Serves 6

Baked Butternut Squash with Nutmeg and Maple Syrup

Winter squash in the market says fall is here. Butternut is my favorite for its smooth, creamy consistency.

1 butternut squash
1 cup apple juice
Nutmeg
¼ cup butter, melted
¼ cup maple syrup

Preheat the oven to 400°. Cut squash in half. Remove seeds. Place squash, cut side down, in baking dish. Pour apple juice around squash and add a few gratings of nutmeg. Bake in the oven for 45 minutes to 1 hour, until fork tender. Cut into serving pieces and pour melted butter mixed with syrup on top.

Serves 6

Butter-Steamed Beets and Carrots

The last remnants of a summer garden: The sweetness of the carrots adds to the earthiness of the beets.

> *4–5 small beets*
> *6–8 small carrots*
> *4 tablespoons butter*
> *½ cup water*
> *Salt and pepper to taste*

Peel beets and cut into wedges. Peel and round-cut carrots. Place in a saucepan with butter and water, and cover with a tight-fitting lid. Simmer gently for 12–15 minutes. Sprinkle with salt and pepper and serve.

Serves 4

Pickled Beets

Serve these chilled during the winter holidays and on summer picnics.

> *3–4 pounds fresh beets, medium sized*
> *2 cups sugar*
> *2 cups water*
> *2 cups vinegar*
> *1 lemon, sliced thin*
> *1 tablespoon cinnamon*
> *1 teaspoon cloves*
> *1 teaspoon allspice   6–8 sterilized pint canning jars*

Cook beets in boiling water until just tender and skins slip off easily. Cut into slices or chunks.

Simmer the rest of the ingredients in a 3-quart saucepan for 15 minutes. Pack beets in the jars.

Bring syrup to a boil and pour over the beets. Process in a water bath for 20 minutes.

Yield: enough for 6–8 pint jars

Beet and Sausage Soup

A hearty, sweet and sour soup that is delicious in the fall.

> 4 tablespoons butter
> 2 medium-sized onions
> 1 clove garlic, crushed
> 2 pounds canned tomatoes, diced (including juice)
> 4 quarts rich beef broth
> 1½ pounds new potatoes
> 1 pound spicy country-style breakfast sausage
> 2 pounds medium-sized beets
> ½ head cabbage
> ½ cup red wine vinegar
> 1 tablespoon sugar
> Sour cream
> Chives

In a large soup pot, melt butter over medium heat, add onions and sauté slowly. Add garlic and cook just until onions are soft. Add tomatoes and beef broth.

Dice new potatoes and add to the pot. In a sauicepan, crumble the sausage, lightly brown and drain. Add to the soup.

Wash, scrape and grate the beets and put them in the pot. Shred the cabbage and stir in. Add the vinegar and sugar and cook for 30 minutes. This soup is best served the same day, because the color of the beets will fade overnight. Serve with sour cream and chives.

Serves 8

Skagit Valley Sauerkraut

My good friend Father Mike Schmidt used to make sauerkraut every fall, which he served at a potluck supper for at least 60 people in October. Everyone loved it! And everyone who knew him misses him.

> *6–8 heads green cabbage*
> *½ tablespoon kosher salt per ½ head of cabbage, or*
> *   3½ tablespoons salt for every 4 to 5 pounds of cabbage*
> *Caraway or dill seed*
> *Small russet potato, grated*

Shred 3 to 4 heads of cabbage into a 5-gallon crock. Add the salt and mix with your hands. Pound the cabbage with your fist until juices start to appear. Add 3 or 4 more heads shredded cabbage and repeat until the crock is almost full. Put a large plate on top and place a heavy rock on top of the plate to weight down the cabbage.

Ferment the cabbage for 10 to 14 days in a 60° room. Skim off any impurities every 2 days. Then can the sauerkraut in quart jars or freeze in milk cartons.

To serve: Simmer 1 quart of sauerkraut with 1 tablespoon caraway or dill seed for 50 minutes. Add grated potato and simmer 10 minutes longer. Serve with good German-style sausage and boiled potatoes.

Sweet and Sour Sauerkraut Slaw

This is a delicious accompaniment to corned beef and makes a great Reuben sandwich.

> *4 cups sauerkraut, well drained*
> *1 cup chopped celery*
> *½ cup chopped red pepper*
> *½ cup chopped green pepper*

1 cup chopped green onion
1 cup sugar
¼ cup salad oil
¾ cup white vinegar

Put sauerkraut, celery, red and green pepper and green onion in a bowl. Mix well. Blend sugar, salad oil and vinegar together and pour over vegetables. Cover and refrigerate overnight.

Serves 8–10

Sweet and Sour Cabbage

Cabbages from the Skagit Valley and crisp apples from the Okanogan region combine to perfectly complement pork, duck or sausage—all of which make a hearty fall dinner. It's also a tradition with Thanksgiving turkey in many homes.

4 tablespoons butter
½ yellow onion, cut into thin slices
1 medium-sized head red cabbage, cut in quarters
½ cup white wine vinegar
½ cup water
2 tablespoons red currant jelly
Salt and pepper to taste
2 Granny Smith apples, cut into thin slices (unpeeled)

Sauté the butter and onions in an enamel pan. Thinly slice cabbage and add to the pan. Add the rest of the ingredients except apples. Stir until well mixed. Cover, leaving lid slightly ajar, and cook over low heat for 25 minutes. Add apples and cook 10 minutes longer.

Serves 6

Potatoes

We have wonderful potatoes in the Pacific Northwest. Small baby red new potatoes the size of walnuts, wonderful half-pound (and larger) russets for baking, yellow Finns, buttery and delicious, the Norgold russets from Ellensburg, which deep-fry so well.

It's important to use the *right* potato for the desired results.

Russets: Use for making baked potatoes, hash browns and mashed potatoes.

For making baked potatoes:

1. Preheat oven to 400°. Scrub potatoes well. Then pat or air-dry completely.

2. Poke several times with a fork to prevent potatoes from exploding in the oven.

3. Bake potatoes in the oven for 1 hour (you can leave them in the oven longer if you are not ready to eat yet). Remember that a good baked potato is like a soufflé—as soon as it is removed from the oven it starts to cool; it starts to steam and collapse inside the skin, and become dense and compact. If you have to wait to serve dinner, leave the potatoes in the oven until everyone's ready. The outer edge of the potatoes will continue to cook and have a wonderful crisp texture. Don't turn the heat down! This will cause the potatoes to collapse inside.

4. To open a potato, cover it with a towel and strike it with your fist. The potato will burst open, fluffy and dry. Let everyone help themselves to lots of butter, sour cream, chopped chives and freshly grated Parmesan cheese—and lots of freshly cracked pepper.

For crisp hash browns: Cook your potatoes the day before as follows.

1. Place unpeeled russet potatoes in a large pot. Cover with cold water, bring to a boil, turn down heat and continue gently boiling. Cook until tender. Drain. Leave in pot until cool. Refrigerate overnight.

2. The next morning, peel and grate potatoes.

3. Heat 3 tablespoons each of butter and oil in heavy 10-inch skillet. Add 6 cups of grated cooked potatoes, lightly pressing

them into pan. Cook one side of the potatoes until golden brown, flip out onto plate. Add additional butter and oil. Return the potatoes to frying pan and cook the other side. Sprinkle with salt and freshly cracked pepper. Serve with crisp bacon and warm applesauce.

For light, fluffy mashed potatoes: Peel russet potatoes. Cut into quarters. Cook in boiling salted water until soft; drain. Shake over low heat, until white and mealy. (I use my heavy enamel pan to cook them in.) Mash with a potato masher. To 3 cups mashed potatoes add ½ cup hot milk and 4 tablespoons soft butter. Continue mashing until smooth and fluffy.

Little red new potatoes: These are so sweet and delicious I could eat them every day a different way.

To boil new potatoes, always start them in cold water, then cook until soft. I test with the tip of a small paring knife. Drain off water, shake in pan over low heat, covered, for several minutes. This tightens the skin and keeps it from falling off in potato salads.

I never peel the red jackets, because the skin is so tender and colorful. Once they are boiled, I love to serve them with a fresh fish dinner, tossed with melted butter and fresh chives from the garden. You can also steam them or simply put them in a casserole with a lid, drizzle them with a little olive oil, sprinkle them with chopped shallots and bake, covered, until tender.

Good hot or cold, they make a delicious cold potato salad using the recipe for Malt Vinegar Dressing, p. 212. Cut up and fry in butter for wonderful fried potatoes, or use in a good hash.

Yellow Finns: These are becoming increasingly more available. They are a buttery yellow color and are best when boiled and then used like a new potato. Do peel after cooking. They make a wonderful salad with sliced Walla Walla Sweet Onions and the Malt Vinegar Dressing. Serve with thick slices of garden-ripe tomatoes and a nice roast chicken.

White rose potatoes (also called boiling potatoes): They make good potato salad, and are also good sliced and pan-fried with onions.

Oven-Roasted Potatoes

These are nice to serve with a roast leg of lamb, roast veal or roast chicken.

4 russet potatoes
½ stick butter
¼ cup salad oil

Preheat the oven to 375°. Peel the potatoes and cut lengthwise into quarter wedges. Melt the butter and add the oil. Place the potatoes in a 9- x 13-inch glass baking dish and pour in the butter–oil combination. Make certain the potatoes are well-coated by turning them over several times. Sprinkle with salt and pepper and bake for 1 hour.

Serves 6

Baby Red Potatoes with Sautéed Walla Wallas, Cougar Gold and Coarse Black Pepper

At the Pike Place Market in Seattle, we can find small red potatoes the size of walnuts. I keep a bin in the refrigerator filled with them. I can use them to make a wonderful potato or German potato salad, or I can boil and then fry them in butter, or I can use them for clam chowder, in hash, or in this recipe, which can serve as Saturday's lunch or a late snack. I like to serve something salty on the side—a dish of imported green olives, smoked hard-shell clams or oysters, and a simple green salad.

6 small red potatoes
½ Walla Walla sweet onion, cut in crescent slices
3–4 tablespoons butter
Coarse ground black pepper
A generous handful of grated Cougar Gold cheese or Yakima
  Gouda or Kasseri

In a saucepan, cover the potatoes with *cold* water (to prevent skins from bursting) and bring to a boil. Reduce heat to a gentle boil and cook until potatoes are tender, 15–20 minutes. Pour off water, leaving potatoes in pan, and cover. Leave covered for several minutes; this plumps the potatoes and makes the skin tight.

While the potatoes are cooking, sauté the onion in the butter until soft and lightly browned.

Remove the lid from the pan, and while still hot, cut potatoes into thick slices. Place in a small shallow bowl, and pour in the onions. Grind coarse black pepper over the top and sprinkle with the grated cheese.

Serves 2

Kelly Beard's Killer Potatoes

This is a creamy potato dish that goes well with baked ham.

> *6 medium russet potatoes, washed, peeled and grated*
> *1 medium white onion, finely chopped*
> *8 ounces cheddar cheese, grated, reserving ¼ cup for top*
> *1½ cups sour cream*
> *½ cup melted butter*
> *Salt and pepper to taste*

Preheat the oven to 350°. Mix together potatoes, onion, cheese, sour cream, butter and salt and pepper, and put into a 3-quart oven-proof casserole. Sprinkle with the remaining ¼ cup grated cheese and bake in the oven for 50 to 60 minutes.

Serves 8

Scalloped Potato and Cheese Casserole

I serve these cheesy, creamy potatoes with a bone-in baked ham and tender baby carrots cooked in butter.

3 pounds russet potatoes
3 teaspoons salt
3 tablespoons butter
2 tablespoons flour
¼ teaspoon freshly grated nutmeg
2¼ cups milk
3 cups grated Swiss cheese
Chopped parsley
4 slices lightly cooked bacon

Preheat the oven to 375°. Peel potatoes and cut into slices ½-inch thick. Place potatoes in a large saucepan and cover with boiling water. Sprinkle in 2 teaspoons salt and cook, covered, for 5 minutes. Drain. Melt butter in saucepan, blend in flour, nutmeg, and the remaining teaspoon of salt. Gradually add milk. Cook, stirring, until mixture thickens and forms a smooth paste.

In a buttered 9- x 13-inch glass baking dish place half the potatoes and pour in half the sauce. Sprinkle with 2 cups of cheese. Add remaining potatoes and sauce. Cover with foil and bake in the oven for 45 minutes. Remove foil and sprinkle with parsley and the remaining cup of cheese. Lay the strips of bacon across the top. Bake uncovered for 20 minutes longer, or until potatoes turn a light golden brown.

Serves 6

Swedish Roast Potatoes

If you put a chicken in to roast at the same time as these potatoes, you'll end up with an easy and delicious dinner.

6 medium-sized potatoes
½ cup butter, melted
Salt and pepper
Paprika

Preheat the oven to 400°. Wash and peel potatoes. Slash them cross-wise and thinly, about ¾ of the way through, leaving the bottoms whole. Coat potatoes with the melted butter and place in a baking pan. Sprinkle with salt and pepper. Bake in the oven until crisp and golden, about 1 hour and 15 minutes, basting occasionally with the butter from the baking pan. Sprinkle with paprika.

Serves 6

Potato Pancakes

I usually serve these with pan-fried pork chops, warm applesauce and a dollop of sour cream.

4 large russet potatoes (6–8 ounces)
3 eggs, beaten
1 teaspoon salt
¼ teaspoon pepper
2 tablespoons flour
2 tablespoons salad oil
2 tablespoons butter

Peel and finely grate potatoes. Put in a large bowl and add all the other ingredients except the salad oil and butter. Mix well. Heat a large Teflon-coated frying pan and add the oil and butter. When oil is hot enough to sizzle, drop in several spoonfuls of potato mixture and form small pancakes. Turn when golden brown. Drain on paper towels. Serve hot.

Serves 4

Irene Hlueny's Potato Lefse

Lefse is Norwegian for a large, thin potato pancake served buttered and folded. Lefse dough needs to be well chilled before rolling, and then you want to be sure to roll it as thin as possible.

> *5 large boiling potatoes*
> *½ cup sweet cream*
> *3 tablespoons butter*
> *1 teaspoon salt*
> *All-purpose flour: use ½ cup to each cup of mashed potatoes*

Boil potatoes, mash very fine, and add cream, butter, and salt. Beat until light, then let cool. Add flour and roll into a ball of dough, kneading until smooth. Form into a long roll and slice into pieces about the size of a large egg, or larger, depending on the size of lefse desired. Chill dough.

Roll each piece round like a pie crust, and as thin as possible. Do not grease griddle. Bake on lefse griddle or pancake griddle at moderate heat, turning once. When baked, place between clean cloth or waxed paper to keep from becoming dry.

Serve with plain butter, or butter, sugar and cinnamon. Cut each lefse in half or fourths and roll up before serving.

Serves 6–8

Cougar Gold Cheddar and Potato Soup

Cougar Gold is a delicious, slightly sharp cheddar cheese, with a wonderful texture developed and sold by Washington State University. It slices, crumbles and melts beautifully. The cheese is sold in a 30-ounce tin.

> *¼ cup butter*
> *1 yellow onion, thinly sliced*
> *¼ cup flour*
> *1 teaspoon dry mustard*
> *3 cups chicken broth*
> *1 cup carrots, peeled and grated*

> 3 cups potatoes, peeled and cut into ½-inch slices
> 2 cups half-and-half
> 3 cups shredded Cougar Gold cheese
> Salt and pepper to taste
> Celery leaves, finely chopped

Sauté onion in butter over moderate heat until soft. Stir in flour and dry mustard. Cook for several minutes, stirring continuously. Transfer to soup pot and stir in broth, whisking until smooth. Add carrots and potatoes.

Simmer over moderate heat for 30 minutes. Add half-and-half. Reduce heat to low and stir in cheese until melted. Season with salt and pepper to taste. Sprinkle with celery leaves.

Serves 6

20-Minute Potato–Sausage Soup

Throughout the winter we always have a large sack of russet potatoes on hand. Baked, mashed or made into this creamy soup, they are a mainstay of our winter menus.

> 6 medium-sized russet potatoes
> 4 cups chicken broth
> 1–2 leeks
> ¼ cup butter
> 2 cloves garlic, chopped
> 1 pint half-and-half
> ½ pound precooked smoked sausage, cut in half and then sliced
> 2½ teaspoons kosher salt
> ¼ teaspoon white pepper
> Dash of cayenne

Peel and dice potatoes. Cook them in chicken broth until tender. Set aside to cool.

Trim off tough tops of leeks. Cut leeks in half lengthwise. Rinse carefully under running water to remove any silt. Cut into ½-inch pieces. Pat dry. Sauté the leeks in butter over moderate heat. Add garlic and cook until soft.

Purée the potatoes with the chicken broth in the food processor, in batches if necessary. Transfer to saucepan, add cream and reheat. Stir in leeks and sausage. Cook 5 minutes. Season with salt, pepper and cayenne.

Serves 6

Baked Yams with Toasted Hazelnuts

Yams are usually served only for Thanksgiving, and yet they are delicious all year round with venison or roast pork.

> *6 yams, cut in quarters*
> *4 ounces soft butter*
> *2 tablespoons maple syrup*
> *1 cup chopped toasted hazelnuts or filberts*

Preheat the oven to 375°. Cook the yams with the skins on until tender. Peel and place in a 2-quart casserole. Mash with fork and mix in butter and maple syrup. Sprinkle with nuts and bake for 25 minutes.

Serves 6

Mom's Baked Beans

Baked beans from scratch do take time, but they will get nice and soft if you cook them in a crockpot. Slow, easy cooking is what they like.

> *1 pound small navy beans*
> *Cold water*
> *1 tablespoon salt*
> *¼ pound uncooked bacon, diced (or end pieces of smoky ham)*
> *½ yellow onion, chopped*
> *¼ cup brown sugar*
> *6 tablespoons molasses*
> *1 teaspoon dry mustard*
> *½ teaspoon powdered ginger*

½ teaspoon ground coriander
16-ounce can diced or stewed tomatoes, with juice
¼ cup ketchup

Cover beans with cold water, add salt and soak overnight. The following day, rinse the beans. Place in a large saucepan, add 2 cups cold water and simmer, covered, for one hour.

Put beans and any liquid leftover into crockpot. Mix in bacon, onion, brown sugar, molasses, seasonings, tomatoes and ketchup. Cover and cook on the low setting 6 to 8 hours, until beans are soft. Remove cover for last half hour of cooking.

Serves 8

Nina's Bagna Cauda

Try this outdoors in the summertime. It's fun to eat and goes well with barbecued meats.

Have on the table a tray or basket of fresh vegetables cut into easy dipping-sized pieces. The following are my favorites: red pepper strips, cauliflower pieces, fresh mushrooms, fresh green beans, rolled Napa cabbage leaves, cherry tomatoes, zucchini strips; a basket of sliced French bread.

1 cup soft butter
⅓ cup olive oil
3 cloves garlic, finely sliced
1 can (2 ounces) flat anchovy fillets, well-drained
Tray or basket of fresh vegetables

Put the butter, olive oil and garlic in an enamel 6–8 cup saucepan. Heat slowly. Chop the anchovies and add to the butter mixture. Stir until mixture bubbles. Keep heat low enough so that mixture doesn't burn.

To serve, set over a warming candle or low flame to keep warm. Swirl vegetable pieces in the "hot bath." (Use bamboo skewers or fondue forks to prevent burning the fingers.)

To catch the flavorful drippings, hold the bread under the vegetables as they are removed from the dip. Then enjoy the bread.

Serves 6

Smoked Bacon and Fresh Corn Chowder

My father likes to add 1 small jar of raw oysters to this recipe for an oyster–corn chowder.

3 strips smoked bacon
¼ cup finely chopped yellow onion
2 cups fresh or frozen corn kernels
2 tablespoons butter
2 tablespoons flour
2 cups milk
1 teaspoon salt
½ teaspoon pepper
2 cups half-and-half

Cut the bacon into ½-inch pieces. Fry until it begins to crisp. Add the onion and sauté until soft. Put corn in a food processor and process lightly, leaving some texture. Add the corn to onion and bacon, and cook until corn is hot. Add butter, then stir in the flour. Cook slowly over low heat for 3 minutes. Add milk, salt and pepper, and cook until thickened. Then add cream and stir over low heat until nice and hot.

Serves 6

Fresh Corn Chowder with Cheddar Cheese and Tomato Salsa

Gilman Village in Issaquah (a town 20 minutes east of Seattle) is a favorite outing for visitors. 1920s small houses, all refurbished, form a village of shops and restaurants. At Sweet Additions restaurant this delicious soup is served during fresh corn season.

½ cup chopped onions
4 tablespoons butter
3 cups fresh corn removed from the cob (or frozen or packaged corn)

1½ cups russet potatoes, peeled and diced
1 cup chicken broth
3½ cups half-and-half
1 teaspoon salt
Freshly cracked pepper
1–2 teaspoons Tabasco
1½ cups finely grated cheddar cheese
1 cup Salsa (p. 344)
Fresh coriander

Sauté onions in butter. Coarsely purée corn in food processor. Add to onions and heat. Transfer to soup pot. Add rest of the ingredients, except the cheese, salsa and coriander. Cook over medium-low heat until potatoes are cooked and soup thickens slightly.

Sprinkle each serving with a little cheese, add a dollop of salsa and some fresh coriander.

Serves 6

Sydney Moe's Chilled Summer Yakima Tomato Gazpacho

In summer, when the tomatoes in Yakima are plump and red and ripe, I make a big pitcher of gazpacho and keep it in the refrigerator.

4–6 ripe tomatoes
1 small green bell pepper
½ white onion
1 English cucumber
1 32-ounce bottle good-quality Bloody Mary mix
4 tablespoons olive oil
6 tablespoons wine vinegar
1 avocado
1 small can salted roasted almonds

Remove stem end from tomatoes. Cut into large chunks. Seed the green pepper and cut into large pieces. Coarsely chop the white onion. Cut cucumber in half. Cut one half into thick slices and save the other half for garnish.

Put two cups of the Bloody Mary mix in the food processor with the oil and vinegar. Add half of the vegetables and process until smooth. Transfer this mixture to a large pitcher. Process remaining vegetables briefly so that they still have some texture, and then add them to the puréed mixture. Stir in the remaining Bloody Mary mix.

When ready to serve, dice the avocado and the remaining half of the cucumber and serve as garnishes for the soup along with the almonds.

Serves 8

Tillamook Cheddar–Beer Soup

We have friends who serve this as their house soup at their ski cabin in the winter. It's hearty and good with Granny Smith apples and giant pretzels.

> ¼ cup butter
> 1½ cups chopped yellow onion
> 1 cup peeled and sliced carrots
> 1 cup chopped celery
> 2 cups diced new potatoes
> 2 cups chicken broth
> ½ cup flour
> 2 cups milk
> 3 cups grated cheddar cheese (or you can use Cougar Gold)
> 1 teaspoon dry mustard
> ⅛ teaspoon cayenne
> ½ can beer (the remaining half is for the cook)

Melt butter in heavy 6-quart saucepan. Add vegetables and sauté briefly. Pour in chicken broth and simmer for 30 minutes. Mix flour and milk together until smooth, then blend into soup. Stir and cook until well blended. Add cheese, mustard and cayenne. Stir until cheese melts, then stir in beer.

Serves 6

Garden Minestrone Soup

This is a variation of a soup developed by Angelo Pellegrini, famous gardener and food enthusiast in Seattle. I serve it with homemade bread and Apple Grunt (p. 270) for dessert.

> *4 slices bacon, cut in 1/2-inch strips*
> *2/3 cup light olive oil*
> *3 cloves garlic, minced*
> *3 cups chopped yellow onion*
> *Freshly ground black pepper*
> *4 stalks celery, chopped (including tops)*
> *4 cups chopped Swiss chard (including leaves and stalks)*
> *1/2 cup chopped parsley*
> *2 cups small zucchini, sliced*
> *2 cups green beans, cut in thirds*
> *1/4 cup fresh basil*
> *2 cups shredded and chopped cabbage*
> *4 carrots, peeled and sliced*
> *2 28-ounce cans chopped or stewed tomatoes with juice*
> *6–7 cups beef broth*
> *2 cups canned, drained and puréed white cannellini beans, or 1
>   or 2 11 1/2-ounce cans of bean with bacon soup (depending on
>   how thick you like your soup)*
> *Fresh parsley for garnish*
> *Freshly grated Parmesan cheese*

In a large pot, sauté bacon until just brown and drain off fat. Add olive oil. Stir in garlic, onion and celery and sauté over medium heat until soft. Add several grinds of fresh black pepper. Stir in all of the vegetables and herbs, and let cook together for 5 minutes. Add tomatoes, beef broth, and beans. Simmer for 30 minutes and serve, sprinkled with fresh parsley and freshly grated Parmesan cheese.

Serves 8

Fresh Mushroom Soup

When I was growing up, my father always had a pot of soup on the stove in winter, which changed day to day according to whatever leftover vegetables he added after dinner. When I came home from school I'd add 1 cup of water to the pot to thin the mixture, boil it for a few minutes, and enjoy Dad's "soup du jour."

1 pound fresh white mushrooms, thinly sliced
2 cups onion, cut into quarters and thinly sliced
1 bay leaf
4 tablespoons butter
3 tablespoons flour
5 cups fresh chicken broth
1 tablespoon uncooked rice
1 cup half-and-half
Salt and pepper
Tabasco to taste
Parsley, chopped

Sweat mushrooms, onions and bay leaf in butter in a 10-inch frying pan by placing a circle of waxed paper directly on mushrooms and weighting with a saucer to prevent excess condensation. Continue cooking over very low heat for another 10 minutes. Remove waxed paper and sprinkle mushrooms with flour. Mix well. Transfer to a 4-quart saucepan and add chicken broth and rice. Simmer over low heat for 15 minutes. Add half-and-half and season to taste wih salt, pepper and a dash of Tabasco. Sprinkle each serving with parsley.

Serves 6

Chinese Vegetable Soup (War Mein)

A light soup that can be served as a first course.

> *¼ pound Chinese noodles*
> *3 cups chicken stock*
> *¼ pound barbecued pork slices*
> *1 cup green vegetables (pea pods, baby bok choy)*
> *4 water chestnuts, sliced*
> *1 green onion, sliced*
> *Soy sauce*

Boil noodles until tender. Rinse in water, drain and set aside.

Bring stock to a boil. Add barbecued pork, vegetables and water chestnuts and boil for 2 minutes. Add noodles just to heat. Serve, garnished with the green onion, and let each person add his own soy sauce to taste.

Serves 4

Lentil Soup from "Alpenland"

We are fortunate to have this cozy Mercer Island restaurant, owned and run by Gunter and Katrin Bonnofsky, in our neighborhood. They serve delicious soups. Lovage is an easy herb to grow and is particularly good in many soups.

> *2 cups lentils*
> *4 cups chicken stock*
> *1 teaspoon salt*
> *1 clove garlic*
> *½ teaspoon pepper*
> *4 bay leaves*
> *2 celery stalks, trimmed*
> *1 carrot, peeled*
>
> *1 leek, washed thoroughly*
> *1 sprig fresh lovage*
> *1 cube chicken bouillon*
>   *(optional)*
> *2 tablespoons vinegar*
> *1 smoked farmer's or*
>   *pre-cooked sausage, cut up*

Soak the lentils in water overnight in an enamel, stainless steel or porcelain-coated soup pot. The next day, drain the lentils, return them to the pot and add the stock, salt, garlic, pepper, and bay leaves. Chop the celery, carrot and leek, and add to the pot. Stir in the lovage, chicken bouillon (if desired), vinegar and smoked sausage. Cook over low heat for 2 hours. This soup will keep well in the refrigerator for up to 3 days.

Serves 6

Glazed Turnips

Root vegetables come to the market in the late fall. Delicious raw, these nicely glazed turnips are a good accompaniment to duck. This is a recipe from Jane Wherrette, a well-known Northwest artist.

> *6 medium-sized white turnips*
> *Water*
> *½ teaspoon salt*
> *3 tablespoons soft butter*
> *1 tablespoon flour*
> *½ cup chicken broth*
> *Salt and freshly ground black pepper to taste*
> *Fresh parsley*

Wash, peel and cut each turnip into 6–8 wedges. Cover with water, add the salt and cook the turnips uncovered just until tender, about 10 minutes. Drain well. Stir in the butter and let melt. Sprinkle with the flour and mix well with the buttered turnips. Add the chicken broth and cook over low heat until a sauce is formed. Season with salt and pepper and sprinkle with fresh parsley.

Serves 4

SALADS AND DRESSINGS

T here is probably no more ubiquitous element demonstrating man's intrusion into the natural world of the Pacific Northwest than the stuff known as "beauty bark." No industrial mall, no suburban subdivision is complete without it. The product comes from sawmills where bark is removed from logs before they are transformed into lumber or plywood for the building industry, or pulp for the paper industry. The metamorphosis of mere tree bark to beauty bark occurs in an industrial chipper where all matter is reduced to manageable size. The stuff simplifies landscaping. While one part of the team from the local nursery rolls out the lawn, another pokes rhododendrons into holes, then covers the garden beds with beauty bark. It makes everything look neat and fresh, and when it's applied in a thick enough layer, the sight of weeds becomes an uncommon thing. Lots of homeowners think they like that.

If Carl Woestendiek and Shery Litwin could have their way, they would banish beauty bark from North America. They are two elements of a landscape design firm—Shery powerhouses the design while Carl oversees the implementation—specifically oriented to edible plants rather than ornamentals. There are few places for beauty bark in their scheme of things. Flavorful weeds are welcome. "What I see all over Seattle," Carl says, "is a lot of people who feel alienated from their own yards. They have a garden. They have grass. They've got a rhododendron. They've got traditional ornamental shrubs. But it doesn't mean anything to them. It's a maintenance problem: They either grudgingly care for the garden themselves or hire someone to come in and make it look nice." The look-nice types use beauty bark and mow the lawn and use motorized air blowers to blow the grass clippings into the street. Carl and Shery would rather see the clippings composted because, as they point out, edible landscaping is a complicated issue, with all elements interconnected.

Carl Woestendiek and Shery Litwin are garden shamans. They

stamp the city ground and make a verdant, country earth appear. Shery is a short, sharp-featured woman with razor-cut black hair and a taste for long earrings that spin and wobble while she moves. She is always moving, walking in careful Tai Chi patterns while she talks. Her moving hands give fleeting, ephemeral shape to the rapid onward roll of her words. At times a look will cross her face that suggests she doesn't know where she is headed. But she will just as quickly break through the thicket of a complex idea and stand knee-deep in the essence of what's on her mind. A rapid-fire smile marks the moment, she exhales in long relief, then catches her breath and is off again.

Carl has been standing by, a long shadow of a man with thinning hair and high knobby cheekbones. His skin is weathered and he has the hands of a laborer. He is a patient man and his movements are spare, considered. His words come slowly and he lays his thoughts out as carefully as a mason, tapping each one into place with the butt of a trowel. Where Shery can wave her hand and make the unbeliever suddenly see the possibility of a small pond in an urban yard, Carl has eyes that see a city with an altered landscape. "Any reason you need this driveway?" he'll ask, staring down at the pavement, and the concrete as good as melts away and filbert thickets spring up between his feet. When Carl shifts his gaze, fence lines fall.

"If what we do in our own yard and other yards were to catch on," Carl says, "you'd see fence lines change. Any new construction in the neighborhood would take sunlight into consideration. You'd see fewer dogs because they don't fit in with this kind of landscape, and you'd see more wild birds, more fowl and poultry and rabbits in backyards. People would share ideas and cuttings. They'd understand the skill it takes to grow food and maybe respect the farmer more than they do now. What you'd see, I think, is more people out in their yards."

Food is the active element in the designs Shery Litwin and Carl Woestendiek create as Edible Landscape Services. "We provide the integration for people who want to change their yards, but who see food production as a separate thing," Shery says. Lawns don't have much meaning for these two. "People too often are tyrannized by a dominant aesthetic that demands a certain amount of lawn or a certain kind of fencing or a certain kind of planting. It is mostly eighteenth- and nineteenth-century fashions," Carl adds. Their design is not only to create beautiful yards for their clients, but to create yards their clients can eat, yards that attract their clients the way nectar attracts hummingbirds to places they've never been before.

The dominant intellectual organic matter that gives their landscape designs a living quality is permaculture, a term coined by Australian environmental scientist Bill Mollison that describes the conscious design of permanent, self-sustaining agricultural ecosystems. "Permaculture," Shery Litwin says, "is the design of landscapes patterned after natural ecosystems. At any scale they are complex—each plant or structure or animal in the design has more than one function; they are efficient—emphasizing good use of space; they are conservative—as in the cycling of nutrients; and they are self-regulating—making minimal use of chemical pesticides and fertilizers. We focus on the quality of the interaction between person and yard, yard and neighborhood, neighborhood and bio-region. This approach is environmentally righteous. It makes for human pleasure. And in the long run, it saves money."

Their own yard, like the teeth of a dentist's child, needs work. Wooden pegs mark the spot where the pond will appear beneath the living room window. The water and the fruiting plants and trees around it will attract birds in close to the house. Last summer Carl managed to find the time and materials to build a small rock wall in front of an expanse of black bamboo that yields bamboo shoots for the kitchen. Paths and other walls, beds, and tree plantings are envisioned. The contours of the yard have been allowed to assert themselves, the rises and dips that deeply trouble a lawn enthusiast. Entry points will change. A structure will emerge. But already the food is there. Even in winter.

The maritime climate of the Pacific Northwest allows for active gardens ten and eleven out of twelve months. In January Shery Litwin picked a salad in her yard that included small leaves of Russian red and Scotch curled kale, green wave and *maizuna* mustard greens, cilantro greens, bok choy, *shungiku* (edible chrysanthemum), scallions, endive, chickweed, parsley, garden cress, arugula, *mache,* rutabaga greens, beet greens, shepherd's purse, sage, rosemary, golden marjoram, and thyme. And dandelion leaves. The winter was mild enough that the dandelions were early and Carl had spotted them. The bold flavors grappled with each other like naked wrestlers and demanded a dressing that could achieve consensus in the bowl. Dressing applied, the salad had all the power of hot winter soup.

It is not an uncommon sight these days in Seattle, this wild salad. Mark Musick at Pragtree Farm north of the city got it rolling with the encouragement of some of the city's more adventurous chefs. So many of the elements of the wild salad are, in fact, wild that weeds—the good, flavorful ones—have been invited into the Pragtree salad garden. Minimal tillage occurs. The only tractor on the farm is the Goose Tractor, two geese in a bottomless, movable pen. They eat everything beneath their feet, scratch up the soil, and leave their high-powered droppings behind.

Perhaps the best exponent of the wild salad today is Fraser Common Farm in British Columbia's Fraser Valley. The farm calls its salad company Glorious Garnish and Seasonal Salad. They supplied the salad at Carl and Shery's wedding reception. Other friends supplied yellow Finn potatoes from eastern Washington, apples and pears, and goat and sheep cheese. It was that interconnectedness of all things appearing on the table. Carl and Shery are as involved with rural food production as they are with food production in the city. "I grew up in Chicago," Carl says, "and I don't think I saw a plant until I was twenty. I'm a city boy at heart, so what I know is how to grow food in the city." Carl has a degree in horticulture from Washington State University. He apprenticed at Pragtree Farm, then worked for seven years as the groundskeeper at the Good Shepherd Center in Seattle, a hilltop Catholic school and estate that was turned over to the city. Carl helped establish the demonstration garden for Tilth, an organization linking urban and rural people devoted to a sustainable regional agriculture. The garden is for city people to see what kinds of planting and composting techniques work well in Seattle.

Carl and Shery's wedding reception was held on the grounds at the Good Shepherd Center. Planning outdoor weddings and receptions in Seattle in September can be a thing of whimsy. You are as likely to bake as you are to soak in a late summer rain. It was Carl and Shery's great fortune, however, that the day could not have been any more perfect. The reception buffet table laid out beneath the enormous old shade trees at the Center was as lovely a statement about Pacific Northwest provender as has ever been made. The requisite baked salmon stuffed with sliced onions and French sorrel was the size of a small seal. The yellow Finn potatoes had been turned into a vinaigrette-covered potato salad. The fruits and cheese fell early victim to the knife. But it was the wedding salad that garnered the most attention. A dozen shades of green frolicked with violas, ox eye daisies, rose petals, calendula petals, and *shungiku* blossoms. A botanist could identify beet greens, certainly, and several kales. The radicchio that is exotic in so many salads had to share its glory with the likes of red orach, wild sorrel, lamb's quarter, chickweed, anise hyssop, fennel, arugula, dill, garlic chives, amaranth, lovage, and yarrow.

The salad, of course, changes with the season, the powerful flavors of winter giving way to greater delicacy come spring when various lettuces, sweet and crisp, can be added. The traditional vegetable garden has been transformed in Carl and Shery's yard. Their food grows where it seems to belong, not isolated in back of the house in a rectangle of turned earth. To pick a salad requires a walk throughout the yard, which of course has been their point all along, an edible yard designed to attract the unwary to its wonders.

Northwest "Waldorf" Salad

A classic salad that's so at home here because of our supply of good apples and walnuts. This is a version, with the addition of flavored nuts, orange zest and a little apple butter in the dressing, that's even more flavorful than the original.

> *2 tablespoons salad oil*
> *1 cup walnut halves*
> *1 tablespoon sugar*
> *1 teaspoon salt*
> *2 tablespoons apple butter*
> *½ cup mayonnaise*
> *1 teaspoon lemon juice*
> *3 or 4 Granny Smith apples, cut in bite-sized chunks*
> *1 cup chopped celery*
> *1 teaspoon orange zest*
> *Finely chopped walnuts for garnish*

Heat the salad oil in a heavy skillet. Add the walnuts. Sprinkle them with the sugar and salt and cook over medium-high heat until the sugar caramelizes and coats the nuts, about 2–3 minutes.

Mix apple butter, mayonnaise and lemon juice in a medium-sized bowl. Add apples and celery and coat well. Chill until ready to serve. Just before serving, sprinkle with orange zest and walnuts.

Serves 6

DEFINING THE PACIFIC NORTHWEST STYLE

> ### Sweetbread Salad with Warm Tarragon Vinaigrette

Marianne Zdobysz from Queen City Grill created this warm salad.

> 4 ounces fresh veal sweetbreads
> 1 tablespoon salt, plus salt and pepper for seasoning
>   lettuce
> Flour
> Olive oil
> 2 tablespoons balsamic vinegar
> 2 tablespoons reduced beef stock
> 1 tablespoon chopped tarragon
> 2 tablespoons cold unsalted butter
> Hearts of romaine and Bibb lettuce

Soak sweetbreads in cold water for at least 1 hour, overnight if possible.

Drain and place sweetbreads in a saucepan, cover with cold water, add salt, and bring to a boil. As soon as water boils, remove sweetbreads and cool under cold running water. Remove nerves and excess fat.

Slice sweetbreads into scallops ½-inch thick, season with salt and pepper, and dust with flour. Sauté in olive oil until brown. Turn and brown the other side.

Remove sweetbreads from pan and deglaze pan with vinegar. Add beef stock and tarragon to pan and reduce liquid to 2 tablespoons. Whisk in *cold* butter to finish. Present sweetbreads on bed of romaine and Bibb lettuce with sauce ladled over.

Serves 2

Oregon Blue Cheese, Bartlett Pear and Hot Walnut Salad

A fall salad that works well as a first course and one that eloquently, if simply, showcases Pacific Northwest products.

> *½ cup walnut oil*
> *3–4 tablespoons sherry vinegar*
> *Salt and a pinch of sugar to taste*
> *1 cup walnuts*
> *3 tablespoons butter*
> *2 heads Bibb lettuce, washed carefully and dried*
> *2–3 Bartlett pears*
> *2–3 ounces Oregon blue cheese*
> *Hot walnuts for garnish*

Make a dressing by beating together the oil, vinegar, salt and sugar.

Sauté walnuts over low heat in butter.

Place lettuce on salad plates. Arrange sliced pears on top. Pour dressing over the fruit and lettuce, and sprinkle with chunks of blue cheese and hot walnuts.

Serves 6

Oregon Blue Cheese Crumble

This recipe, a winner in the *Mercer Island Reporter* recipe contest, has become the most popular hors d'oeuvre I serve. It's also delicious on grilled steaks or hamburgers and as a topping for salads. Or serve the crumble with sliced Granny Smith apples and wheat crackers as the fruit-and-cheese course at dinner.

> *8 ounces crumbled blue cheese*
> *2 cloves garlic, mashed*
> *⅓ cup olive oil*
> *2 tablespoons red wine vinegar*
> *1 tablespoon lemon juice*
> *½ cup chopped red onion (or chopped green onion)*
> *½ cup minced parsley*
> *Freshly ground black pepper*

Sprinkle cheese into a shallow 6- to 8-inch dish. Mix together garlic and olive oil and drizzle over cheese. Combine remaining ingredients and pour over the cheese. Refrigerate for 1 hour. Sprinkle with pepper.

Serves 8

Dad's Potato Salad

This was a fixture of my childhood in Spokane, Washington, a traditional potato salad best made with French's mustard and Best Foods' mayonnaise. You can add celery, pickles, or anything else you like. The most important thing is to use enough mayonnaise. That makes the salad moist and flavorful.

> *2 pounds boiling potatoes, peeled after cooking (or leave skins on small red potatoes)*
> *½ pound Walla Walla sweet onions or other sweet onions, sliced in crescents*
> *4 eggs, hard-boiled*
> *1–1½ cups mayonnaise*
> *3 tablespoons mustard (I like the flavor of prepared yellow best)*
> *Kosher salt and freshly ground black pepper*

Cook the potatoes until tender. Cool to room temperature. Break up into bite-sized pieces using two forks. Sprinkle potato with chopped onions and refrigerate, covered with plastic wrap. Chill well. When ready to serve, cut up eggs and add to potatoes. Moisten well with mayonnaise and mustard. Season to taste with salt and pepper.

Serves 6–8

Yellow Finn Potato Salad

Add freshly cracked pepper just before serving so that it retains its aroma and flavor.

2 pounds yellow Finn potatoes (or small red potatoes)

Malt Vinegar Dressing:
⅓ cup malt vinegar
⅔ cup salad oil
1 teaspoon Dijon mustard
1 teaspoon kosher salt
1 clove garlic, minced
1 bunch green onions
Freshly cracked pepper

Gently boil potatoes about 20 minutes until fork tender. Drain and cool slightly. Then peel.

Combine well the remaining ingredients, except onions and pepper, to make a dressing.

Slice the potatoes, pour on dressing, and marinate at room temperature 1 hour. Mix carefully again. Sprinkle with green onions and several grinds of freshly cracked pepper.

Serves 6

Marinated Mushrooms and Walla Walla Sweet Onions

A great accompaniment to hamburgers and steaks.

½ pound fresh mushrooms, cut in thick slices
1 Walla Walla or other sweet onion, cut into crescents
⅓ cup salad oil
⅔ cup tarragon vinegar
1 tablespoon fresh tarragon, or 1 teaspoon dried
½ teaspoon kosher salt
2 tablespoons sugar

Mix mushrooms and onions together in a bowl. Combine the rest of the ingredients to make a marinade. Pour on the marinade. Let marinate for several hours, then serve.

Yield: 1 quart

Wilted Lettuce Garden Salad

The dressing for this is equally good over spinach or boiled and sliced new potatoes.

> *1 head red leaf lettuce, or equivalent amount of green leaf*
> *lettuce*
> *8–10 pieces bacon*
> *¼ cup sugar*
> *¼ cup cider vinegar*
> *2 tablespoons water*

Break red leaf lettuce leaves in quarters, green leaf lettuce in half, but no smaller as lettuce will shrink. Place in large bowl.

Cut bacon in half-inch pieces and cook until crisp. Remove pieces, but keep the fat. Put heat on low. Add sugar and vinegar. Dissolve sugar. Add water. Turn heat up to medium. Just as dressing starts to bubble, remove from heat and pour over greens. Add bacon. Toss and serve immediately.

Serves 4

Romaine, Carrot, Blue Cheese and Walnut Salad

When you select romaine, find a head that smells sweet and fresh, not bitter, at the stem end. Your salad will taste much better.

> *1 head romaine*
> *2 carrots, peeled and very thinly sliced on the bias*
> *4 ounces blue cheese*
> *½ cup large walnut pieces*
> *¼ cup red wine vinegar*
> *1 teaspoon kosher salt*
> *½ teaspoon sugar*
> *1 teaspoon Worcestershire sauce*
> *1 teaspoon freshly cracked pepper*
> *½ teaspoon Colman's mustard*

Cut romaine into bite-sized pieces. Put in a large salad bowl. Mix in carrots. Sprinkle blue cheese and walnuts over top. Cover with plastic wrap and refrigerate until ready to serve. Whisk together the remaining ingredients, or shake them vigorously to make a dressing. Toss the salad with dressing before serving.

Serves 6

Tomato, Cucumber and Green Pepper Salad

This salad is excellent with barbecued fish or meat. I think you'll find that the tomatoes taste much better when served at room temperature.

> *¼ cup white or red wine vinegar (tarragon vinegar works well, too)*
> *¼ cup light olive oil or salad oil*
> *1 teaspoon sugar*
> *½ teaspoon kosher salt*
> *½ green pepper, cut into thin strips*

1 English cucumber, very thinly sliced
Fresh parsley, minced
Freshly cracked pepper
3 tomatoes, cut into large chunks

Combine the vinegar, oil, sugar and salt. Layer green pepper and then cucumber in a shallow dish. Pour on the vinegar mixture and marinate, refrigerated, for 1 hour. Sprinkle with parsley and freshly cracked pepper.

When ready to serve, put sliced tomatoes in a serving dish. Top with marinated peppers and cucumbers.

Serves 4

Great Greek Salad with Anchovy Dressing

The anchovies in the dressing give this salad much flavor and character.

Salad:
½ small head romaine lettuce, shredded
1 English cucumber
3 tomatoes
½ red pepper (green if red is not available)
8 ounces feta cheese
12 Greek olives

Dressing:
1 small tin flat anchovies
1 clove garlic, cut in half
1 teaspoon oregano
¼ cup red wine vinegar
¾ cup olive oil

Wash lettuce and place in shallow salad bowl. Cover with moist paper towel and plastic wrap. Refrigerate.

Put dressing ingredients in processor and process until smooth. Trim ends off cucumber. Cut in half lengthwise. Scoop out seeds with spoon. Cut into ¼-inch slices and place in small bowl. Cut tomatoes into large chunks. Seed red pepper and cut into thin strips.

To serve: Sprinkle cucumbers over salad greens, then tomatoes, feta cheese, pepper strips and Greek olives. Pour dressing on salad and serve immediately.

Serves 6

Sweet and Sour Cucumbers

I like to serve this in the summer with barbecued salmon.

> *3 nice firm cucumbers (or 1 English cucumber)*
> *1 cup water*
> *¼ cup sugar*
> *2 teaspoons kosher salt*
> *⅓ cup white vinegar*
> *Chopped chives*

Peel cucumbers and cut into thin slices. Mix water, sugar, salt and vinegar, and let sit until sugar and salt dissolve. Pour over sliced cucumbers and refrigerate for 1 to 2 hours. Sprinkle with chopped chives and serve cold.

Serves 6

Broccoli, Mushroom, Avocado and Tomato Salad

The flavors and textures in this salad blend extremely well together.

> *1½ pounds broccoli*
> *½ pound mushrooms, sliced*
> *8 slices thick-sliced bacon cut in ½-inch pieces and cooked until crisp*
> *1 avocado, thinly sliced*
> *½ pound cherry tomatoes*
> *¾ cup mayonnaise*

> ½ *teaspoon sugar*
> ½ *teaspoon salt*
> 1 *tablespoon lemon juice*
> 1 *clove garlic, minced*
> 1 *teaspoon chopped shallots*
> ½ *teaspoon paprika*
> 1 *tablespoon grated carrot*
> 1 *tablespoon finely diced green pepper*

Prepare broccoli for salad by cutting off flowerettes and breaking into small pieces. Peel stalks and cut into thin slices. Put in salad bowl along with mushrooms, bacon, avocado and tomatoes. Combine the remaining ingredients to make a dressing.

Mix the salad with the dressing and refrigerate for at least 4 hours.

Serves 8

Tomato Salad with Fresh Basil

Spread in a glass dish and sprinkle with minced parsley to serve.

> 1 *clove garlic, minced*
> 1–2 *tablespoons wine vinegar*
> ½ *teaspoon sugar*
> *Salt and freshly ground pepper*
> 5 *tablespoons olive oil*
> 2–3 *tablespoons finely chopped fresh basil*
> 4 *tomatoes*

Just before serving, mix together all of the ingredients except the tomatoes to make a dressing. Slice tomatoes ½-inch thick. Overlap slightly on serving plate. Spoon on the dressing and serve.

Serves 4

Marnie's Chutney–Spinach Salad with Red Delicious Apples

I like to serve this salad in the fall when the apples and walnuts are fresh. The dark green spinach leaves and the red apple slices make a pretty combination.

3 tablespoons lemon juice
⅔ cup salad oil
4 to 6 tablespoons mango chutney
1 teaspoon curry powder
1 teaspoon dry mustard
Salt to taste
2 bunches spinach
3 red Delicious apples
⅔ cup fresh walnuts
½ cup raisins
½ cup thinly sliced green onion

Mix together the lemon juice, oil, chutney, curry powder, mustard and salt in a pint jar with a lid and shake well. Let stand at room temperature for several hours. Shake again before mixing with salad.

Wash spinach well to remove any dirt or sand. Remove stems and tough ribs and cut into bite-sized pieces. Pat dry, or spin dry in salad spinner. Cover with plastic wrap and chill in refrigerator until ready to serve.

Just before serving cut apples in half and then crosswise into thin, crescent-shaped slices. Mix spinach, apples, walnuts, raisins and green onion and toss gently with dressing, coating the greens well.

Serves 6

Orange, Red Onion and Cilantro Salad with Pomegranate Seeds

This is the sort of salad we love in a fall dinner that includes Pacific Northwest game birds. In the fall oranges are just in season and pomegranates are still available.

> 6 *oranges*
> 1 *red onion*
> 1 *bunch cilantro*
> 1 *teaspoon chili powder*
> ¼ *cup orange juice*
> ¼ *cup red wine vinegar*
> ½ *cup salad oil*
> ½ *cup pomegranate seeds*

Peel and slice oranges. Arrange on shallow serving dish. Cut onion in half lengthwise and slice thinly crosswise. Scatter the onion over oranges.

Wash and shake dry cilantro. Tear off leaves and reserve

Beat together the chili powder, orange juice, vinegar and oil, and pour over oranges and onion. Scatter cilantro leaves and pomegranate seeds on top of salad and serve.

Serves 6

Couscous Salad with Fresh Corn, Sweet Red Pepper and Cilantro

This colorful salad is terrific with roast chicken.

> 1½ *cups water*
> 2 *tablespoons butter*
> 1 *cup quick-cooking couscous*
> ⅓ *cup salad oil*
> *Juice of 1–2 limes*
> 4 *green onions*
> 1 *cup cooked fresh corn kernels*
> 1 *small red bell pepper*
> ½ *jalapeño pepper*
> ¼ *cup fresh cilantro*
> *Salt*
> *Tabasco*

Put water and butter in a 2-quart saucepan. Bring to a boil. Add couscous, cover and remove from heat. Let sit for 5 minutes. Transfer to small salad bowl. Stir in salad oil and lime juice.

Chop the green onions and, with the corn, add to the couscous. Dice the red pepper and add to the salad.

Carefully remove the seeds from the jalapeño and finely dice. (Be sure to wash your hands afterwards. Remember, the smaller the pepper, the hotter it is and you can burn your eyes easily.) Add the pepper to the salad. Coarsely chop the cilantro and sprinkle over the top. Mix gently until well blended. Season to taste with salt and a little Tabasco.

Serves 4

Mushroom–Bacon Salad

This is a perfect salad to serve with a delicious roast beef and twice-baked potatoes.

> *12 slices bacon*
> *1 pound medium-sized mushrooms*
> *⅔ cup olive oil*
> *4 tablespoons lemon juice*
> *1 teaspoon Worcestershire sauce*
> *½ teaspoon salt*
> *¼ teaspoon pepper*
> *½ teaspoon dry mustard*
> *Butter lettuce leaves*
> *½ cup chopped green onion*

Cut bacon into ½-inch pieces and cook until just crisp. Drain on paper towels.

Clean mushrooms and slice ¼-inch thick. Whisk together olive oil, lemon juice, Worcestershire sauce, salt, pepper and dry mustard until well blended. Pour over mushrooms. Marinate for 30 minutes to 1 hour, but no longer.

Arrange lettuce cups on individual salad plates. Fill with marinated mushrooms. Sprinkle with bacon and green onion.

Serves 6

Japanese Cucumber Salad

Refreshing as a light salad. Wonderful for picnics.

> *1 English cucumber*
> *Kikkoman seasoned rice vinegar*

Peel cucumber. Remove seeds with a spoon. Cut into very thin crescent-shaped slices and put in small serving bowl. Pour over seasoned rice vinegar. Chill.

Serves 6

Chilled Orange, Date and Fresh Coconut Salad

In mid-January and February the large navel oranges appear in the markets. At the same time you will see plump, moist large dates. The combination of the two makes a very refreshing winter salad.

> *5 large oranges*
> *½ pound fresh dates*
> *½ cup freshly grated coconut*

Peel the oranges with a small, sharp knife. Cut into the flesh of the orange slightly as you peel to remove any of the white pith. Carefully cut into each section so that you remove the orange segment with as little membrane attached as possible. Place segments in a shallow salad bowl.

Pit the dates and cut into ½-inch pieces. Add the dates to the oranges and mix. Chill for several hours to let the sweetness of the dates blend with the oranges. Just before serving, sprinkle with the coconut.

Serves 6

Chicken and Apple Salad with Chutney–Lime Dressing

This simple recipe meets every expectation for a clean, fresh-tasting chicken salad.

> *2 pounds chicken breast*
> *2–3 Granny Smith apples*
> *1 cup homemade mayonnaise, or your favorite brand*
> *Juice of ½ lime*
> *3 tablespoons mango chutney*

Poach chicken and cool. Skin bone, and cut chicken into ½-inch strips (or use oven-roasted chicken). Put in 2-quart serving bowl. Cut apples into thin slices and add to chicken. Blend together the mayonnaise, lime juice and chutney and mix thoroughly with the chicken and apples. Serve on individual pieces of green leaf lettuce.

Serves 4

Than's Shrimp and Shredded Cabbage Salad

This delicious slaw comes from a young Vietnamese man who works for Gretchen Mathers, a popular Seattle caterer. The unusual combination of flavors, both exotic and different, is a real treat.

> *1 head red cabbage, finely shredded*
> *1 head green cabbage, finely shredded*
> *1 bunch coriander, chopped*
> *½ cup chopped fresh mint*
> *1–2 fresh jalapeño peppers (seeded)*
> *½ cup Tiparos (or Vietnamese-style) Fish Sauce*
> *3 cups white wine vinegar*
> *½ cup sugar*
> *Juice of 2 limes*
> *1 teaspoon freshly ground pepper*
> *1½ pounds fresh baby shrimp (or smallest available shrimp cut in half), cooked*

Mix cabbages, coriander, fresh mint, and peppers together in a large bowl. Beat the remaining ingredients together to make a dressing and pour over salad. Toss well. Top the salad with shrimp just before serving.

Serves 10–12

Mother's Coleslaw

My mother says that shredding the cabbage is the most important part of making a good coleslaw.

Coleslaw, baked beans and barbecued chicken are another way of saying summer in the Pacific Northwest.

> *4 cups shredded green cabbage*
> *½ cup mayonnaise*
> *2 tablespoons lemon juice*
> *1 tablespoon grated onion*
> *½ teaspoon celery seed*
> *1 teaspoon sugar*
> *½ teaspoon salt*
> *¼ teaspoon black pepper*
> *1 cup dry roasted peanuts*
> *½ cup red pepper, diced*
> *½ cup green pepper, diced*

Crisp the shredded cabbage in ice water for 1 hour. Drain well.

Combine mayonnaise, lemon juice, grated onion, celery seed, sugar, salt and black pepper. Mix the well-drained cabbage with the dressing and the dry-roasted peanuts. Garnish with the diced red and green bell pepper.

Serves 6

Lynnie's Coleslaw

A nice tart slaw that's even good the next day.

> 1 large head green cabbage
> 1 large head red cabbage
> Walla Walla sweet onion (or mild white salad onions),
>   chopped
> 1 cup chopped green onion
> 1 red pepper, seeded and cut into thin strips
> 1½ cups pimiento-stuffed olives, sliced
> 2 cups red wine vinegar
> 2 cups light, fruity olive oil (or salad oil)
> 2 teaspoons sugar
> 2 teaspoons celery seed
> 2 cloves garlic, minced
> 1 teaspoon salt
> 2 teaspoons freshly ground black pepper

Finely shred cabbages. Put in large bowl with onions, pepper, and olives. Mix together vinegar, oil, sugar, and seasonings. Pour over cabbage mixture and mix well.

Serves 8–10

Dad's Hot Slaw

An assertively flavored slaw that holds its own with a good grilled steak. The anchovies dissolve in the hot dressing, which is poured over the crisp cabbage, wilting it slightly.

> ½ head green cabbage, shredded
> 6 thick slices bacon
> ⅓ cup olive oil
> ⅓ cup red wine vinegar
> 1 small tin flat anchovies
> 2 cloves garlic, thinly sliced
> Freshly ground pepper

Put cabbage in salad bowl. Cut bacon into ½-inch pieces and cook until crisp. Drain and reserve.

Warm olive oil in small frying pan over medium heat. Add vinegar, anchovies and garlic. Mash anchovies with fork until dissolved. Turn up heat just until mixture begins to boil. Pour over shredded cabbage.

Sprinkle with bacon and serve. Lots of freshly ground pepper brings all the flavors together.

Serves 4

Dad's Anchovy Dressing

This is my house dressing, which works particularly well on a simple romaine salad with croutons. I give bottles of this as Christmas gifts.

1 ounce blue cheese (or Parmesan)   *¾ cup olive oil*
1 small tin anchovies   *¼ cup red wine vinegar*
1 clove garlic

Whirl ingredients in blender. Chill.

Yield: 1½ cups

Honey–Lime Dressing for Fresh Fruit

Prepare a large bowl of fruit in the middle of summer and serve this dressing on the side.

⅔ cup sugar   *5 tablespoons cider vinegar*
1 teaspoon dry mustard   *1 tablespoon lime juice*
1 teaspoon paprika   *1 tablespoon grated onion*
1 teaspoon celery seed   *1 cup salad oil*
⅓ cup honey

Mix ingredients together well. Chill for several hours before using.

Yield: 1¾ cups

Dungeness Crab Louie

A classic Northwest Salad.

> 1 head iceberg lettuce
> 2 cups mayonnaise
> ½ cup milk
> 2 tablespoons vinegar
> ½ cup cocktail sauce
> ¼ cup grated Walla Walla sweet onion (or white salad onion)
> 1 pound Dungeness crabmeat (shrimp may be substituted)

Garnish:
Tomato wedges   Hard-boiled egg quarters
Avocado slices   Jumbo black olives

Just before serving, line salad bowl with outer leaves of the head of lettuce. Shred remaining lettuce to form a salad bed. Combine well all other ingredients, except for the crabmeat and garnish, and pour over salad bed. Top with crab and garnish.

Serves 4

My Favorite Oil and Vinegar Dressing

A tart and lively dressing that came to me from my good friend Ann Wells. Her father was a great chef in London at Buckingham Palace and Ann gave me his recipe 20 years ago. I have enjoyed it ever since whenever an assertive dressing is called for, such as for large, fat spears of cooked, chilled asparagus.

> ⅓ cup malt vinegar   1 teaspoon salt
> 2 teaspoons chopped shallots   ⅔ cup salad oil
> 1 teaspoon Colman's mustard

Mix vinegar, shallots, mustard, and salt together. Slowly whisk in salad oil.

Yield: 1 cup

Oregon Blue Cheese Dressing

Make this ahead. You can double the recipe and keep it on hand in the refrigerator. This is a heavy dressing, best with romaine lettuce and other strong greens to support it.

4 ounces Oregon blue cheese, crumbled into very small pieces
1 cup buttermilk
½ teaspoon dry mustard
1 teaspoon coarse black pepper
1 teaspoon Worcestershire sauce
1 clove garlic, minced
1 teaspoon kosher salt
1–2 tablespoons lemon juice
1⅓ cups mayonnaise

Place all the ingredients in a medium-sized mixing bowl. Stir together. With an electric mixer set at low speed to prevent splashing, mix together half the quantity at a time, until well blended. Don't overmix. Refrigerate overnight. This dressing must sit 24 hours before serving.

Yield: 2½ cups

Honey–Tamari–Sesame Dressing for Winter

This complements the sturdy, colorful kales mixed with winter salads.

1 tablespoon honey
1 tablespoon tamari
1 teaspoon pure (not filtered) sesame oil
⅓ cup safflower oil
⅓ cup rice vinegar

Blend ingredients together.

Yield: 1 cup

Lemon Herb Dressing for Summer

Delicate and light for tender, summer garden greens.

> ⅔ cup light, fruity olive oil
> ⅓ cup lemon juice
> ½ teaspoon freshly cracked pepper
> ½ teaspoon kosher salt
> 1 teaspoon fresh lemon thyme
> ½ teaspoon dried basil
> 1 tablespoon minced shallot

Blend ingredients together.

Pear Vinegar, Walnut Oil and Roasted Walnut Dressing for Fall

This dressing works well on a salad of mixed greens—a light sprinkle of blue cheese adds flavor.

> ⅓ cup walnut oil
> ¼ cup pear vinegar
> Salt and pepper
> 1 cup roasted and salted walnuts

Blend oil, vinegar, salt and pepper. Sprinkle walnuts over salad after dressing has been well tossed with the greens. (This keeps them crisp and adds texture to the salad.)

BERRIES

W | hen she started, back in the early '70s, all Ann Franklin meant to do was harvest berries at the u-pick farms down near Portland, then sell her goods out of the trunk of her car in The Dalles at the Saturday market. She lived in The Dalles, a Columbia River town in Oregon and the last stop on the old Oregon Trail, with her husband Ken and his three boys and her three boys. Ken ran the marina, selling boats and repairing motors.

After a few years Ann discovered she could buy fruit wholesale, though she liked the idea of picking her own. "I'm a country girl," Ann says, harking back to a hard-work childhood on a Sacramento Valley farm in the '30s and '40s. Her berry business grew beyond the capacity of her car and settled into her garage. Farm wives would drive from as far away as Grass Valley out in the high desert wheat land, to buy their canning and jam fruit from Ann. Then they convinced her to start driving out to them. And when she did, and word spread, people in one town after another asked Ann if she wouldn't stop for them as well. Today, from June to September, Ann Franklin drives a fruit and produce route in eastern Oregon that would weary a veteran UPS delivery man.

In late summer she loads her van with 300 ears of Golden Jubilee corn picked by Ken that morning, 250 pounds of sweet Roadside cantaloupe, 850 pounds of Bartlett pears, 250 pounds of vine-ripened tomatoes, 250 pounds of Red Haven peaches, 300 pounds of Alberta peaches, 250 pounds of Hale peaches, 30 pounds of Little Red nectarines, 120 pounds of Gravenstein apples, 75 pounds of green beans, a case of green peppers, a box of Satsuma plums, and a case of dry land Tilton apricots, the last of the season. With each new box, the van groans under the weight. "Either one of us or the other," Ann Franklin says, "the van or me, is going to have to get a girdle."

Ken and Ann Franklin now live on 10.9 acres of farmland downriver from The Dalles outside the town of Hood River. The Hood River Valley is famous in Oregon for apples and pears. The Franklins bought the place in 1978 when the boys had pretty much gone their own ways. They now run a little cattle like the other pocket farmers in the area. And Ken still puts in a full day at the marina. But fruit is the big issue, mostly berries. In spring, when she's putting the thorny berries up on wires, Ann Franklin will go through seven pairs of heavy work gloves. Ken gets home from work and is already changing clothes by the time he hits the front door, headed for the bedroom. He'll move irrigation pipe or roto-till new beds until it is dark, then come back to the house with the blood pressure of a young, relaxed man. He leaves the fruit selection up to Ann, figuring that after her many years of picking berries she knows what she wants.

"Our only conflict was the thornless blackberry," Ann recalls. "I only wanted 100 plants because I knew from picking them how prolific they were. So he got 500 plants and we put in ten rows, 450 feet long. About three years ago we had a real hard frost and a freeze and we got Arctic winds blowing on the river for about 30 days and it killed the crowns of the thornless blackberries and when they came up that spring, they had reverted back to thorns. We pulled them all out, but we're still fighting them."

The Franklins grow marionberries. blueberries, tayberries, rasp-berries, boysenberries, and most recently kotata berries, a delicious new blackberry hybrid from the Oregon State University breeding station. It is a big, black, glossy berry, similar in many ways to the marion, though sweeter. "I like it because I can hold it a few days without refrigeration and it doesn't fall and get all weepy," Ann Franklin says, "and that's something you want for the fresh fruit market. A lot of people haven't heard of the berries I'm growing now, but they will. Next year we'll have plenty of kotatas."

The Franklins grow peaches as well: Early Gold, Sunbright, Hale Haven, Alberta, and Hale-Berta. Ann swears by the Hale Haven and whenever any of her trees need to be replaced that is the peach that goes in. "They're solid," she says. "They don't mush up, and they have that full, syrupy Red Haven flavor, so that makes a good peach. It bruises: Don't get me wrong. But when you can it, if it's got marks on it, it will come back to its natural form, just like it was fresh picked." Ann calls that "bounce back."

Ann Franklin is an attractive woman who counts her fifty-seven years as a proud accomplishment. Her hair is blond gone to white. She parts it on one side of her head, taking full advantage of a natural curl and wave. She is warm, friendly and good-natured, and radiates a certain shine because of it all. Maureen Stapleton could walk right in and play her part, though she would have to learn to move with the stiffness that comes from numerous back surgeries and no kneecaps, the result of a tumble down a flight of stairs. "We don't do strawberries," Ann says, "because I can't get down and pick them. If I get down on the ground ,ike that, I have to crawl over to something so I can pull myself up." She says all this while bent over in the back of her van, stacking cases of fruit.

Strawberries mark the beginning of her season. "Usually June twelfth," Ann says, "then raspberries by the twentieth, and tayberries. The marionberries come in by the 4th of July, and boysenberries ten days later. I figure six weeks from bloom to harvest and I keep it all written down in a little calendar book each year so I can tell my customers what to expect."

Ann Franklin's day begins sometime before six. By seven she's on the road in a white Chevy van that has seen its full complement of wear and tear. The engine roars like a bulldozer. Inside the van the gentle odors of fruit take turns asserting themselves until the day is warm enough for the cantaloupe to become most apparent of all. The top of the dashboard is a landscape of road maps, old gas receipts, notebooks, scrap paper, and a carton of Kents. Ann is a serious smoker. She travels with a thermos of coffee and adds Cremora to her cup as she drives. The coffee cup and the overflowing bean bag ashtray rest on top of an engine cover crusty with the stains of spilled coffee mixed with cigarette ash.

The countryside around Hood River is forested with tall conifers, but as Ann drives east on a highway hugging the contours of the Columbia River, the impressive evergreens give way to scruffier pines made of the stuff that can endure an arid climate and barren soil. The lay of the land shrinks down from the steep, waterfall-wetted escarpments that characterize the Columbia where it cuts through the Cascade Mountains, a stretch of river called The Gorge. Coarse, blackened, volcanic rock begins to show up at the side of the highway in a waving lava ribbon of anticline and syncline. And the heat increases. Farther east than Ann will drive, Lewis and Clark called the land the most God-forsaken piece of country they had seen since heading west.

The Lewis and Clark party reached the stretch of the Columbia River now known as The Dalles in October 1805. William Clark describes mighty rapids and "bad whorls and suck" in the river. "Nor could I See where the water passed further than the current was drawn with great velocity to the Lard. Side ˙of this rock at which place I heard a great roreing . . . The whole of the Current of this great river must at all stages pass thro' this narrow channel

of 45 yards wide . . . I determined to pass through this place not-
withstanding the horrid appearance of this gut swelling, boiling
and whorling in every direction, which from the top of the rock
did not appear as bad as when I was in it."

These were confident young men—Clark was thirty-five; Lewis
thirty-one—who had the crossing of an entire continent lending
them a certain credibility when they decided to run the rapids in
their cargo canoes. They knew their limitations. When they made
their move through The Dalles, an appreciative Indian audience
gathered to watch. The word that a bunch of crazy white men were
going to try to kill themselves on the worst part of the river had
spread from the fishing camps on both sides of the Columbia.

All that wild river is gone now. The riparian memory of what it
was lies submerged under deep, placid water backed up behind
dam after dam producing the cheapest electricity in the nation.
Where Lewis and Clark once pushed their luck on the water, tug-
boats now nudge barges up and down the river. The tugs have
distinctive pilot towers rising high above their decks, giving the
man at the wheel a view of the water ahead.

Ann heads in-country at Arlington where the Columbia River is
wide and flat and motionless in the morning. The town is hidden
off the highway by sagebrush-covered wind-rounded bluffs with
exposed pockets of black basalt that look like bad tooth decay in a
fruit tramp's smile. She parks the van in the shade in the parking
lot of the Pheasant Grill Drive-In, a roadside café she will return to
at the end of the day for a maple pecan ice cream cone. Ruby, the
cook, is a big woman who waddles over to the open van door. She
wears shorts, a polo shirt and apron. Ann sells her several canta-
loupes.

"I've got some nice Golden Jubilee corn picked this morning,"
Ann says, but Ruby answers that she's on a new diet and corn isn't
part of it. Al, the Shell gas station owner, pulls up in a long car
with his wife. Al has a flat-top haircut with a thin spot in the middle
on top. He's looking for peaches. "There are only two of us," Al
says, "so all we need is a half dozen. We just want 'em to eat." Al
ends up buying cantaloupe and corn as well. "They're only the two
of us," he repeats like an apology while handing over his money.
He picks up the sacks, and ambles back to the car and his wife. Ann
slams shut the van door and climbs into the driver's seat. She
pauses to light a cigarette before starting the engine.

It is all uphill between Arlington and Condon, and then Condon
to Fossil, from near sea level to 3,366 feet at Cummings Hill. Local
high school students have no open rock faces or concrete bridge

abutments to paint with their graffiti, so they use the two-lane highway in one long section out of Arlington. The messages are written to be read both driving uphill and coming back down.

The landscape takes on a visual counterpoint of juniper, sagebrush, and carefully scribed wheat fields. This is a long-settled piece of country with grain elevators standing beside abandoned railroad track, and farm machinery lined up in careful rows next to weathered outbuildings: an open land with all the signs of people, but no people to be seen. Hay has been baled in some fields, bundled into giant shredded wheat biscuits in others. The fields are not flat, but roll steadily uphill on an angle and drop down into draws, then rise up and slant away like fast jets sucked over the horizon. Where the wheat has been harvested the golden brown stubble sticks up like a worn-out old brush that has lost too many bristles to be of much use. In some fields circular irrigation rigs with electric motor-driven wheels pivot too slowly to be noticed by the passing eye. In other fields old Aeromotor windmills pump water for lazy cattle too dumb to know their market is all but gone. The symmetry of the land is constant, broken only by clusters of old farmhouses that have been in the same family for three generations, houses surrounded by stately shade tree windbreaks.

Ann Franklin points to the trees and calls them "populars" instead of poplars. She calls the line of them a "windbreaker," and she wishes she had such big trees on her own land where the wind so constantly howls off the Columbia that Hood River has become a wind-surfing center on the West Coast. Ann Franklin understands farmers and their hard times and their instinct for the land. She has seen her own crops destroyed by weather and worries about this coming winter. The ducks and geese have been flocking up too early on the river, and Ann fears the worst. Bad weather isn't going to help the economy in the area. "Last year we got rain when we shouldn't have and it ruined the wheat, or they couldn't harvest. This year we got too much wheat with an early heat wave and the grain didn't mature. A lot of these farmers plowed their crops under. These people want my fruit, but they don't know where the next dollar is coming from. Same's true in town."

An empty canning cupboard is something Ann Franklin would rather not imagine. Each year she cans enough pears to last two years, and the next year she does peaches. That way she doesn't have to contend with all the fruit at once. She freezes her berries when they come in, then makes her jams and jellies in the winter.

"I lived in the country growing up," Ann says. "Near Chico,

California. In the '30s, Dad would move the wood stove out under the cherry trees in summertime and my mother did the canning: 180 quarts each of peaches, pears, and tomatoes. We didn't have back then the kind of peaches we have now. We had the old Cling and you'd have to dip them in lye water and then in cold water to get the skins off. I just wonder what the younger generation would think if they had to go back to fruit like that. They always ask for the same peaches their mothers used, but I tell them different."

Ann Franklin's father died when she was thirteen. She had an older brother and six younger siblings, and her mother had to go to work at night. So Ann grew up cooking the evening meal, then getting everyone up in the morning and feeding them breakfast. She was eighteen when she married the first time, and twenty when she first tasted milk out of a bottle. "We had our own barnyard animals—ducks, turkeys, chickens, a milk cow—butter and cream, our own eggs; I remember what things used to taste like." She was pushing thirty when she moved to Hood River, a single mother with three boys. She and her first husband had driven through the country years earlier, and when it came time to pull out of California and a marriage gone sour, she knew which direction to head. "I'd have to have one foot on the banana peel and the other in the grave to go back to California to live," Ann says today.

She was working in a Hood River restaurant when she met Ken. He was always driving down from The Dalles for boat motor parts, and made a point of stopping at the restaurant. He'd been coming in for a year before he asked her for a date. "The way he did it, I had to say I'd go out with him," Ann recalls. "I wasn't interested in dating. I had three kids to raise. I was thirty-four and if you had been burnt like I had, you'd have been gun-shy too." She told Ken she got off at 9, then asked her boss if she could leave at 8. "Ken was down there at 7:30," Ann says with a little laugh, "but he was such a nice guy. Just great. I wouldn't trade him today for a million dollars."

"I love to fish," Ann says, "and we do that a lot together. I learned to fish as a kid and it taught me to be patient. It helps you relax and gives you time to meditate on things. I'd take the boys fishing when they were babies, tie them in the stroller so they could splash their feet in the water. When I hurt my back and knees Ken gave up a lot. We used to bowl three nights a week in three different leagues, and he gave that up. His average was 235 a game. And for seven or eight years he gave up hunting. Now, he picks a spot where I can fish and he can hunt the hills."

The two-lane highway rises and drops and careens right and left. It rarely settles down and stretches out. A sudden drop and turn takes the van through the thick shade of cottonwoods growing in a dry, rocky creek bottom where several old houses huddle. It's a town called Olex and it is behind the van and disappearing in the rearview mirror with the next turn and rise in the road.

Ann Franklin leaves the highway for a smaller side road that takes her to Mikkalo, a general store and post office surrounded by black locust trees that date back to the turn of the century. The Mikkalo family has farmed all the nearby country for generations and the land is littered with Mikkalo brothers and cousins and wives and children. Some of the Mikkalo women had asked Ann if she wouldn't drive in to them rather than making them drive all the way to Condon, and Ann complied. "The people are so nice," she says ingenuously, "you can't turn them down. I could drop all my routes and just stay in The Dalles, but I like all the people where I go."

Ann Franklin's van once broke down in Arlington with 150 crates of berries. The water pump had burned out and the mechanic said he would have to drive all the way back to The Dalles to look for a replacement. Ann had the phone number of a woman in Condon who had placed an order, so she called and explained her dilemma and asked the woman to go down to the parking lot and tell all those waiting that she wouldn't be making it. An hour later the woman pulled up in a station wagon. Another followed behind. The ladies loaded all the berries into the two cars, and Ann as well, and drove back to Condon to sell the fruit.

Condon is the Gilliam County seat and, with all the brick buildings on the main street, has a suitably substantial look. It isn't a town ever likely to dry up and blow away. Ann drives past the Buckhorn Tavern, the Liberty Theater, Cooney's Garage, the Roundup, Sweeney Mortuary, and the C and J Shoestring Drive-In. She parks in a gravel-covered lot on a side street. Some customers are waiting. Others pull in. They all drive American cars.

Ann takes her time getting organized, setting out the cash box, arranging the scale so the customers can read the needle, moving empty boxes out of the way, opening the back doors for easy access to the corn and cantaloupe. Everyone crowds around the side doors to examine the goods, but when it comes to doing business, there is an order to things. The older ladies are first, then the young moms with wiggling kids. "Look at those green peppers," one woman remarks. "Aren't they just beautiful? Mother and Dale love them stuffed." Another asks Ann if she got the Gravenstein apples, and Ann replies that indeed she did. There are forty pounds in a box.

A thin old man with chipped, rimless bifocals approaches the van. He works nearby and wants to buy a few peaches. He wears an old denim work apron over his coveralls and the cap on his head is threadbare on the edges and shiny with an ancient patina of grime. "How are you today?" Ann asks him, and he replies without much enthusiasm that he is OK. He is there for the peaches, not the conversation. "What'd the doctor say?" Ann persists and the old man looks at her for a moment and answers, "He said, 'Come back.' I guess I'll be going down there all winter."

Stout old iron-haired ladies, stiff-hipped and tight-lipped, count their cash out of government envelopes. They buy peaches and pears and apples by the box and regret out loud that berry season is over and gone. They are church-basement women, farm wives who have aged with the land around them. They speak with each other in the full, unspoken knowledge of where each one stands in the community. When they leave, a woman completely unlike them shows up just before Ann slams her doors.

She is a tough, lean old bird wearing a gimme hat, T-shirt, and new jeans. Her arms are farmer-tanned a deep brown and the squint wrinkles around her eyes are deep and well defined from a summer of looking out for cattle from the back of a horse. She wears old mud- and manure-spattered cowboy boots that are cracked along the toes. One has split open across the top of her foot. She drives a pickup truck with a water spray tank mounted in the back as a range fire precaution. When she pays for her peaches and the box of Little Red nectarines, she finds her money in a leather purse ornamented with hand-tooled roses and horses. She is a friendly woman, quick to smile, but shy. She doesn't have much to say. She probably thinks of herself as a rancher, not a farmer. "Between Condon and Fossil," Ann will say a little ways up the two-lane, "I've run into a 1,000-head herd of cattle on the road moving from one dry land pasture to another. It took twenty minutes to clear, so I had nothing to do but ease back and watch."

As Ann nears a farmhouse built close to the highway she explains that in summer, when the black Bing cherries are in, the farmer stands next to his mailbox waiting for her van to appear at the crest of the hill. "He knows about when I'll show up," Ann says, "and as soon as he sees me he starts waving this big red flag. Every week the cherries are in, he buys a box. Twenty pounds. He's convinced his wife that they are good for his gout. I prefer the Rainier cherry myself. I think it's the up-and-coming cherry. The flavor's great. You can eat them, and you can bake them, and they hold up in a cool place with a wet gunny sack over them and they taste just picked. When you bite in you get that crunch and snap of a fresh picked apple."

Fossil is the county seat of Wheeler County. Five hundred thirty people live there, a lot of them retired. Hunters come through in the fall. Fishermen and rockhounds show up all through the summer. The two garages seem to account for the majority of the business in town, though a sign in front of a house on the way into Fossil indicates that dew worms and night crawlers are for sale on the premises. Ann Franklin parks her van under a tall old cottonwood tree, one among many planted long ago around the Fossil town park. The senior citizen center is nearby, and soon after lunch has been served, men and women wander over to see what Ann has today.

Her stops on the route have all lasted between fifteen and thirty minutes. But not Fossil. Ann spends the better part of the afternoon under the cottonwood, and she rarely has time to sit down for lunch. Cars continually drive up, some from sixty miles away. If the crowd gets too big, as often as not someone will jump into the van with Ann and help bag fruit, take orders, weigh up produce, and make change. Without Ann Franklin these people would have no fruit to put up, no berries for jam and jelly. Certainly not of the quality and variety that she supplies. The growing season is too short for them to do a lot of it themselves, and what the deer don't eat, the grasshoppers finish off. "I've been over here after the 4th of July," Ann says, "and it was so cold it was raining and sleeting and there was snow in the grain in the fields."

The drive home is a straight shot in a near empty van. Fresh rain looks like steel wool hanging off in the distance. Ann looks windblown, her hair springing off in several directions. It has been a long, hot day and the ice cream cone she buys when she gets down out of the high country and back onto the river at Arlington barely revives her for the last stretch home. "Ken," she says, "won't let me go out much past October. It gets rainy and the roads ice up. Condon can have icy fogs that last for weeks. It's just too dangerous. People'd like me to keep coming with the fall apples, but I only do the Transparent, Lodi, and Winter Gravenstein. The rest are just too late."

Just past The Dalles the air changes. It is cooler, more moist, and feels close to home. The tall evergreens appear, and out on the

Columbia, Indian fishermen have set their nets for salmon the way they have done for countless centuries past. Fall is close.

"My little guy won a blue ribbon with his tayberry wine," Ann says with transparent pride. She is speaking of a longtime customer in Fossil who is either pushing eighty or has already gone over the edge. Whenever Ann shows up with a new fruit, the red Bartlett pears for example, he's the first to latch on. He recognized the kotata berry for the blue ribbon potential it has, but held off on jam in deference to kotata berry wine. It won't be ready until next year's county fair. "I was out until all hours picking him the last of those kotatas so he'd have enough for his wine," Ann Franklin says. "Ken had wanted them, too. But I just couldn't say no to that little guy. And Ken understood. Aren't too many men out there as understanding as my Ken."

Fruits

Strawberries: Shuksan, Puget Beauty, Hood, Rainier.
Raspberries: Meeker, Willamette, Golden.
Blueberries: Bluecrop, Dixie, Jersey, Collins.
Blackberries:

Boysenberry: Reddish-black fruit. Blackberry–raspberry cross. Large, sweet, and juicy.

Marionberry: A cross between wild and domestic blackberries, named for Marion County, Oregon, where it was developed. Medium-sized fruit that is longer than it is wide. Bright black.

Loganberry: Red raspberry–wild blackberry cross. Large fruit with unique flavor and quality.

Tayberry: From Scotland, a red berry similar in shape to the boysenberry. Cross between loganberry and black raspberry.

Wild Blackberry: The large Himalayan is an import that now grows everywhere. The fruit is black and juicy and seedy, and is used best in cobblers. The diminutive Coast Trailing blackberry is a native with an intense, sweet flavor. It is a tiny black berry that is prized for pies and jams. It takes forever to fill a bucket, so pickers are known to keep their best patches top secret.

Currant: Both red and black. Used in sauces, jellies and juices.

Gooseberry: A round, green berry protected by vicious thorns. The tart fruit is used in pies, jams and sauces.

Lingonberry: Red, tart berry on low-lying evergreen plant. Swedish pancakes without lingonberry syrup and without lingonberries stirred into whipped cream are simply not Swedish pancakes.

Huckleberry: For the Indians in the Northwest, this berry constitutes a major wild crop and its arrival is celebrated with First Berry rituals. Sweet, musky blue huckleberries are found at higher elevations on the mountainsides, particularly where there has been fire or logging activity. The red, tart huckleberry is found in the Puget Sound lowlands.

Grapes
Interlaken: Golden berry, good for drying as raisins.
Schuyler: Extremely productive, sweet, juicy black grape for eating fresh and using as a juice.
Canadice: Red seedless with spicy flavor.
Red Flame: A red seedless variety.

Cantaloupe:
Some of the sweetest, richest-tasting varieties come from Oregon and eastern Washington. Soft fruit that doesn't travel well. Short season.

Cranberries:
A big crop on the coast of Washington and Oregon.

Rhubarb:
One of those vegetables that always gets stuck in among the fruits. The majority of the U.S. crop is grown in the Puyallup Valley in the shadow of Mt. Rainier. First come the hothouse varieties, then the field-grown rhubarb.

Hood River Cream Sauce with Berries

This is a light custard sauce that complements but doesn't overpower the fruit. Serve fresh berries in cut glass dishes, then pass around a pitcher of this wonderful sauce.

> ¼ plus ⅓ cup sugar
> 2 pints freshly sliced strawberries, fresh raspberries or
>   blackberries
> 1 cup milk

½ cup cream
1 vanilla bean
4 egg yolks
2 teaspoons cornstarch

Sprinkle ¼ cup of the sugar over berries and chill.

Meanwhile, in a medium-sized saucepan combine milk, cream, and vanilla bean, and bring just to a boil. Remove from heat and let sit for 10 minutes. Using an electric mixer, gradually beat ⅓ cup sugar into egg yolks until mixture is light and lemon-colored. Beat in cornstarch. Stir milk mixture into beaten yolks. Return to saucepan. Cook until mixture is thick enough to coat a metal spoon, then cool. Remove vanilla bean. Chill thoroughly.

Yield: 1½ cups

Tukwila Blackberry Jam

We have a bank near our house that is covered with blackberry bushes. The fruit comes on in the late summer. These are the large, juicy blackberries that don't work in pies because they are simply too juicy. These berries work best in cobblers and jam. (The smaller wild blackberry is the best for pies.)

3¼ cups crushed blackberries
¼ cup freshly squeezed lemon juice
1 package powdered pectin
1 cup light corn syrup
4½ cups sugar

Lightly rinse blackberries in cold water, then crush but don't purée in a food processor. Put the blackberries and lemon juice into a 4-quart kettle. Slowly pour in the pectin, stirring vigorously until it is dissolved. Let the mixture sit for 45 minutes, stirring occasionally. Add the syrup and mix well. Over very low heat, stir sugar gradually into the crushed berry mixture. Using a candy thermometer, slowly warm to 100 degrees, but no warmer. When sugar is dissolved, pour into clean glass jars with tight lids. Will keep in refrigerator for 2 to 3 weeks or will store for longer periods of time in freezer.

Yield: 8 cups

Overlake Farm's Spiced Blueberry Jam

Every August we look forward to fresh blueberries at the Overlake Farm near Seattle. Five varieties grow there, and they all freeze well.

> *6 cups blueberries*
> *2 tablespoons lemon juice*
> *1 box powdered pectin*
> *½ teaspoon each cloves, cinnamon and allspice*
> *5 cups sugar*

Crush washed berries (should measure 4 cups). Put into a 5-quart kettle. Add lemon juice, pectin and spices; mix well. Bring to a full boil over high heat, stirring constantly. Immediately stir in sugar. Boil hard 1 minute stirring constantly. Remove from heat and skim off foam. Stir and skim for 5 minutes to get rid of floating fruit. Ladle into sterilized glasses. Cover with paraffin.

Yield: 10 cups

Forgotten Torte with Fresh Berries and Whipped Cream

If you gradually add your sugar *after* the soft peak stage when beating egg whites, they form a light, lovely meringue. My favorite fruit topping for this is a combination of peaches or nectarines and two or three different kinds of berries mixed together in a bowl and sprinkled lightly with sugar and a dash of kirsch.

> *1 cup egg whites (about 7 eggs)*
> *¼ teaspoon salt*
> *½ teaspoon cream of tartar*
> *1 teaspoon vanilla*
> *½ teaspoon almond extract*
> *1½ cups granulated sugar*
> *4 cups marionberries, raspberries or strawberries, or sliced*
> * peaches, lightly sprinkled with ⅓ to ½ cup sugar*
> *1 cup whipping cream, lightly sweetened*

Preheat oven to 450°. Put egg whites in a large glass or stainless metal mixing bowl and bring to room temperature. Beat until soft peaks form. Sprinkle in salt, cream of tartar, vanilla and almond extract and continue beating. Slowly add sugar while continuing to beat egg whites until all the sugar is added and a nice meringue has formed. Transfer to a standard-sized angel food cake pan buttered on the bottom only. Place in oven and turn off heat at once. Leave in oven overnight. Next morning, turn out onto a serving plate. Chill, lightly covered with plastic wrap, in refrigerator.

An hour before serving, whip the cream and use it to frost the meringue cake. Spoon berries and/or peaches on each serving.

Serves 8

Blueberries and Cream Muffins

A moist blueberry muffin with golden brown "cracked" tops and filled with plump blueberries.

> *4 ounces butter, at room temperature*
> *¾ cup sugar*
> *2 extra large eggs, at room temperature*
> *1 teaspoon lemon zest*
> *¾ cup sour cream*
> *1 teaspoon vanilla*
> *2 cups fresh or frozen blueberries*
> *2 cups flour*
> *½ teaspoon baking soda*
> *½ teaspoon salt*

Preheat the oven to 375°. Cream butter and sugar together. Add eggs, one at a time, beating well after each addition. Add lemon zest, sour cream and vanilla. Stir in blueberries.

Mix together the flour, baking soda and salt, and fold into the sour cream mixture with a spatula, being careful not to overmix.

Fill 12 paper-lined muffin cups. Bake in the oven for 25 to 30 minutes.

Yield: 12 muffins

Strawberry–Rhubarb Jam

This is my idea of a morning wake-up jam, the tart rhubarb mixing with the sweet strawberries on bread hot from the toaster.

> *3 cups chopped rhubarb*
> *2 cups crushed strawberries*
> *¾ cup water*
> *1 package powdered pectin*
> *5 cups sugar*

Cut rhubarb into small pieces. Add ¾ cup water. Bring to a boil, then turn down heat and simmer in a large covered pan over low heat for about 3 minutes, or until the rhubarb gives up its juices. Add strawberries. Stir in powdered pectin. Over high heat, stirring constantly, bring mixture to a full boil. Add sugar, continuing to stir and bring to a boil. Boil hard 1 minute, remove from heat. Skim off foam, stirring occasionally, for 5 minutes. Pour into sterilized jars. Seal with paraffin.

Yield: 9 cups

Cranberry–Apple Relish

I like the fresh tart taste of the cranberries in this recipe. It stands up well to turkey and dressing, and leaves you wondering about all those years you spent worrying over cranberry sauce.

> *2 Granny Smith apples, with skins on*
> *1 orange with skin on*
> *1 bag cranberries*
> *1 cup sugar*

Wash all fruit. Quarter orange and core apples. Coarsely chop cranberries, then apples, and then orange in a food processor. Add sugar, stir, and chill for several hours in the refrigerator before serving.

Yield: 4 cups

Cranberry Conserve

This goes well with a roast pork or game dinner.

6 cups cranberries
2 oranges
orange zest
½ cup chopped walnuts

1 cup golden raisins
4 cups sugar

Put cranberries in a large saucepan. Cover with water and cook until tender. Drain and mash well with a potato masher.

Grate the rind from the orange, orange part only, then remove the white membrane. Chop the oranges in a food processor.

Mix cranberries, orange zest, chopped oranges, nuts and raisins in an enamel pan and cook slowly for 15 minutes. Add sugar and bring to a boil. Turn heat down and cook for 5 minutes over low heat, stirring continuously, until mixture thickens.

Yield: 6–8 cups

Steamed Cranberry Pudding with Butter Cream Sauce

Cranberries give a tart flavor to this moist holiday dessert. Serve warm with the hot butter cream sauce poured over the top.

Pudding:
¼ cup shortening
⅔ cup sugar
1 egg
1½ cups flour
½ teaspoon salt
3 teaspoons baking powder
⅔ cup milk

1 cup chopped cranberries
½ cup seedless raisins
½ cup chopped walnuts
1 teaspoon orange zest

Cream the shortening and sugar together. Add the egg and continue mixing. Add all of the remaining ingredients and stir until completely mixed.

Pour into a greased and sugared 1-quart mold. Cover. Put 1 inch of water in a pot with a tight-fitting cover. Place the mold on a rack in the pot and cover. Bring to a boil and then reduce heat to low. Steaming should be slight. Add water as needed. Steam for 1½ hours. Remove mold from steamer; let stand several minutes before unmolding. Spoon on the butter cream sauce.

> Butter Cream Sauce:
> *1 cup sugar, mixed with 1 tablespoon flour*
> *1 cup butter*
> *½ cup half-and-half*
> *1½ teaspoons vanilla*

Place all of the ingredients in a heavy saucepan. Stir until well mixed. Simmer over low heat for 12 to 15 minutes, until thickened.

Serves 4

Cranberry–Orange Muffins

The tart cranberries are complemented by the orange. The muffins are moist and rise well.

> *1 teaspoon orange zest*
> *1 cup orange juice*
> *½ cup honey*
> *2 extra-large eggs, beaten*
> *¼ cup vegetable oil*
> *2 cups cranberries, coarsely chopped in food processor*
> *2 cups all-purpose flour*
> *1 tablespoon baking powder*
> *½ teaspoon salt*

Preheat the oven to 375°. Mix together zest, juice, honey, eggs and oil. Stir in cranberries.

Mix flour and baking powder together and fold into orange–cranberry mixture, until just mixed. Don't overmix.

Drop the batter into paper-lined muffin tins. Bake in the oven for 25 minutes.

Yield: 12 muffins

Blueberry–Apple Chutney

This spicy, fresh-tasting condiment complements roast pork or roast chicken.

> *2 pounds blueberries*
> *Zest of 2 lemons*
> *1 pound sugar*
> *3 Granny Smith apples, peeled, cored and finely chopped*
> *1 cup cider vinegar*
> *Juice of 2 lemons*
> *1 tablespoon red pepper flakes*
> *1 tablespoon mustard seed*
> *4–6 sterilized pint jars*

Wash fruit. Combine blueberries, lemon zest and sugar, and leave overnight in refrigerator. The following day peel and chop apples. Combine apples, vinegar, lemon juice, red pepper flakes and mustard seed with blueberry mixture. Cook in heavy enamel saucepan over low heat until mixture thickens, about 30 minutes. Pour immediately into sterilized jars and seal.

Yield: enough for 4–6 pint jars

Fresh Berry Syrup

I like to keep this in the freezer to enjoy over vanilla ice cream in the winter, or to make berry ice cream or fruit fools.

> *1 pound fresh or frozen berries*
> *1 cup sugar*

Warm berries and sugar gently over low heat, stirring until sugar is dissolved. Remove from heat and push the mixture through a strainer. Scrape bottom of strainer to get as much berry pulp as possible without seeds. Freeze in plastic container with tight-fitting lid.

Yield: 2 cups

Tamara's Raspberry Sauce

This is a very simple, but very elegant, sauce. You may leave the seeds in (for instance, when you are pouring it over yogurt) or strain them out for sauce to serve with chocolate cake. The sauce freezes well and keeps for months in the freezer. (This also works well for blackberries.)

> *9 cups raspberries*
> *2 cups sugar*

Put the berries in a saucepan and mash slightly. Add the sugar and bring to a moderate heat. Cook for five minutes. Cool, and transfer to containers.

Yield: 1½ quarts

Vanilla Ice Cream

This is my favorite ice cream recipe, a rich French-style vanilla that is the best accompaniment to perfect berries. (You don't have to cook it!)

> *2 cups sugar*
> *4 eggs*
> *4 cups whipping cream*
> *1 teaspoon vanilla*
> *Seeds from 2 vanilla beans (split each bean and remove seeds*
>   *with the tip of a knife)*
> *4 cups whole milk*
>
> *Ice*
> *Rock Salt*

Beat sugar and eggs together until light-colored and creamy. Add whipping cream and stir. Add vanilla and vanilla seeds. Add milk. Pour into container of your ice-cream maker and cover. Layer ice and rock salt according to the manufacturer's instructions on your machine. When hard to stir, remove dasher. Put the lid on and pack with more ice and rock salt, and cover for 1 hour.

Yield: generous half gallon

Blueberry Sauce

Very nice on blintzes for brunch.

> 1½ cups blueberries
> ½ cup orange juice
> ¼ cup sugar
> 1 tablespoon cornstarch
> 1 teaspoon orange zest

Cook all ingredients over low heat until thickened.

Yield: 2 cups

Strawberry Butter

This is good on breakfast scones (*very* Northwest).

> ½ cup butter
> 1 cup sliced strawberries
> 1 tablespoon lemon juice
> Honey to taste

Cream butter. Add strawberries, lemon juice and honey. Continue creaming until well blended.

Yield: 1½ cups

Glazed Strawberry Pie

A beautiful pie that tastes like strawberries and cream.

> *3 cups sliced strawberries*
> *1 9-inch baked pie crust, p. 305*
>
> Topping:
> *2 cups mashed strawberries*
> *½ cup cold water*
> *1 cup sugar*
> *3 tablespoons cornstarch*
> *Whipping cream*

Arrange sliced berries in baked pie shell. Meanwhile, make the topping: Put mashed strawberries, water, sugar and cornstarch into a medium-sized saucepan. Stir over medium-high heat until mixture thickens. Pour over uncooked strawberries in shell. Chill until set.

Serve with whipped cream.

Yield: 1 9-inch pie

Strawberry–Rhubarb Pie

For me, strawberries and rhubarb complement each other like no two other ingredients.

> *1½ cups sugar*
> *¼ cup flour*
> *¼ teaspoon salt*
> *Several gratings of fresh nutmeg*
> *3 cups rhubarb, sliced in ½-inch pieces*
> *1 cup sliced strawberries*
> *Pastry for 2-crust pies, p. 305*
> *2 tablespoons butter*

Preheat the oven to 400°. Combine sugar, flour, salt, and nutmeg.

Add fruit, mixing well; let stand 20 minutes. Line a 9-inch pie pan with enough pastry dough to form a crust; spoon in the fruit mixture. Dot with butter. Roll remaining pastry dough ⅛-inch thick and cut into ¾-inch strips. Arrange a lattice crust over the fruit. Turn edges of the bottom dough up and flute with fingers to make a standing rim. Bake in the oven for 40 to 45 minutes.

Yield: 1 9-inch pie

Orange Scone Berry Cakes

This is a gold-medal recipe, my favorite in the book. It was given to me by a dear friend who couldn't remember the source, but has been making these for many years. She made 200 once and froze them for a garden reception.

> *2 cups all-purpose flour (less 2 tablespoons)*
> *1 tablespoon baking powder*
> *1 teaspoon salt*
> *2 tablespoons plus ½ cup sugar*
> *⅓ cup butter*
> *1 extra-large egg, beaten*
> *½ cup cream*
> *2 tablespoons melted butter*
> *1 tablespoon orange zest*
> *1 quart sweetened strawberries*
> *Whipped cream*

Preheat the oven to 425°. Stir together the flour, baking powder, salt and 2 tablespoons of sugar. Rub in the butter until well blended. Combine egg and cream and add to flour mixture. Mix until just blended together.

Turn out on lightly floured board and knead for 1 minute. Roll out to a rectangle 8 inches wide and ¼-inch thick. Brush with melted butter. Sprinkle with ½ cup of sugar and orange zest. Roll up jelly-roll fashion, sealing edge. Cut into 1 inch slices.

Bake in the oven on ungreased baking sheet for 12 to 15 minutes. Serve with strawberries and whipped cream.

Serves 8

Huckleberry Cream Cheese Pie

I first tasted this at a roadside restaurant in huckleberry country and returned home determined to make one of my own. I think you'll find that huckleberries and cream cheese were made for each other.

Crust:
1 cup all-purpose flour
2 tablespoons powdered sugar
½ cup butter

Filling:
3 ounces cream cheese
½ cup powdered sugar
½ teaspoon vanilla
1 cup whipping cream

Topping:
3 tablespoons cornstarch
½ cup sugar
2 cups fresh huckleberries

Preheat the oven to 425°. Blend crust ingredients together until they just crumble. Pat evenly into a 9-inch pie pan. Prick well with a fork and bake in the oven for 8 to 10 minutes. Cool.

Make the filling by beating together cream cheese, sugar, and vanilla. Whip the cream until stiff and fold into cream cheese mixture. Turn into pie shell. Cover with plastic wrap and chill.

Make the topping by mixing cornstarch and sugar together. Stir into the berries and cook over medium heat in heavy enamel saucepan until mixture thickens and looks shiny and clear. Cool and spread evenly over chilled pie.

Yield: 1 9-inch pie

Jan's Huckleberry Nectarine Pie

This is a great treat for a Labor Day weekend gathering. The lattice crust allows some steaming to occur, but not too much, and is good for soft tree fruits which overcook easily, as well as for berries.

Pastry for 2-crust pies, p. 305
½ cup sugar
2½ tablespoons cornstarch
½ cup cold water
4 cups sliced nectarines, unpeeled
1 tablespoon lemon juice
1 cup huckleberries

Preheat the oven to 425°. Line a 9-inch pie pan with enough pastry dough to form a crust. Combine sugar and cornstarch in a saucepan, add water and bring to boil, cooking for 1 minute. Cool.

Mix sugar–cornstarch mixture with nectarines, lemon juice and huckleberries. Pour into pastry-lined pan. Roll remaining dough ⅛-inch thick and cut in ¾-inch strips. Arrange a lattice-style crust over top of fruit. Turn edges of bottom crust up and flute with fingers to make a standing rim. Place pie on cookie sheet to prevent spills on the oven floor. Bake on lower rack in the oven for 30 to 40 minutes, until crust is golden and you can see fruit bubbling slightly.

Yield: 1 9-inch pie

Wild Blackberry Pie

You have to use the small wild blackberries for this pie. The big blackberries, while more abundant and easier to pick, simply yield too much juice.

Pastry for 2-crust pies, p. 305
4 cups small wild blackberries
4 tablespoons flour
1 cup sugar
4 tablespoons butter

Preheat the oven to 425°. Roll out half of pastry and fit into 9-inch pie pan. Fill shell with berries. Mix flour and sugar and sprinkle over berries. Dot with butter. Roll out upper crust and fit over top of pie pan. Seal edges. Make 6 to 8 slits in top crust. Bake on lower shelf of oven for 35 to 45 minutes.

Yield: 1 9-inch pie

Blackberry Cobbler

This is a good way to use the big blackberries. In August we make this daily on Vashon Island, where the berries are wildly abundant, and enjoy it for breakfast and lunch.

> *4 cups blackberries*
> *½ cup granulated sugar*
>
> Topping:
> *1½ cups flour*
> *2 teaspoons baking powder*
> *¼ cup plus 2 tablespoons sugar*
> *⅓ cup butter*
> *1 cup half-and-half*

Preheat the oven to 425°. Put blackberries in a deep-dish pie plate that is at least 3 inches deep to prevent berry juices from overflowing in the oven. Sprinkle berries with sugar.

To prepare the topping, mix together flour, baking powder, and ¼ cup sugar. With fingertips, blend in butter completely. Stir in half-and-half, being careful not to overmix. Spoon topping over berries, not quite covering completely. Sprinkle topping with 2 tablespoons sugar and bake for 30 minutes, or until golden brown on top.

Serves 4–6

4th of July Raspberry Summer Pudding

Sprinkling a little sugar over your berries and letting them sit in the refrigerator for several hours brings out the juice. Served with cream, they are just fine. This was the dessert James Beard had his class serve for the 4th of July picnic at Seaside, Oregon, where the classes were held.

> *¾ cup sugar*
> *2 pints raspberries*

Thin-sliced white bread, crusts removed
¾ cup water
Whipping cream

Sprinkle sugar over raspberries. Let sit for 30 minutes. Line a 6-cup flat-bottomed bowl with white bread. Transfer berries to medium-sized saucepan. Mix in water. Bring to a boil. Remove immediately from heat and let cool. Pour half into bread-lined bowl. Add another layer of bread, then the remaining berry mixture, and finally cover with bread. Lay a plate that will fit inside the bowl on top to add the necessary weight to press mixture into bowl. Refrigerate for 4 to 6 hours. Invert onto serving plate. Serve with whipped cream.

Serves 6–8

Huckleberry Slump

This is a colonial New England specialty that has become a part of the culinary tradition of the Pacific Northwest.

6 cups huckleberries (blueberries can be substituted)
1 cup sugar
1 teaspoon cinnamon
½ cup water
1½ cups all-purpose flour
¼ teaspoon salt
1½ teaspoons baking powder
½ cup milk
Sweetened heavy cream mixed with a dash of fresh nutmeg
and lightly whipped

Combine huckleberries or blueberries, sugar, cinnamon, and water in a saucepan. Mix together flour, salt, and baking powder to make a soft dough. Add milk and mix lightly. Bring huckleberry mixture to a boil. Drop dough by spoonfuls onto huckleberry mixture. Cover. Turn down heat and simmer for 30 minutes. Serve warm with sweetened heavy cream.

Serves 6

Gooseberry Fool

It takes time to pick the fuzzy ends off gooseberries, not to mention the needle-sharp jabs you suffer harvesting the fruit. But they are so wonderfully tart that a treat like this fool makes it worth the trouble.

1 quart ripe gooseberries (or raspberries, huckleberries,
  rhubarb, marionberries, blackberries or boysenberries)
½–1 cup sugar, depending on sweetness of fruit
¼ cup water
1½ cups heavy cream (the richer the better)

Combine the berries and sugar with the water in a saucepan. Cook over low heat until fruit is soft. Taste for sweetness and add more sugar if needed. Remove from heat and work through a strainer to make a smooth purée. Chill.

Whip cream. Fold chilled fruit purée into whipped cream, just barely mixing them together to get a well-marbled appearance. Chill and serve in champagne-style dessert dishes with nice, crisp shortbread cookies.

Serves 6

TREE FRUIT

T om and Cheryl Thornton sat each other down in the fall of 1986 for a serious talk about the future of their farm. They had lost 400 apple trees the winter before, victims of an exceptional freeze and misguided planting procedure. In an orchard 5,000 trees strong, having to pull 400 trees doesn't sound too damaging at first. But those apples were six years old. "By the time we get new trees up to that age," Tom Thornton says, his jaw muscles working rhythmically beneath a neatly trimmed, rufous beard, "we will have lost close to $100,000. It was our profit, our black." He looks out the window at twenty acres of farm rising like debt up the hillside behind the house. "I began to feel a little self-indulgent about all this."

He named it Cloud Mountain Farm nine years ago when he found the property outside Everson, a small farming town in Whatcom County in the northwest corner of Washington State, and decided he wanted to have a serious run at agriculture. He had only dabbled before. Tom was just back from the Cloud Forest Zone of Central America, a would-be anthropologist who had found himself enthralled not so much by the Maya's agrarian culture as by their strong sense of community. "I realized I had never been part of a community before," Tom says, "and back in this world the one institution that maintains a community of sorts is agriculture." He settled on tree fruit over other crops because he much prefers perennials to annuals, and trees to vines. In nine years Tom Thornton has emerged as one of the most knowledgeable modern orchardists in western Washington, a man responsible in part for bringing commercial apple orchards back to the western slope of the Cascade Mountains.

Eighty years ago there were 5,000 acres of orchards in Whatcom County, fertile land that stretches from Bellingham Bay off the Strait of Juan de Fuca east to Mount Baker, northernmost peak in a string of snow- and glacier-covered volcanoes. The north side of the county shares a frontier with British Columbia. Ten thousand acres of apples and pears once grew on the San Juan Islands west of

Bellingham Bay. The orchards were never big. In the Nooksak Valley of Whatcom County, where it is possible to keep more milk cows per acre than anywhere else in the world, every dairy farmer grew one to five acres of tree fruit to diversify. Government-stabilized milk prices allowed the farmers to specialize, and so they pulled their orchards to expand their herds. Besides, the trees were getting old and the cannery equipment was old, and everything over on the east side of the Cascades was new and aimed at what would become apple farming for a mass economy.

Washington was among the top apple-producing states in the late 1800s. It took the lead in 1910 and has never relinquished it. The state could claim 29.5 percent of the national fresh apple market in 1970. By 1980, it had climbed to 48 percent with production doubling and FOB prices nearly tripling. The Winesap used to be the apple of choice and Spitzenburgs and Arkansas Blacks could be found among the varietals shipped out of state. Pioneer apple farmers discovered early on that apples growing in the rain shadow on the eastern slope of the Cascade Mountains grew bigger and better tasting than they did anywhere else.

The apples grown in Washington State today set the standard for high quality on the international market and demand an equivalent price. Those are Red Delicious apples for the most part, 68 percent of the state crop. Golden Delicious accounts for another 25 percent of the 55.5 million boxes of fresh market apples sold last year at $650 million. Another twenty million boxes worth $150 million went to the apple processors. Up until 1982 the Winesap held on to third place but was overrun by the Granny Smith, now 5 percent of the crop. Romes, Winesaps, and Newtowns fill in 1 to 2 percent of the crop, and "all others" finish up the last "less than 1 percent."

Cloud Mountain Farm specializes in "all others": Akane, Spartan, Jonagold, Melrose, Idared, Mutsu, Gravenstein, Discovery, and Tydeman among them. Tom Thornton calls them "new varieties," which in apple terms means they are less than one hundred years old. The Melrose was released in 1955, the Jonagold right behind it, and they are only just beginning to attract attention in any meaningful way. Where the average apple orchard in eastern Washington runs around thirty-five or forty acres, with fifty to seventy acres as the most economically efficient unit, Thornton has planted his trees on eight acres of Cloud Mountain Farm land. He doesn't intend to expand. On the east side of the Cascades apple farmers plant 250 trees to the acre, letting them grow to a size that requires pruning and picking from a ladder.

Thornton has never had an apple ladder on the farm. His trees are all full dwarfs that grow no higher than six or seven feet. He prunes them in a style developed at Penn State called oblique palmette. Where an espaliered fruit tree looks like it has been carefully tortured to grow limbs parallel to the ground at precise intervals the length of the trunk, the oblique palmette allows the tree to assume a more natural shape, the limbs angling up and away from the trunk like the barbs of a feather. The trees are pruned to grow flat against four rows of supporting wires. At maturity, when they are full of fruit, Thornton's trees are no more than a foot-and-a-half deep, but the foliage and the fruit are so thick it is impossible to see through the hedgerow. Depending on the variety, he believes he can pick 1,000 boxes, or 40,000 pounds of apples, to the acre.

Thornton plants 900 trees on an acre of land. "The Dutch," he says, "will plant 1,800 trees in the same space. They're the best, but they have so little land they have to be. The Dutch figure that the apple marketing scene is changing so fast that they have developed a system where they can earn money on an orchard for most of its life, then pull the trees if they want to in fifteen years. They are talking about planting a two-year-old tree and paying for their expenses to that point the first year. By the second year they have 80 percent production, and the third year they are going strong. The Dutch just planted five million Jonagolds and in the next five years it will be the most planted apple tree in Europe."

Americans want their apples big, sweet, juicy, and red. What the consumer demands, the industry supplies. There are strains of the Red Delicious grown today that reveal a bright red pea-sized apple from the moment the petals fall off the blossom. The Red Delicious apple has never been as popular in Europe as its golden cousin. Europeans are far more interested in how a thing tastes than how it looks, which explains their loyalty to the Cox, a small, homely apple that is hard to grow but well worth the effort. The Jonagold is likely to displace the Cox. It's an easy tree to grow. It fruits heavily. And its combination of Golden Delicious dessert qualities with Jonathan tartness and cooking characteristics makes it just about perfect for the commercial grower.

Cloud Mountain Farm looks more like a vineyard than a traditional apple orchard. Long rows of wire and cedar fencepost-supported trees staircase their way up the hill behind the Thornton house and the big red barn. An evergreen forest fronted by a thin line of stark white birches delineates where farmland stops and mountain foothills begin. A creek divides two fields, the one planted in trees, the other alternately fallow and planted in nursery stock and the Italian silver skin garlic that Tom and Cheryl grow and pull themselves and then braid for the specialty food market. In spring skunk cabbage strains to bloom in the creek bottom, and a skittish pair of bufflehead ducks rest up on the pond used for drip irrigation six weeks in the summer. "We could have drilled a well," Tom says, standing by the pond and worrying about a leak, "but you can't swim in a well."

Dairies remain the big farming venture in the surrounding countryside. Pea farming and raspberries are big too. The people are descended from Dutch settlers, and many have relatives engaged in dairy farming across the border in Canada where the Nooksak Valley noses north. Credible Gouda cheese can be found in the neighborhood. When Tom Thornton speaks of community, living among Dutch descendants and growing tree fruit in a Dutch style is part of what he means, even though many of the farmers have no idea what he's up to.

He and Cheryl are alone in their endeavor. No one has preceded them in quite the way they grow and sell their fruit. Had there been modern orchards in the area Tom might have been warned away from following the Dutch a little too blindly and planting his dwarfing rootstock-grafted trees with the graft high above the ground. The Dutch think that this practice enhances the dwarfing characteristics of the tree and increases fruit production, but in Tom's case it left 400 trees open to killing freeze. Now he plants dwarf trees with the graft at ground level.

It is not farm size and planting style but marketing that is probably the greatest difference between Cloud Mountain Farm and the commercial orchards on the east side of the Cascades. Traditional apple farmers attend to their fruit production, then sell to the warehouse. Everyone between the farmer and the customer takes a piece of the apple and what's leftover is the change the farmer sticks in his pocket and calls income. When the apple industry has problems, so do the farmers. The grower today actually makes less money on apples than he did fifteen years ago. Tom and Cheryl Thornton avoid all that. They take responsibility for selling what they grow. They deal directly with the public and with grocery store produce buyers—and on their own terms. Cloud Mountain Farm in many ways is the family farm of the future.

Cheryl Thornton manages the marketing. She and Tom have been married for three years, good friends for a dozen. Like Tom,

Cheryl grew up in a city family, not on a farm. She arrived at Cloud Mountain by way of the Alaskan Arctic, where she had worked on a pre-Alaska pipeline field biology survey for the National Oceanographic and Atmospheric Administration. Cheryl loves the Arctic as much as Tom loves the tropics. She named her nine-year-old daughter Cara after the Kara Sea, a body of water in the Russian Arctic Ocean where the northern tip of the Ural Mountains disappears from land.

Marine biology, the kind that demands fieldwork in the Arctic, has tempted Cheryl for a long time, first in Norway where she worked for a while to get a sense of herself and her direction, then at Western Washington State College in Bellingham where she met her first husband and people like Tom Thornton. But she didn't like the way biologists either conducted research or taught. There had to be more to it, she thought; less isolation, more involvement with people and their practical needs. As her interest in marine biology waned, her interest in gardening and agriculture, in food production, grew. And the more she became involved with food production, the more she found herself in a position of translating for a lay community what scientists had discovered but had never been able to adequately communicate. She spent six years working with low-income families on food-related issues, like nutrition, in the food program of a community action agency.

At Cloud Mountain Farm she has come to realize that she and Tom have the opportunity to sell information as much as high-quality fruit. They are educators as well as farmers. "We'll give you the tree," Tom will say to his nursery customers, "and sell you the information you'll need to plant it right." The big problem by last fall was how to keep the farm going. Or to keep it going at all. "I could see how the farm had been in a development stage for eight years," Cheryl says, her dark, black eyebrows keeping an easy cadence with her words. "Now we are in transition and we had some hard-line decisions to make to get the product out and make the farm a business. We had to re-evaluate where we stood philosophically, where we want to go, where we stand economically, how we want to relate to the public. And then how we are going to do it."

They established marketing priorities. The first one is on-farm sales. "We have an open grounds rule, an open farm," says Cheryl. "If people want to come here for a picnic and watch the apples grow through a season, they can come. We don't romanticize farming for them. We don't run a pony show, you know, pumpkin carving contests for the kids in fall. People aren't looking for that this far out in the country. What they really want is to feel connected, if only for a little while. So people experience this place for what it is and keep a little bit within them when they go home. They know farming is a difficult task, and coming out here is a way for them to better integrate with where they get their food."

When the apples are ripe the educating begins. Many customers find themselves experiencing for the first time apples that taste like those of their childhood memories. Cloud Mountain customers, like most mass economy, supermarket shoppers, have become used to disappointing apples. They have all the looks and all the juice, but are picked so green and stored so long and waxed so well, they have no taste, certainly not the exciting taste of an Akane fresh from the tree. "When I eat an Akane at peak season," Tom says, "it's my favorite apple. Then you pick that first Discovery and it's just perfect and you haven't eaten any apples since April and you wonder how anything could be better than this. And then you get a Mutsu at just the right time, or a Jonagold." The Thorntons have a difficult time with customers who want to be told which apple is the best one to buy.

They send out flyers with approximate harvest dates, beginning with Akanes in mid-September and continuing almost until Christmas. Many customers accustomed to buying apples year-round find themselves learning the real season the fruit is ripe. "We tell them to call before they drive all the way out here," Tom says. "If it has rained for four days or if the temperature has dropped, the apples aren't ripe and we don't pick them. Or we can sell out of some apples on a single weekend. People will drive up and buy ten boxes, 400 pounds. That's their winter supply. A lot of these new varieties store much better than the old ones. They keep until spring in an outbuilding or a carport."

The Thorntons have discovered that their most stable market is the on-farm customer, the people who have come to identify with the orchard on the hillside, with Tom and Cheryl, and with the name. Their second marketing priority is to extend the Cloud Mountain name throughout the county. For two years now Cheryl has labored at the re-education of Whatcom County produce buyers. She insists that if they are going to sell Cloud Mountain apples and pears in their stores, then the name must appear above the product. "We want people identifying good fruit with our name," Cheryl says. "They'll see the name and know what the quality is going to be. The produce buyers kept telling me that no one would notice the name, that an apple is an apple. Then customers began asking for Cloud Mountain apples when the stores ran out. 'When you gonna get some more of those Cloud Mountain apples?' They didn't know which apple they had been eating, which variety, but they remembered our name and they remembered how good the apple tasted. Most of the buyers have come around. We don't deal with the rest.''

Last fall in their knee-to-knee, Tom and Cheryl decided to rebuild the barn into a packing shed with cold storage. A front room will be used for sales, and an office is going in on the upper floor. They also decided that the nursery deserved more attention. "It has paid the bills for the last nine years," Tom says. "It's time to make more of a business out of it." They will expand the nursery planting, leasing nearby land from a dairy farmer who went along with the government dairy buyout; he can't have a cow on his property for five years. Twenty percent of Whatcom County's 500 dairy farms closed up with the same program, so land is available.

The Cloud Mountain Farm Nursery mail order catalog says as much about Tom and Cheryl Thornton as anything. It reads like a short textbook on tree fruit production. The fruit trees, the nuts, the grapes and blueberries and currants and kiwis, all grow at Cloud Mountain Farm. Customers don't just buy trees to plant in their yards. They buy the body of experience and information the Thorntons represent. Planting Cloud Mountain fruit trees, in a way, extends Cloud Mountain Farm into every customer's backyard. When Tom Thornton speaks about community, that's part of what he means.

Tree Fruit

Apples:
Though Washington and Oregon are famous for Red and Golden Delicious apples, there are many other locally grown varieties available in markets and roadside fruit stands. Old favorites like McIntosh, Rome Beauty, and Jonathan are common enough. Some other varieties include:

Melrose: A big, round, red apple with a flavor balanced between tart and sweet. The Melrose is harvested between mid- and late October, but will keep until March when properly stored. As good for cooking as it is for eating. Best for eating around Christmas when it has had time to sweeten up in storage.

Mutsu: A Japanese eating apple that in some ways is like the Golden Delicious. This apple grows to enormous size and density. It weighs heavily in the hand. It is crisp and sweet, a great eating apple. Mutsu is harvested mid- to late October and will store until March. Yellow skin with occasional red blush.

Summerred: This is not a keeper. Harvested from early to mid-September, Summerred should be used immediately, either as an eating apple or for cooking. It is fine textured, firm, with a rich flavor. Solid red background, speckled with dots.

Jonagold: Harvested mid- to late October, Jonagold is great for eating, cooking and drying. The crisp, juicy flesh is sweet and rich. It keeps until Christmas. Red stripes over yellow-green skin.

Gravenstein: One of the all-time classics. The Gravenstein is harvested from early to mid-September. It is a large, crisp, juicy apple that is good for eating and for sauce. A summer apple, it doesn't keep. Red-striped skin over light green.

Akane: Another apple from Japan. The Akane is harvested in mid-September and keeps about a month. This is an all-time favorite eating apple with crisp flesh and a flavor that is balanced between sweet and tart. Bright, solid red.

Gala: Harvested in early October, the Gala is a hard, crisp apple that keeps well and cooks well. The flesh is aromatic and semi-sweet. Bright scarlet striped over yellow.

Idared: Transplanted from the eastern United States, a beautiful red apple of classic shape and color. Polishes up like glass. Harvested in late October, it keeps until spring. Idared is tart when first picked, but sweetens with storage. A good cooking and eating apple.

Some other interesting varieties include *Chehalis, Lodi, Yellow Transparent,* and *Newtown Pippin.*

Pears:
The *Bartlett* is ubiquitous. The Red Bartlett is coming on strong. Other Northwest pears of interest include:

Bennet: A Bartlett-type harvested in late August. It is a big pear with smooth skin and a buttery, sweet flavor.

Comice: Harvested in early October, the Comice stores until

Christmas. A large fruit that is greenish-yellow when mature. Very aromatic and buttery.

Bosc: Harvested mid- to late October. A good keeper. Fine texture. Long neck. Spicy flavor.

Seckel: A small, sweet pear that is good fresh or in preserves. Intense flavor. Reddish-brown over yellow.

Asian pears (also called *pear-apples*): This fruit remains firm and crisp and juicy when ripe, much like an apple. The flavor and the texture, however, are nothing like an apple, and only vaguely resemble a pear. Go figure. Asian pears can be eaten either fresh or cooked; they retain their crispness after cooking. Colors range from light yellow to russet. Flavors range from light and sweet to highly aromatic and cinnamon-like. The most popular varieties planted in the Pacific Northwest include *Chojuro, Nijisseiki (Twentieth Century), Hosui, Kikisui, Seuri, Shinsui* and *Kosui.*

Apricots:

Riland: A round, peach-colored fruit with a distinct red blush. The flavor is strong.

Moorpark: Large fruit. Brownish-red skin. Yellow to orange flesh. Aromatic, sweet, rich flavor.

Royal Blenheim: Good either fresh, canned or dried. Sweet, aromatic yellow flesh.

Figs:

Brown Turkey: Rich flavor. Best fresh.

Desert King: Cool-climate fig. Large fruit. Dark-green skin.

Mission or Black Mission: Large fruit with purplish black skin. Excellent flavor. Good fresh, canned or dried.

Peaches:

Halehaven: Red over greenish-yellow skin. Yellow flesh.

Freestone: Best of the canning peaches. Good for cooking or when eaten fresh.

Red Haven: Brilliant red skin. Juicy, sweet yellow flesh.

Roza: Large, round fruit with excellent flavor. Good fresh or canned.

Nectarines:

Red Gold, Sun Gold.

Plums:

Stanley: Italian prune-type. Large, dark-blue fruit. Good dried, fresh, cooked.

Shiro: Yellow skin and flesh. Juicy and sweet. Most popular of the Japanese plums.

Quince:

Pineapple quince: A Luther Burbank original. Aromatic. Excellent in sauces and preserves.

Cherries:

Bing: Crisp, wine-red to black. Great for eating fresh. When dried, these work well in sauces.

Rainier: Yellow-red in color. Sweet, apple-crisp. For cooking and canning as well as eating fresh.

Lambert: Smaller than Bing. Later harvest. Bold flavor.

Montmorency: Best of the pie cherries.

Bing and Lambert comprise 95 percent of the Northwest cherry crop. But other cherries that show up in the market include *Black Republican, Black Tartarian, Royal Ann, Chinook, Burlat* and *Deacon*.

How to Select Fresh Fruit

Buy in season, in your local area. Soft tree fruit is the hardest to get when it's just right. Peaches and apricots don't ripen off the tree, so if you buy them green they will only get mealy as they soften. Buy tree-ripened fruit and can it, freeze it packed in orange juice, or dehydrate it. Nectarines are excellent dehydrated.

Pears, on the other hand, ripen nicely off the tree, so they mature successfully at home.

If you aren't going to eat apples or melons that you bring home immediately, refrigerate overnight, but always let sit at room temperature for several hours before serving. Ice-cold fruit has little flavor.

Cloud Mountain Apple Soup

This is a delicious soup served cold as a first course. A Northwest specialty.

> 1 pound Jonagold or Spartan apples, peeled, cored and sliced thin
> 3 cups water
> 1 teaspoon grated lemon rind
> 1 teaspoon grated orange rind
> 1 tablespoon lemon juice
> 1 tablespoon orange juice
> 1/2 cup honey (more or less to taste)
> 1/2 teaspoon cinnamon
> 1/4 teaspoon nutmeg
> 1/2 cup sour cream blended with 1/4 cup milk

Place all but last ingredient in an enamel or stainless steel saucepan, cover, and simmer about 20 minutes, until apples are mushy. Purée in a food processor or blender. Serve hot or cold with a little of the sour cream mixture drizzled over the top.

Serves 2

Apple Butter

I have a Gravenstein apple tree on Vashon Island that is a prolific producer. This is an easy way to preserve the bounty.

> 3 quarts apple cider
> 8 pounds juicy, ripe apples, washed, cored and quartered
> 2 1/2 cups brown sugar
> 2 teaspoons cinnamon
> 1/2 teaspoon powdered allspice
> 1/2 teaspoon powdered cloves
> 1/2 teaspoon cloves
> 1/4 teaspoon salt
> 8–12 sterilized pint jars

Boil cider in a large enamel kettle until reduced by half (approximately 30 minutes). Add apples and cook over low heat until tender, about 30 minutes. Stir often with wooden spoon. When completely cooked, force through a large mesh strainer. Return to kettle, add sugar, spices and salt. Cook over low heat until sugar is dissolved. Then continue cooking very slowly for 30 minutes. (Put a flame-tamer under the kettle to prevent sticking and burning.) Stir almost constantly at the end of the cooking time. Pour at once into hot sterile jars and seal.

Yield: enough for 8–12 pint jars

Baked Apples with Walnuts and Vanilla Cream Sauce

A good winter dessert. Cozy and delicious.

> *6 medium-sized Rome Beauty apples*
> *1 cup crumbled macaroon cookies*
> *6 tablespoons butter, softened*
> *½ cup brown sugar*
> *12–18 walnut halves*
> *1½ cups apple juice*
>
> *1 pint good vanilla ice cream*

Preheat the oven to 375°. Wash and core apples. Remove about 1 inch of peel from the stem end. Place apples in glass baking dish. Mix together cookie crumbs, butter and brown sugar to form the filling for the apples. Fill the apples, mounding some of the filling over their tops. Press 2 or 3 walnut halves into the mounded filling of each apple.

Heat the apple juice to boiling and pour into baking dish. Bake in the oven for 1 hour, basting 3 or 4 times during the hour. While apples are baking, remove ice cream from the freezer and let it melt. Transfer to a pitcher to serve as a sauce for the warm apples.

Variation: Stuff 3 mini-marshmallows or several raisins to the bottom of each apple cavity when the apples are firmly resting in the baking dish to seal the opening and prevent filling from running out during baking.

Serves 6

Apple Grunt

This is one of my favorite recipes from James Beard's classes at Gearhart, Oregon. I have used it over and over again because it is so easy to prepare and is so well received at the table.

> *3–4 large Granny Smith apples, peeled and sliced*
> *4 tablespoons butter*
> *4 tablespoons sugar*
>
> Topping:
> *⅓ cup white sugar*
> *1 cup self-rising flour*
> *1 cup whipping cream, whipped*
>
> *Vanilla ice cream*

Preheat the oven to 400°. Place apple slices in a well-buttered 9- x 5-inch bread pan, filling it ⅔ full. Dot with butter and sprinkle with sugar. Mix together sugar and flour for topping, fold in whipped cream, and spread over apples. Bake in the oven for 40–50 minutes, or until golden brown and bubbly. Serve warm with vanilla ice cream.

Serves 6

Apple–Mincemeat Pie

The apples help to lighten the mincemeat. This is good served warm with vanilla ice cream.

> *4 cups peeled and sliced apples*
> *2 cups mincemeat*
> *1 tablespoon lemon juice*
> *¼ cup brown sugar*
> *Pastry for 2-crust pies, p. 305*

Preheat the oven to 400°. Mix apples, mincemeat, lemon juice and sugar, and spoon into pastry-lined pie dish. Put on top crust and seal edges. Cut 4–6 vent holes on top crust. Place pie on baking sheet and bake in the oven for 40 to 50 minutes.

Yield: 1 9-inch pie

Pear Marmalade

This is a fresh-tasting fruit topping for toast in the morning, and is a favorite on toasted English muffins.

> *3 cups pears, peeled and diced*
> *1 cup canned crushed pineapple, well drained*
> *1 small orange, chopped and then processed in food processor*
> *1 package powdered pectin*
> *4½ cups sugar*
> *6 small sterilized jars*

Bring pears, pineapple, orange, and pectin to a boil, stirring constantly. Add sugar and boil 2 minutes longer. Pour into hot sterilized jars and seal.

Yield: enough for 6 small jars

Neil's Cranberry Pears

The winter pears take on a beautiful blush color and a nice tart flavor when poached in cranberry juice instead of red wine.

> *6 pears, peeled and cored*
> *4–6 cups cranberry or cran–raspberry juice*
> *3–4 tablespoons honey (depending on how sweet the*
> *pears are)*
> *1 2-inch piece of cinnamon stick*

Preheat the oven to 375°. Put the pears in a 2½-quart casserole with a lid. In a saucepan, bring the juice, honey and cinnamon stick to a boil. Pour over the pears and bake in the oven for 1 hour (until pears are tender but not mushy and have a nice pink color). Let pears cool in juice. Serve in dessert dishes with a little of the juice and a pitcher of cream to pour over.

Note: To make a syrup to pour over the pears, you can reduce the cooking juices in the saucepan.

Serves 6

Pear and Cranberry Crunch

Gretchen's of Course, a Seattle restaurant and catering company, developed these fruit crunches. You can use apples or peaches. One of my favorites is nectarine and blueberry. They are fast and simple to make. You can prepare a large batch of the topping and keep it in the refrigerator, all ready to go.

> *6–8 Bartlett pears*
> *1½ cups cranberries*
> *1 teaspoon orange zest*
> *½ cup granulated sugar*
> *4 tablespoons butter*
>
> Topping:
> *1 cup all-purpose flour*
> *½ cup brown sugar*
> *½ cup butter or margarine*
> *1 cup oatmeal*
> *1 cup chopped pecans*

Preheat the oven to 350°. Peel, core, and cut the pears into 1-inch pieces. Mix together with cranberries, orange zest and sugar, and put in a 9- x 13-inch glass baking dish. Dot with butter.

Mix topping ingredients together, rubbing through fingers until well blended. Pack on top of fruit. Bake in the oven for 45 to 55 minutes until pears are soft and juicy.

Yield: 1 9 x 13 baking dish

Pear Streusel Pie

This is a favorite winter pie recipe that was given to me years ago and is always a showstopper. Use Bartlett pears.

3 tablespoons all-purpose flour
¼ cup brown sugar
¼ cup white sugar
3 tablespoons lemon juice
5–6 peeled and sliced pears
¼ teaspoon fresh grated nutmeg
3 tablespoons melted butter
1 unbaked 9-inch pie crust, (p. 305)

Streusel Topping:
½ cup all-purpose flour
¼ cup brown sugar
¼ cup white sugar
⅓ cup butter, softened
½ teaspoon cinnamon

Vanilla ice cream

Preheat the oven to 400°. Mix together the flour and sugars. Add the lemon juice, pears, nutmeg and melted butter, mixing well. Arrange in pastry shell.

Mix ingredients for topping until crumbly and sprinkle over pears. Bake in the oven for 40–50 minutes. Serve warm with vanilla ice cream.

Yield: 1 9-inch pie

Pear Butter Cake

The buttery richness of this cake makes it just right for a breakfast coffee cake.

> *½ cup butter or margarine, softened*
> *¼ cup sugar*
> *1 teaspoon vanilla*
> *1 egg*
> *1 cup all-purpose flour*
> *½ teaspoon baking powder*
> *¼ teaspoon salt*
> *3 pears, peeled, cored and cut into 1-inch pieces*
> *½ teaspoon cinnamon mixed with ¼ cup sugar*
> *1 cup whipping cream, whipped and lightly sweetened*

Preheat the oven to 350°. Grease a 9-inch springform pan. Cream butter and sugar together until light and fluffy. Add vanilla and egg and mix well.

Combine flour, baking powder and salt. Stir into butter mixture until well combined. Spread dough in pan. Arrange pears on top. Sprinkle with cinnamon sugar and bake in the oven for 40 minutes. Cool. Remove outside rim of springform pan and cut into serving pieces. Transfer to individual dessert plates. Serve with a dollop of lightly sweetened whipped cream on top.

Serves 8–10

Peach Shortcake

I think shortcake should always be served in a shallow bowl so that you can get plenty of fruit around the cake. When James Beard made peach shortcake he always added a little bourbon to the sliced peaches.

> *8–12 ripe peaches, sliced and sugared lightly ahead of time,*
> *with a little lemon juice squeezed over to prevent*
> *discoloring*

1¾ cups cake flour
½ teaspoon salt
1 tablespoon baking powder
¼ cup sugar
½ cup butter, cut into 6–8 pieces
¾ cup milk
Whipping cream, whipped and lightly sweetened

Preheat the oven to 425°. Mix together dry ingredients. Add butter and blend until mixture resembles coarse crumbs. Add milk. Mix until dough follows fork around bowl. Pat out into a circle (½-inch thick) on a buttered baking sheet. Bake in the oven for 20–25 minutes. Cut into 6 wedges. Split and fill with sugared peaches. Save a few slices for topping, together with lightly sweetened whipped cream.

Serves 6

Fresh Peach Melba with Raspberry Sauce and Homemade French Vanilla Ice Cream

I like tree-ripened peaches best in uncooked desserts. The texture and flavor of the fruit seem to disappear during cooking.

French Vanilla Ice Cream
1 cup sugar
¼ teaspoon salt
8 large egg yolks
4 cups milk
2 cups heavy cream
2 tablespoons vanilla

4 peaches

Tamara's Raspberry Sauce (p. 248)
Whipped cream (optional)

To make the ice cream: Mix together sugar, salt and egg yolks. Pour in milk. Cook in double boiler until mixture coats spoon. Cool, strain and add cream and vanilla. Freeze in your ice cream maker according to directions.

Blanch peaches for 1 minute in boiling water. Remove skins and cut in half. Serve a scoop of ice cream with a peach half and pour raspberry sauce over the top. Whipped cream can be offered on the side.

Serves 8

Burnt Sugar Peach and Blueberry Pie

The glazed topping on this pie gives it that wonderful peaches-and-cream flavor.

> 4 peaches, peeled and sliced
> 1 unbaked 9-inch pie crust (p. 305)
> 1 cup sugar
> 1½ cups sour cream
> 3 eggs, beaten
> 1 cup blueberries
> ⅛ cup cinnamon
>
> Burnt Sugar Topping:
> 4 tablespoons brown sugar
> 4 tablespoons white sugar

Preheat the oven to 450°. Place peach slices in pie shell. Mix sugar, sour cream and eggs together. Pour over peaches. Sprinkle with blueberries, then cinnamon. Bake in the oven for 10 minutes at 450°, then for 30 minutes at 350°. Let cool and then refrigerate.

To glaze: Mix together brown and white sugars. After pie has cooled, sift sugar mixture over the top and put under the broiler for several minutes until the topping begins to bubble and form a glaze. It is best to do this just before serving.

Yield: 1 9-inch pie

Jackie Clark's
Peach Dumplings

These fruit dumplings are baked in a delicious sauce and served warm with a pitcher of chilled nutmeg cream to pour over.

> *3 peaches (or apples), peeled and cut in half*
>
> Pastry:
> *1½ cups flour*
> *1 teaspoon baking powder*
> *½ teaspoon salt*
> *½ cup shortening*
> *½ to ¾ cup milk*
>
> Sauce:
> *¾ cup dark brown sugar*
> *1½ cups water*
> *¼ cup butter*
> *¼ cup sugar*
> *½ teaspoon cinnamon*
>
> *1 cup chilled half-and-half, sweetened with 4 tablespoons sugar*
> *and ½ teaspoon freshly ground nutmeg*

Preheat the oven to 375°. Peel peaches and cut in half.

To make the pastry, mix together flour, baking powder, and salt. Blend in shortening. Add just enough milk to hold the mixture together. Roll out on floured board to ¼-inch thick. Cut into 6 squares. Place peach half in middle and bring corners together and pinch to seal. Try to enclose fruit completely.

Put the first 3 sauce ingredients in heavy oven-proof 10-inch skillet and boil for 5 minutes. Place dumplings in skillet with sauce. Sprinkle with sugar and cinnamon and bake in the oven for 25 to 35 minutes.

Serve with chilled cream flavored with fresh nutmeg.

Serves 6

Plum Sauce Cake

This is a wonderful fall cake. The touch of cloves is a nice surprise. I like to serve Hot Spiced Cider (below) with it.

> *½ cup butter*
> *1¼ cups brown sugar*
> *1 egg, beaten*
> *½ teaspoon each of cloves, cinnamon and nutmeg*
> *1 teaspoon vanilla*
> *1½ cups Plum Sauce (recipe follows)*
> *1 cup raisins*
> *½ cup chopped walnuts*
> *2 cups flour*
> *2 teaspoons baking soda*
> *½ teaspoon salt*

Preheat the oven to 350°. Cream butter, sugar and egg. Add spices and vanilla. Stir in plum sauce, raisins, and nuts. Sift together flour, baking soda and salt, and add to plum mixture. Pour into lightly greased 9- x 5-inch bread pan or 9- x 13-inch cake pan, depending on what shape you want. Bake in the oven for 50 minutes in loaf pan or 35–40 minutes in cake pan.

> Plum Sauce:
> *12–16 Italian plums*
> *½ cup water*

Stew plums in a small saucepan with water until soft. Remove seeds and purée in food processor. (In winter use canned plums.)

Variation: Cut the cake into bars and put a dollop of Cream Cheese Frosting on each one.

> Cream Cheese Frosting:
> *3 ounces cream cheese*
> *4 tablespoons half-and-half*
> *1 teaspoon vanilla*
> *2–2½ cups powdered sugar, sifted*

Mix cream cheese and cream together until soft. Mix in vanilla. Gradually add enough powdered sugar to get a good consistency for spreading.

Yield: enough frosting for 1 9- x 13-inch sheet cake or 1 dozen cupcakes

Hot Spiced Cider

We have wonderful fresh cider in the Northwest. I like it served icy cold, or I make this spicy hot cider to take in a thermos when we go skiing.

> 2 quarts apple cider
> ¼ cup lemon juice
> 1 teaspoon whole cloves
> 1 cinnamon stick
> ¼ cup brown sugar
>
> Orange slices

Bring first 5 ingredients to a boil. Simmer and serve with orange slices.

Yield: ½ gallon

GRIDDLE CAKES, SCONES AND COFFEE CAKES

T here is nothing quite like a perfectly fried egg. Take the process too far and the white of an egg goes rubbery while the yolk turns the color of yellow chalk. Hit it just right and the white shines with the blush of firmness while the yolk remains hot and syrupy and darkens to the color of rich mustard. The physics are pure, the formula so simple, and yet every time I fry an egg or order fried eggs I always feel like I am taking a chance. But not at The Dunes restaurant out on Washington's coast. LaRene Morrison, best breakfast chef in the state, fries perfect eggs. "I just stick them on the grill," she says in her froggy voice, "and I tell them to behave."

When LaRene and her husband John Morrison got started at The Dunes in 1964, LaRene cooked three meals a day. "We started with nine tables and no money," she says. "I'd do a home meal every night and it wasn't long before customers would line up on the porch to get in. And they'd watch me work which gave me a case of nerves, so I put newspapers on the windows." Now LaRene limits herself to breakfast. "I wake up feeling like a bundle of joy and ready to work, but when that first lunch order comes in, I quit."

She didn't know how to cook until she was first married when a fine sister-in-law and a good neighbor helped her along. She got rolling with *Fannie Farmer,* the *Joy of Cooking,* and James Beard, and relied on her farm upbringing to remind her of the way things taste. "I once tried cake mixes when I started having kids," LaRene explains. "I thought it would be great, saving time and all. But I gave them up fast. They didn't taste like anything." LaRene had seven children. Ask her about her training for the restaurant and she will tell you she learned to cook for seven hungry kids and no money. LaRene had never worked in a restaurant when she opened The Dunes. John had waited tables in The Mirror Room at the St. Francis in San Francisco as a young man, which made him the experienced one.

The restaurant grew as an extension of the Morrison house, a small bungalow which John and LaRene moved from the main road, the county two-lane that runs through Grayland down to the salt grass-covered dunes bordering the Pacific Ocean. There is a beach between the dunes and the water, a wide, flat expanse running forever in either direction, north or south. It is the kind of beach that gets an old Marine excited. It is a beach with treasures lying in wait, like sand dollars and the occasional Japanese glass float. A long walk can last all day on the beach at Grayland and wash away the burdensome thoughts of a lifetime. During clamming season, when the razor clams are choice, the lowest tides come at night and the legion of clam diggers scour the edge of the water, lighting their way by gas lantern. From back at The Dunes it looks like the opening scene of a Chinese fairy tale.

Razor clam fritters appear on LaRene's breakfast menu, along with squid fillets and Hangtown Fry, that Gold Rush mix of breaded fried oysters, fried eggs and bacon. She likes to cook omelettes and lists thirteen on her menu, ranging from crab, shrimp or oyster omelettes on through to wild mushroom omelettes when the chanterelles and *matsutakis* are in season. She'll cook eggs poached on a bed of spinach any old time, but eggs poached on fresh asparagus is strictly a seasonal thing. LaRene is a big woman, a formidable presence in the kitchen, and though she breaks into the sweetest imaginable smile at the least provocation, she does have the voice of a truck driver and the bearing of a woman who, having raised seven children, has seen and heard it all and laid down the law more than once.

The portions she serves are not skimpy. She loads an oval plate with toast made from delicious bread baked on the spot, hash browns, eggs and ham, if you order it, or bacon. The preserves are a pinnacle experience, as well as pear and apple butters and compotes like dark dreams. Flavor is a guiding principle. Everything tastes not only just the way it should, but is somehow heightened above that level. The cause of this pleasant culinary turn of phrase is no doubt LaRene's enthusiasm for good food. It leaks in and flavors the pot.

Some meals can be successfully dished up with little or no enthusiasm or emotional warmth on the part of the cook. But not breakfast. It is the one meal that suffers when the cook, no matter how talented a technician, doesn't care. That's the difference between LaRene Morrison and too many cooks today: Before she was ever a technician in the kitchen, she was an eater. She likes good food and a day is not complete without at least one new recipe catching her eye. On a trip into Seattle or Portland she heads right for the bookstore and spends her time browsing through and buying cookbooks. She fell in love with James Beard because she agreed with the way he said food should taste. For years his newspaper column ran in the local paper.

She can't eat most of what she serves for breakfast: no bacon, no egg yolks, no sweets. "I like the toast made from homemade bread," LaRene says, "and beautiful high rolls." But she doesn't do much of the baking anymore, particularly the bread, because of all the labor involved. LaRene is nosing around in her early 70s, though by presence alone she seems younger. With all the trouble in her knees she isn't quite as steady on her pins as she would like to be. It is a pleasure, she admits, to take off the apron at lunch and ease into a nap.

"Good American cooking," LaRene'll tell you. "Boy, there's nothing like it. I had a girl in here working for me who had gone to one of those French cooking schools and she did just wild things. Put sauces on everything. And all she was doing was covering up the bad flavor of bad food." The way a thing should taste is not a complicated, sophisticated issue. It's as simple a thing as frying an egg for breakfast. Some always struggle along. Others, like LaRene Morrison, hit it right every time.

Oatmeal Griddlecakes

The oatmeal gives the hotcakes great texture. They go well with fried ham, and nothing beats the flavor of maple syrup when it collides on a plate with ham.

> 1½ cups oatmeal
> 2 cups buttermilk
> ½ cup flour
> 1 teaspoon sugar
> 1 teaspoon baking soda
> 1 teaspoon salt
> 2 eggs, beaten

Mix together the oatmeal and buttermilk and let sit for 15 minutes to soften the oatmeal. Then stir in the remaining ingredients. Bake on hot griddle.

Yield: 12 griddlecakes

Blueberry Buttermilk Pancakes

You will find these aren't caky pancakes, what we call sinkers, but are light and tender. The berries pop open and the juice mingles with the syrup on your plate.

> 1½ cups flour
> ½ teaspoon salt
> 2 teaspoons baking powder
> ½ teaspoon baking soda
> 1 egg
> 1½ cups buttermilk
> 2 tablespoons butter, melted
> 2 cups blueberries
> Maple syrup or powdered sugar and melted butter

Mix dry ingredients together; add beaten egg, buttermilk and butter. Mix well. Stir in blueberries. Drop by spoonfuls onto hot, lightly greased griddle. Turn only once and serve with maple syrup or powdered sugar and melted butter.

Yield: 12–14 pancakes

Priest Lake Waffles

When I was growing up my family spent the summers at Priest Lake, Idaho. The special breakfast was waffles and huckleberry syrup.

> *2 cups flour*
> *¼ teaspoon baking soda*
> *½ teaspoon salt*
> *1 tablespoon sugar*
> *2 cups milk*
> *3 extra-large eggs, separated*
> *¼ cup butter, melted*
> *Fresh Berry Syrup (p. 247)*

Mix flour with baking soda, salt, and sugar. Combine milk, egg yolks and melted butter, and stir until well mixed. Add to dry ingredients. Mix just until well blended.

Beat the egg whites until stiff but not dry, and fold into the batter just before baking. Lightly brush cold waffle iron with solid shortening *then* heat (to prevent sticking). Serve with Fresh Berry syrup.

Note: After making waffles, always leave your waffle iron open to cool to avoid batter sticking to the iron.

Yield: 6–8 waffles

Ricotta Pancakes

Tender and light. I like to serve these with fresh fruit that has been lightly sugared and allowed to sit for 30 minutes. Fresh strawberries or peaches are the best.

> *½ pound ricotta cheese*
> *3 eggs, separated*
> *⅛ teaspoon salt*
> *⅔ cup milk*
> *½ cup flour*

Mix together all the ingredients except the egg whites. Beat the egg whites stiff but not dry and fold into the batter. Bake on a hot griddle. The pancakes should be small, 2 to 3 inches around.

Yield: 12–14 pancakes

Sourdough Apple Pancakes

My good friend Larry Brown is a sourdough expert. He served these to me once and I have been making them ever since.

> ⅔ *cup yellow cornmeal*
> 1⅓ *cups unbleached flour*
> ¼ *cup sugar*
> 1 *teaspoon baking powder*
> 2 *teaspoons baking soda*
> 1 *teaspoon salt*
> ½ *teaspoon freshly grated nutmeg*
> ¼ *teaspoon cinnamon*
> 2 *apples, preferably Golden Delicious, grated*
> 3 *eggs*
> 4 *tablespoons butter, melted*
> 1 *cup Basic Sourdough Starter (p. 333)*
> ½ *cup buttermilk*
>
> Syrup:
> ¼ *cup butter*
> ½ *cup maple syrup*
>
> *Breakfast pork sausages*

Grind the cornmeal in a blender or food processor for a few seconds. In a medium-sized bowl stir together the cornmeal, flour, sugar, baking powder, baking soda, salt, nutmeg and cinnamon. Stir in the grated apple.

In another bowl, blend together the eggs, melted butter, sourdough starter, and buttermilk. Combine with the apple mixture and set aside for 30 minutes.

At the end of 30 minutes, pour ⅓ cup batter onto a hot, lightly oiled griddle. Cook until small bubbles appear on the surface, then flip. Repeat until all the batter is used.

To make the syrup, melt butter over low heat and stir in maple syrup. Pour over pancakes. Serve with nicely browned pork sausages.

Note: Remember, when cooking with sourdough starter, do not use metal bowls or spoons.

Yield: 16–20 pancakes

Challah French Toast

I don't like the skin that forms on French toast when the egg mixtures cooks. I found that by creaming the eggs and sugar, the skin does not develop. Brioche, as well as any other good egg bread, works well here.

> *2 large eggs*
> *⅓ cup granulated sugar*
> *1 cup half-and-half*
> *½ teaspoon cinnamon*
> *6 pieces challah or other egg bread*

Cream together eggs and sugar until light and fluffy. Add half-and-half and cinnamon, and mix well. Pour into shallow dish. Coat bread slices and then cook until lightly browned.

Serves 4

Buttermilk Scones with Currants and Orange Zest

Crusty on the outside and soft on the inside, these scones are wonderful split open and filled with soft butter and raspberry jam. Close them up again so that the butter can melt.

> *3 cups all-purpose flour*
> *⅓ cup sugar*
> *2½ teaspoons baking powder*
> *½ teaspoon baking soda*
> *¾ teaspoon salt*

¾ cup chilled margarine, cut into 6–8 pieces
¾ cup currants
1 teaspoon grated orange zest
1 cup buttermilk

Topping:
1 tablespoon cream
¼ teaspoon cinnamon
2 tablespoons sugar

Preheat the oven to 400°. Using a mixer, mix first five ingredients together. Add margarine and cut into flour mixture until well blended. Add currants and orange zest. Pour in buttermilk and mix only until blended.

Gather into a ball and divide in half. Roll into two circles ½- to ¾-inch thick, then cut each circle into 8 wedges. Bake in the oven for 12–15 minutes. Mix together cream, cinnamon, and sugar and brush over tops of hot scones.

Yield: 16 scones

Dutch Babies

These were made famous at a restaurant in Seattle called Manca's. It's no longer open, but say "Dutch babies" in Seattle and everyone says, "Manca's." I like to serve them on Saturday mornings with the traditional toppings of melted clarified butter, lemon juice and powdered sugar.

4 tablespoons butter
3 extra-large eggs
½ cup all-purpose flour
½ cup milk

Topping:
4 ounces clarified butter
Juice of 1 lemon
½ cup powdered sugar

Preheat the oven to 425°. Melt butter in a 10- or 11-inch black skillet over low heat (here a cast iron skillet works better than any other kind of pan). Mix eggs, flour, and milk in blender. Pour batter in skillet with melted butter. Bake in the oven for 25 minutes. Before serving, pour on the topping: first the butter, then the lemon juice and, finally, the powdered sugar.

Yield: 1 Dutch baby

Blackberry Blintzes

These are worth the effort for special occasion brunches. You can make them ahead, except for the final sautéing, and refrigerate for 2 days.

Batter:
4 eggs
¼ teaspoon salt
1½ cups all-purpose flour
2 tablespoons butter, melted
2 cups milk

Filling:
½ pound cottage cheese
½ pound cream cheese
1 egg, beaten
2 tablespoons butter, melted
2 tablespoons sugar
1 teaspoon vanilla

Blackberry Sauce (p. 248)
Sour cream

To prepare batter, beat eggs until lemon-colored. Add salt, flour, melted butter and milk. Let rest for 30 minutes while preparing filling. Combine all the filling ingredients in food processor and blend until smooth.

For each pancake ladle ⅓ cup batter into lightly buttered 6-inch crepe pan. Cook until lightly browned on one side (you don't have to turn it) and slip out of pan onto paper towels. Fill each pancake with 2 tablespoons filling on brown side. Fold in envelope fashion. Sauté flat side in butter, and serve warm with Blackberry Sauce and sour cream.

To prepare ahead, refrigerate blintzes after sautéing. To serve, cover with foil and heat in a 350° oven for 20–25 minutes.

Yield: 12 blintzes

Swedish Pancakes with Huckleberry Syrup

Another treasure and tradition from our Scandinavian community.

> *3 eggs, separated*
> *2 cups milk*
> *⅛ teaspoon salt*
> *1 cup all-purpose flour*
>
> *2 tablespoons butter, melted*
> *Fresh Berry Syrup (p. 247)*

Beat egg yolks, milk, salt, flour and melted butter together. Beat egg whites until stiff and fold in. Make small pancakes, 2 to 3 inches. Serve with melted butter and huckleberry syrup.

Serves 4

Cinnamon Rolls

These rolls stay soft as they sit, though it is unlikely they will last long enough for anybody to tell.

> *2 packages yeast*
> *1 cup warm water*
> *¼ cup sugar*
> *6 tablespoons butter, softened*
> *¼ cup powdered milk*
> *2 eggs*
> *4½ cups all-purpose flour*
>
> Filling:
> *¼ cup butter, melted*
> *2 teaspoons cinnamon*
> *½ cup sugar*
> *2 cups raisins and 1 cup chopped nuts (optional)*

Preheat the oven to 425°. Dissolve yeast in warm water. Let rest for 10 minutes. Add sugar, butter, milk and eggs. Mix together. Add 4 cups of the flour and mix well. Turn out on floured board, using remaining ½ cup flour. Knead until smooth and elastic. Cover and let rise until doubled.

Roll into rectangular shape, 10 x 15 inches. Mix filling ingredients and spread over dough. Roll up like a jelly roll, then cut into 1½-inch cross sections by sliding a thread under the roll, crossing the ends over the top and pulling tight. This way the dough isn't compressed. Place the sections in a buttered 12 x 18-inch baking dish. Let rise 30 minutes. Bake in the oven for 20 minutes.

If you like, you can add raisins (soften first in hot water) and chopped nuts to the filling.

While still warm, spread with confectioner's frosting.

> Confectioner's Frosting
> *2 cups powdered sugar*
> *2 tablespoons hot water*
> *1 teaspoon vanilla*

Add hot water to powdered sugar and mix well. Then add vanilla. Add a few more drops of hot water if necessary to achieve desired consistency.

Yield: 1 dozen

DEFINING THE PACIFIC NORTHWEST STYLE

> ## *LaRene Morrison's*
> ## *Breakfast Sticky Buns*

This great way to start the day comes from The Dune's Restaurant in Grayland on the Washington coast—home of LaRene Morrison, the best breakfast cook in the states.

Dough:
¾ cup milk, scalded
½ cup sugar
2 teaspoons salt
1 stick butter
½ cup warm water
2 packages dry yeast
1 egg
4 cups all-purpose flour

Buns:
1½ sticks butter
2 cups brown sugar
1½ cups chopped pecans or black walnuts
4 tablespoons butter, softened

Preheat the oven to 350°. To make the dough, combine milk, sugar, salt, and butter, and cool to lukewarm. Measure water into large, warm bowl, sprinkle in yeast, and stir until dissolved. Then stir in the milk mixture, the egg, and 2 cups of the flour. Beat until smooth. Stir in remaining flour to make a stiff batter. Cover tightly with waxed paper. Refrigerate for at least 2 hours. (Dough can be kept in refrigerator for 3 days.)

To make the buns, melt the butter, stir in 1 cup brown sugar and 1 cup nuts. Spoon into a big 12- x 18-inch pan. Combine remaining sugar and nuts and set aside. Divide dough in half and roll out each half to 12 inches square. Spread each square with 2 tablespoons butter, then sprinkle with half the sugar and nut mixture. Roll up like a jelly roll and cut into 1-inch pieces. Place the pieces in the pan, pressing them down into the nuts, sugar, and butter. Cover, let rise 1 hour and then bake in the oven for 25 minutes.

Yield: 24 buns

Blueberry Sour Cream Coffee Cake

The plump, juicy blueberries add pockets of flavor to this moist coffee cake.

> *¼ pound margarine*
> *1 cup sugar*
> *2 extra-large eggs, beaten*
> *½ cup milk*
> *1 teaspoon vanilla*
> *2 cups flour*
> *2 teaspoons baking powder*
> *2 cups blueberries*
>
> Streusel Topping:
> *⅓ cup flour*
> *¼ cup sugar*
> *3 tablespoons butter*
> *¼ teaspoon cinnamon*

Preheat the oven to 325°. Cream together margarine and sugar in an electric mixer. Add eggs and continue beating until light and fluffy. Sift dry ingredients together and add alternately with milk to egg mixture. Fold in blueberries. Spread batter in greased and floured 9- x 13- x 2-inch pan. Mix together flour, sugar, butter, and cinnamon until crumbly to form topping. Sprinkle with streusel topping and bake for 50 minutes.

Serves 8

Sour Cream Cardamom Coffee Cake

I think you should always serve a nice coffee cake for brunch. This is a favorite of mine. It has a good moist texture.

> *1 cup margarine*
> *2 cups sugar*
> *2 eggs*
> *1 cup sour cream*
> *½ teaspoon vanilla*
> *2 cups all-purpose flour*
> *1 teaspoon baking powder*
> *¼ teaspoon salt*
> *½ teaspoon crushed cardamom*
>
> Topping:
> *1 cup chopped nuts*
> *2 teaspoons cinnamon*
> *½ cup brown sugar*
> *¼ cup all-purpose flour*
> *1 tablespoon butter, melted*

Preheat the oven to 350°. Cream together margarine, sugar, and eggs. Stir in sour cream and vanilla. Fold in flour, baking powder, salt and cardamom.

Pour half of batter into a greased tube pan, lightly dusted with flour.

To make the topping, combine the nuts, cinnamon, sugar, flour and melted butter, and sprinkle half over half the batter. Cover with remaining batter, sprinkle with the rest of the topping. Bake in the oven for 55 minutes.

Serves 8–10

Apple Morning Cake

My aunt in Montana served this on Sunday mornings with pork sausages and applesauce.

1¼ cups all-purpose flour   *½ cup sour cream*
½ cup sugar   *½ cup sugar*
1 tablespoon baking powder
½ teaspoon salt
½ teaspoon cinnamon
½ cup chopped walnuts
2 tart green apples with skins on, grated
½ cup milk
1 egg, beaten
3 tablespoons vegetable oil

Preheat the oven to 400°. Mix together dry ingredients. Add walnuts and apples. Mix together milk, egg and vegetable oil and add to batter, being careful not to overmix. Put in 9-inch lightly greased cake pan.

Mix sour cream with sugar and drizzle over top of batter. Bake in the oven for 30 to 35 minutes.

Serves 6

Finnish Coffee Bread

I like to make this on Christmas Eve to serve the next morning.

1 package yeast   Topping:
¼ cup warm water   *2 eggs, beaten*
2 cups warm milk   *¼ cup chopped, slivered almonds*
¾ cup sugar   *Coarsely crushed sugar cubes*
2 eggs, beaten
2 teaspoons crushed cardamom
1 teaspoon salt
8 cups all-purpose flour
½ cup butter, melted

Preheat the oven to 425°. Dissolve yeast in water. Add milk, sugar, eggs, cardamom, salt and 5 cups flour. Mix well. Mix in melted butter. Add 3 cups flour to make dough stiff. Turn out onto floured board and knead for 15 minutes.

Divide dough into 3 parts, then divide each part into 3 pieces. Roll each piece between hands, forming a cord 12 to 14 inches long. Braid the 3 cords together, repeating the process for each loaf. Place on greased baking sheet. Let rise 45 minutes.

Gently brush tops of loaves with beaten egg. Sprinkle with chopped almonds and coarsely crushed sugar. Bake in the oven for 25 to 30 minutes, until golden brown.

Yield: 3 braided loaves

Rosemary's Pear Claws

Rosemary Pflugrath owns Rosemary's Kitchen in Wenatchee, Washington. She produces applesauce, fruit butters, and other items right out of her orchard.

¾ cup milk	3 large eggs
½ cup sugar	6 cups all-purpose flour
1 teaspoon salt	2 cups Pear Butter, (below)
½ cup butter	
2 packages dry yeast	Powdered sugar icing
⅓ cup warm water	Chopped walnuts

Preheat the oven to 350°. Warm the milk. Stir in sugar, salt, and butter. When butter has melted, remove milk from heat and cool to lukewarm.

Dissolve yeast in warm water, then add to lukewarm milk mixture. Whisk in eggs. Add flour and form a soft dough. Knead until smooth. Cover dough and let rise 1 hour in a warm place.

Punch down dough, divide in half. On a lightly floured board, roll each half into a rectangle 6 x 18 inches. Spread 1 cup pear butter in center of dough. Fold dough in half lengthwise. Press together edges to seal. Slice off individual rolls every 3 inches. With scissors, make 2 cuts halfway into roll on folded side, not the sealed edge.

To make claws, place rolls on a greased baking sheet and let rise 20 minutes. Bake in the oven for 25 minutes, until golden brown.

Frost with powdered sugar icing and sprinkle with chopped walnuts.

> Pear Butter:
> *2 pounds pears* *¾ cup sugar*
> *¼ cup butter* *¼ teaspoon cinnamon*

Peel, core, and dice pears. Melt butter in a heavy bottomed, medium-size saucepan. Add diced pears, cover, and simmer until soft, for about 10 minutes. Mash the pears. Then add sugar and cinnamon and simmer over low heat, partially covered, for 30 minutes, or until extra liquid has evaporated and pear butter has a shiny, glazed look.

> Powdered Sugar Icing:
> *1 cup powdered sugar*
> *2–3 tablespoons cream*

Mix sugar and cream together. Drizzle over hot pear claws.

Serves 6–8

Cloud Biscuits

A moist biscuit. The key to having them rise nicely is not rolling them too thin.

> *2 cups flour* *½ cup shortening*
> *1 tablespoon sugar* *1 egg*
> *1 tablespoon baking powder* *⅔ cup cream*
> *½ teaspoon salt*

Preheat the oven to 450°. In a bowl mix together flour, sugar, baking powder and salt. Blend in the shortening with your fingers until mixture resembles coarse crumbs.

Beat egg and cream together and add all at once to flour mixture, stirring gently with a fork just until blended.

Turn out onto a well-floured board, then pat into a circle ⅔-inch thick. Cut into 2-inch rounds and place on an ungreased baking sheet. Bake in the oven for 12 to 14 minutes, until tops are golden brown.

I serve them with melted butter and honey.

Serves 6

BAKING

B efore the ranchers and their cattle and their plows, the south-eastern corner of Washington State was covered with varieties of bunch grass that grew, according to an oft told tale, as high as a horse's belly. That has disappeared, most of it replaced by wheat, particularly in areas like the Palouse where the soil is rich and the land rolls in upon itself like a steep, confused sea. Just to the west, in country called the Big Bend, the last of the state's native grasses grow on ground called scab land. It is a haunting landscape where wheat farms command the hilltops and down low —where a glacial-era flood swept out of Montana and scoured the land clean of any topsoil—coarse, black volcanic rock appears in long patches like slow-healing, crusty wounds. The land is too broken up into draws and hollows to run cattle, so there the bunch grass continues to grow.

The Gray farm looks out at the scab land of the Big Bend country. Walter J. Gray—an Englishman who bought the farm in 1914 to retire from the dry goods business he had built up in Sprague, just to the north—oversaw 1,700 acres of cropland and 1,600 acres of pasture. Gray was, by any estimation, a gentleman farmer. He wore jodhpurs and puttees and a tattersall vest, and rode the horse while his hired man attended to the actual labor of farming. He built his Ionic column-fronted house to look out over a formal orchard and farm buildings that could be lifted and dropped into the Devonshire farm country of his youth. He ran sheep more as a visual counterpoint than for any practical purpose, such as profit.

Walter J. was never without a pair of gloves or a riding crop, but that had more to do with his profound stutter than any kind of British colonial bearing. He would beat time in the palm of one hand with the gloves or the crop to get out his words. Some say he was the black sheep of his family. Others say he knew well enough that as the younger son he would never inherit the family farm, their ownership stretching back to Norman times, and instead sought his fortune elsewhere, first in Canada and then in the Washington Territory. One thing is known for sure: Walter J.

didn't like wet weather and thus picked the arid climate of eastern Washington.

Sometimes in the summer a hot northeast wind blows down on the Gray farm near the town of Washtucna and even the casual observer can watch the wheat shrivel on the stalk. It can happen just before harvest, when the wheat needs another week or two to come to full fruit. This is not rain country, like the west side of the Cascades.

It must have come as a shock to Walter J. when his two sons, John and Joe, decided on careers as farmers rather than business-men. They had been sent off to England as little boys dressed in the style of Little Lord Fauntleroy, for an early education. In later years governesses were shipped in to Sprague from Boston and England. Both the boys attended Washington State College in Pull-man, though John managed only a year while Joe finished. But none of the obvious attributes of British breeding stuck. To see John and Joe as old farmers out in the wheat fields, the one wearing striped coveralls, the other solid blue denim, and both with baseball caps against the sun as they rubbed wheat kernels in the palms of their hands to determine if the time was right to start the harvest, the newly arrived would never guess the two men had such a background. Not with the farmer tan showing.

Their Britishness, particularly John's, the eldest of the two brothers, showed in more subtle ways, like John's bearing with hired hands. He knew how to treat them like servants on the verge of dismissal. That the Gray brothers relied on hired hands at all set them apart from other farmers in the area who approached the business of farming as a family ordeal. John's son Walt now runs the Gray farm. He maintains his own machinery, giant combines and the latest no-till seed drill. His father would have hired a me-chanic.

Food and tradition also set the Grays apart. Chutney was a com-mon condiment on the table, and continues to be in current gener-ations of the family. So too are various curries, and Yorkshire pudding when beef is served, and mint sauce for lamb, made with wild mint and vinegar. The strange puddings common in British households are not unknown in the Gray family. John's wife Lilian baked rice pudding in individual cups. Rice, tasting like it had been slow-cooked in cream, filled three-fourths of the cup, and a rich custard, browned on top from the heat of the oven, curled up and over the lip. To this dessert the lucky diner added a spoonful or two of rich heavy cream, fresh from the family cow.

Lilian may have learned her Yorkshire pudding and curry when she married into the Gray family, but she brought with her cooking skills unparalleled in the surrounding community. Her mother had learned her way around a kitchen from her own mother's Chinese cook in a Portland society home, and passed her lessons on to her daughters. There were five of them, Lilian the youngest. It is said that Lilian began baking bread for the entire family when she was 12, and her baking skills were greatly appreciated on the Gray farm, particularly at harvest time. She cooked on a coal-burning stove until the late '30s when Roosevelt-era programs like the Rural Electrification Administration forever changed the American farm kitchen. Lilian wasted no time switching to an electric stove and oven, and moving in refrigeration and a freezer. Before that she had relied on a locker in the freezer of the butcher shop in Washtucna.

It was the food that brought the same stiffs back to work the wheat harvest year after year under the baleful eye of John Gray. Lilian Gray served the best food around, and plenty of it. Other wheat farmers would pile on the steaks and sausage and bacon, the pancakes and eggs and biscuits, but it was cooked up carelessly and served like slopping hogs. Lunch was delivered to the field, and the men ate it sitting in the dirt. If they didn't like it that way, they could clear out. There were plenty of men looking for work in the Depression years.

But at the John Gray farm the standing order was feet under the table three times a day. Lilian set a proper table, positioned herself at the door, and sent away any man who had not washed the wheat fields out of his ears and off his forearms. She was white-haired even then, the snowy white hair that can come on a woman at an early age and increase her beauty tenfold. Her brown eyes could fill with backlighted mirth or, when she was crossed, snap out at the unsuspecting with summer heat lightning, something John Gray would discover from time to time when he lumbered into his wife's domain. Dinner was to be served at 12:30 each day, and if John Gray got in a little early and started badgering Lilian in the kitchen about laying out the meal on time, sparks would fly.

Her way was to have everything perfect. It didn't matter if the man at the dinner table was near toothless and smelled of body odor and Bull Durham tobacco, a stiff hired off the streets of Spokane for the six weeks of harvest that started in mid-July. Lilian was determined to set a perfect table and produce a meal that was special. She cooked for a dozen hired hands and family men during harvests through the '30s: roasts and fried potatoes and creamed onions fresh from her garden. She had her daughters out picking vegetables before the sun came up because she had read somewhere that fruits and vegetables were the most nutritious at dawn. She didn't just churn butter and form it into a rough block. Lilian pounded the water out of her butter and shaped it until the edges were sharp and the sides were square. The ones who remember get quiet and misty when they try to explain the effect of Lilian's butter melting into one of Lilian's rolls. She was a proud cook, a fine baker.

John Gray started Lilian's stove each morning when he got up. Then he would milk the cow and harness the twenty-eight mules that pulled the combine during harvest. The Gray brothers didn't sell the mules and switch to tractor-pulled machinery until 1937. Generally the stove would be hot enough to bake biscuits by breakfast time. After breakfast Lilian would bake pies for the noon meal, using homemade lard for the crust. Her lard was always as white as her hair, not the beige color taken on by the lard of the careless cook who has let her mind and interest wander in the long rendering process. Patience and low heat and the determination to produce the best lard in the county: such was the energy Lilian brought to her baking. In spring she would bake berry and cherry pies, and through the summer she would change to apple and peach. She baked bread as it was needed, but biscuits and muffins and rolls and hot cross buns were a constant. There were no measuring cups and spoons in her kitchen, and the best of her ingredients came from just outside the kitchen door. Lilian's sour cream was just that. And the sour milk wasn't buttermilk but true clabber. Eggs came fresh from the chicken house. Her oldest daughter, Kathrine, complained that when she left the farm for college she had to learn to cook all over again, and food has never tasted quite the same since. Lilian's cream didn't simply pour from the pitcher. It finally plopped out after a good long wait.

In the days when John Gray drove a combine pulled by twenty-eight mules, whipping the ones nearest him with the driving reins and making free use of the can of rocks at his side to attract the attention of the mules too far away to know what he had in mind, wheat was sewn into sacks on the combine and the sacks were dropped in clusters in the fields. The sack sewer was an important man on the combine, as was the jigger, the man who nudged the filling sacks with his knees to get that full 153-pound measure before lifting the sack over to the sewer. The header puncher, usually a local farm kid, manned an apparatus like a ship's wheel to raise and lower the combine's cutting blades. A good header puncher would leave behind an evenly cut field with a foot-tall wheat stubble. The sacks of wheat were picked up by men in the field, loaded onto the back of a truck, and hauled down to a warehouse by the railroad tracks. Some of those sacks were handled eight times between the field and the train car. So the men who came to sit at Lilian's table were hungry and thirsty. They downed tall glasses of iced tea, refilling them over and over again. And they cleaned their plates. But no one gained weight during harvest.

The size of the crew diminished with the change from mule to tractor, then shrank again when John Gray switched from sacked wheat to bulk. By then he had grandchildren who drove the wheat into town to the grain elevator. He would hire only one or two men who would sit with the family at the noon meal and eat off fine china with silver utensils. Lilian and John Gray left the farm after 45 years and settled in a retirement complex in Portland, where Lilian continued baking. The year before she went into the hospital, never to return, she still baked hot cross buns for the entire complex. She lived to see eighty-three.

Today, Walt Gray stores the wheat he harvests right there on the farm. The big noon meal, like Lilian's cooking and fine baked goods, is a thing of the past. "We were about the last farmers around here to have a noon meal in the house," Walt Gray says. "We quit this year. Our crew is down to three men and the work they do isn't physical, it's boring. They don't need the calories like the old days. The guy on that combine is sitting in an air-conditioned cab with the stereo going and a console over here telling him what's going on in front of him and in back of him and beside him and everywhere around him. His job is just boring and stressful."

There's no money in wheat, and the Gray farm, like so many others in the country, is in trouble. Oddly enough, if anything saves it, it will be bunch grass. The government pays farmers $50 an acre a year to take marginal land out of production for ten years and plant native grasses, and a lot of farmers have signed on. Walt Gray has the no-till seed drill to do the seeding. All he needs is a couple of mild winters when the ground freezes but the snow doesn't pile high, which is asking a lot in his part of the Pacific Northwest. No one is likely to ever see bunch grass growing as high as a horse's belly in the Big Bend country, but it's coming back.

Pie Crust

Here are 2 pie crust recipes—one very traditional, one very easy, and both very light and flaky.

Pie Crust for 2-Crust Pies

My mother bakes the most wonderful pies. This is her technique for a tender, flaky pie crust.

⅔ cup vegetable shortening, such as Crisco
2 cups all-purpose flour
½ teaspoon salt
6–8 tablespoons ice water

Drop the shortening by spoonfuls into the well-mixed flour and salt. Cut the shortening into the flour with a table knife, then blend well, picking up the flour with your fingers and rubbing the thumbs across the fingers, letting the flour fall back into the bowl. This is a picking and lifting motion, the fingers and thumbs working gently and smoothly. With this sensual process you achieve a thorough blend and cornmeal consistency. Pick up handfuls of dough, squeeze, then let crumble apart back into the bowl.

Add water, 1 tablespoon at a time, mixing in lightly with fork. Stop adding water when mixture holds together. Divide dough in half, form into 2 balls, flatten slightly, wrap in plastic wrap, and chill for 30 minutes.

Roll dough into circle on lightly floured board. Once you start to roll, don't flip dough over or too much flour will be absorbed into the dough.

Roll from center of dough circle to outsides, pressing down with heel of hands on center of rolling pin.

Keep flour on rolling pin.

(I still like the Foley ball-bearing rolling pin and pastry cloth with stocking cover for the rolling pin, the best for rolling pie crusts. The pastry cloth and well-chilled dough guarantee a much easier job of rolling out your crust and eliminate the problem of adding too much flour.)

Keep dough floured underneath.

Be patient. Take all the time in the world. Roll a paper-thin crust.

Fold crust in half and lift into pie plate (up to 10 inches). Fill crust with fruit or berries according to recipe. Roll out other half of crust and place loosely over pie. Trim edges and seal with fingertips. Cut several slits in top.

Yield: crust for 1 9-inch, 2-crust pie.

Alice Stroh's Never-Fail Extra-Flaky Pie Crust

This is an easy dough to handle and makes a delicious, flaky crust. I especially like it for pumpkin pies.

> *3 cups all-purpose flour*
> *1½ teaspoons salt*
> *1½ cups shortening*
> *1 egg, beaten*
>
> *5 tablespoons carbonated soda*
> *water*
> *1 tablespoon vinegar*

Using an electric mixer, mix together flour, salt, and shortening until dough resembles cornmeal. Stir in egg, soda water and vinegar all at once. Divide dough into three pieces, cover with plastic wrap, and chill.

Yield: 3 single 9-inch crusts

Shoo-Fly Pastry Snacks

> *Brown sugar*
> *Butter*
>
> *Chopped nuts*
> *Raspberry jam*

Preheat oven to 425°. Gather up pastry scraps left over from making pie crusts. Roll out ¼-inch thick. Cream equal parts brown sugar and butter until fluffy and spread on top. Sprinkle with chopped nuts. Cut in strips. Place on baking sheet. Bake in the oven for 12 to 15 minutes.

Or spread scraps with raspberry jam and roll up like a cigar and bake. Let cool before eating or you will singe your tongue.

Yield: enough for snacks

Chocolate Chip Walnut Pie

The Gallery restaurant in Sisters, Oregon, served this pie and we liked it so much that now it is a favorite dessert.

2 eggs	6 ounces chocolate chips
½ cup flour	1 cup walnuts, chopped
½ cup white sugar	1 unbaked 9-inch pie crust (p. 305)
½ cup brown sugar	Vanilla ice cream
1 cup butter, melted	

Preheat the oven to 325°. Beat eggs. Add flour and sugars. Mix well. Stir in butter. Fold in chocolate chips and walnuts. Pour into pie shell. Bake in the oven for 50 minutes.

Serve warm with vanilla ice cream.

Serves 8

Christmas Pie

Café Sport, at the Pike Place Market in Seattle, serves this delicious cranberry–raisin pie at Christmastime every year. Its sweet–tart flavor is a hint of spring in the middle of winter.

2 cups raw cranberries	Grated zest of 1 orange
½ cup golden raisins	Pinch of ground allspice
½ cup sugar	Pinch of ground ginger
¼ cup honey	3 grinds of fresh black pepper
½ teaspoon vanilla	2 tablespoons butter
1 tablespoon brandy	

Preheat the oven to 425°. Combine all ingredients thoroughly and spoon into your favorite 9-inch pie crust. Use a lattice top.

Bake at 425° for 15 minutes; turn heat down to 350° and continue baking for 35 to 40 minutes.

Serves 8

DEFINING THE PACIFIC NORTHWEST STYLE

> ## *Walnut and Rose Petal-Infused Honey Tart*

This tart comes from Bruce Naftaly and Robin Sanders of Restaurant Le Gourmand.

> *1 cup aromatic rose petals*
> *½ cup mild honey*

To make rose petal-infused honey, add the petals to the honey and gently simmer for 10 minutes. Steep for at least 1 hour. Strain and reserve honey.

> Crust (prebaked shell):
> *¼ pound cold, unsalted butter*
> *1½ cups flour*
> *⅓ cup sugar*
> *⅛ teaspoon salt*
> *1 egg yolk*

To make the crust, combine all ingredients in a bowl except egg yolk. Add yolk and, if necessary, 1 to 2 tablespoons cold water to hold dough together. Roll out to ⅛-inch thick to fill an 11-inch tart pan. Prick dough in tart pan with a fork, then line with waxed paper and fill shell with dried beans or their metal equivalent to keep sides of tart shell from collapsing. Bake shell at 450° for 10 minutes. Bake blind at 450° for 10 minutes, then remove beans and waxed paper and finish at 350° for 10 minutes or until done and just golden brown.

> Filling:
> *1 cup fresh shelled walnuts, broken into pieces*
> *3 eggs*
> *½ cup rose petal-infused honey*
> *⅓ cup corn syrup*
> *1½ tablespoons unsalted butter*
> *¼ teaspoon vanilla*
> *1 tablespoon dark rum*
> *Whipping cream, whipped and lightly sweetened*

Preheat the oven to 350°. Combine filling ingredients. Pour into the tart shell and bake in the oven for 35 minutes. Serve with slightly sweetened whipped cream.

Serves 8

Fresh Rhubarb Pie

Of all pies, this is my favorite. The tart rhubarb tastes so fresh at the beginning of spring.

> *Pastry for 2-crust pie (p. 305)*
> *1¼ cups sugar*
> *5 tablespoons flour*
> *½ teaspoon cinnamon*
> *4 cups diced rhubarb*
> *2 tablespoons butter*
> *2 tablespoons milk*
> *1 tablespoon sugar*

Preheat the oven to 425°. Prepare pastry and roll out undercrust; fit into a 9-inch pie pan. Combine sugar, flour and cinnamon. Spread half of this mixture over pastry-lined pan. Add rhubarb and sprinkle remainder of mixture over the fruit. Dot with butter. Roll upper crust and fit over pie, sealing edges carefully. Brush with milk and sprinkle with sugar.

Bake on lower shelf in the oven for 30 to 40 minutes.

Serves 8

Rhubarb Custard Pie

Aunt Marje Kramis has a lovely garden in her backyard in Missoula, Montana. This is her recipe for rhubarb pie. I like the way the custard seals in the juices from the rhubarb.

> *3 cups thinly cut rhubarb*
> *1½ cups sugar*
> *3 eggs, beaten*
> *½ teaspoon nutmeg*
> *1 unbaked 9-inch pie crust (p. 305)*

Preheat the oven to 425°. Stir all of the ingredients together and then pour into the pie shell. Bake in the oven for 15 minutes and then at 350° for 35 to 45 minutes, until custard is set and light golden-colored.

Serves 6

Anita's Swedish Lemon Tart

The crust is a crisp shortbread—a little difficult to roll out, but worth it. Halfway through baking time, put foil around edges of crust to prevent excess browning.

> Crust:
> *1½ cups flour*
> *8 ounces butter*
> *2 large eggs*
> *¼ cup sugar*
> *1 teaspoon salt*

Preheat the oven to 375°. Mix all ingredients together in a food processor or mixer. Chill for 30 minutes. Roll out on a well-floured board to fit a 10-inch tart pan.

> Filling:
> *1 cup whipping cream*
> *2 large eggs*
> *Zest and juice of one large lemon*
> *⅓ cup sugar*

Beat all ingredients together. Pour into the unbaked tart shell and bake in the oven for 35 minutes. Serve at room temperature.

Serves 8

Lemon Butter Tarts

My neighbor Eve Currie used to have a Christmas tea every year, when she would serve the most wonderful lemon tarts. She would make the lemon butter in advance, keep it in the refrigerator in a glass jar, and the day of the tea would fill small tart shells with it and offer the finished tarts with hot tea to her guests. I have never seen a recipe like this for lemon filling and think it is a real treasure.

> *4 egg yolks*
> *1 pound sugar*
> *¼ pound butter*
> *4 egg whites, well beaten*
> *Juice and grated rinds of 2 large lemons*

Cream the egg yolks, sugar and butter together until very light and fluffy. Fold in the beaten egg whites and cook in a double boiler until mixture thickens (about 15 minutes). Then add the juice and grated rinds of the lemons. Turn into a glass dish to cool. Use to fill small tart shells or as a filling for cakes.

Note: This also makes a wonderful filling for coconut cake.

Yield: 1 pint

Adam's Graham Cracker Birthday Cake

The graham cracker crumbs make this cake moist and coarse-textured.

Cake:
3/4 cup shortening
3/4 teaspoon salt
1 1/2 teaspoons vanilla
1 cup sugar
3 eggs, separated
1 cup sifted flour
1 tablespoon baking powder
1 2/3 cups graham cracker crumbs
  (21 graham crackers, crushed)
1 cup milk

Frosting:
2 cups whipping cream
3/4 cup cocoa
4 cups powdered sugar
2 teaspoons vanilla

Preheat the oven to 350°. Combine shortening, salt, vanilla and sugar. Add egg yolks and beat well.

In a separate bowl, sift together flour and baking powder and stir in graham cracker crumbs. Add alternately with milk to creamed mixture.

Beat egg whites until stiff, then carefully fold in. Pour into 2 greased 9-inch cake pans (lined with waxed paper). Bake in the oven for 25 to 30 minutes. Cool for 5 minutes, then remove from pans.

Blend together all frosting ingredients and let stand 1 hour in refrigerator. Whip. Frost cake between layers, and on the top and sides. Refrigerate.

Serves 10

Christmas Lemon Pecan Pound Cake

This is good to make ahead and keep in your freezer.

1 pound butter
2 1/3 cups sugar

6 eggs
2 ounces lemon extract

4 cups flour	*1½ cups chopped pecans*
1½ teaspoons baking powder	*1 tablespoon lemon zest*
½ teaspoon salt	

Preheat the oven to 300°. Cream together the butter and sugar until light and fluffy. Add the eggs, one at a time, beating well after each addition. Add the lemon extract. Fold in the flour, baking powder, salt, pecans and lemon zest, being careful not to overmix.

Line three 1–pound loaf pans with brown paper. Lightly butter sides of pan and paper. Bake in the oven for 1 to 1½ hours until firm in center.

Yield: 3 cakes

Coconut Cake with Lemon Filling

James Beard served this in his home and I could have eaten the whole thing. The lightness of the whipped cream frosting with the lemon filling is a classic combination. It's a wonderful Easter cake.

Cake:

1 cup flaked coconut	*3 cups sifted cake flour*
1 cup warm milk	*4 teaspoons baking powder*
¾ cup butter	*¾ teaspoon salt*
1½ cups sugar	*4 egg whites*
1 teaspoon vanilla	

Lemon Cream Filling:

¼ pound butter	*1½ cups sugar*
Grated rind of 1 lemon	*3 egg yolks*
Juice of 3 large lemons	*3 eggs*
¼ teaspoon salt	*1 teaspoon vanilla*

Frosting:

2 cups whipping cream, whipped	*1½ teaspoons vanilla*
½ cup powdered sugar	*1½ cups flaked coconut*

Preheat the oven to 350°. Put the coconut in a small mixing bowl and pour in the warm milk. Let cool. Drain through a strainer, pressing the coconut with the back of a wooden spoon. Reserve milk.

Cream the butter. Add the sugar and beat until very light and fluffy. Add the vanilla.

Sift the flour with the baking powder and salt, and add alternately with the milk from the coconut (1 cup). Fold in the coconut.

Beat the egg whites until stiff and fold into the cake mixture. Turn into two 9-inch cake pans which have been buttered, floured, and lined with waxed paper. Bake in the oven for 30 minutes. Cool on a rack.

Meanwhile, prepare the filling. Melt the butter in a double boiler. Add the grated rind, lemon juice, salt and sugar. Add the egg yolks, eggs, and vanilla beaten together, whisking continuously until the mixture thickens. Cool. You can cover with plastic wrap and refrigerate until ready to frost the cakes and serve them.

Split the two cakes in half. Place one half on a cake plate and spread with a thin layer of lemon filling. Place the other half on top and spread with filling. Continue with the remaining halves.

To make the frosting, whip the cream. Add the sugar and vanilla and continue whipping until stiff peaks form. Frost cake and sprinkle with coconut.

Serves 8

Marianne's Lemon Tea Cookies

These are real showstoppers. The surprise of the fresh lemon taste makes it impossible to stop eating them.

1½ teaspoons vinegar	1 teaspoon grated lemon zest
½ cup milk	1¾ cups flour
½ cup butter	1 teaspoon baking powder
¾ cup sugar	¼ teaspoon baking soda
1 egg	¼ teaspoon salt

Lemon Glaze:

¾ cup granulated sugar	¼ cup lemon juice

Preheat the oven to 350°. Stir vinegar into milk. Cream together butter and sugar until fluffy. Add egg and lemon zest and beat well.

Sift all dry ingredients together and add alternately with liquid to butter–sugar mixture. Beat smooth after each addition. Drop from teaspoon 2 inches apart onto ungreased baking sheet. Bake in the oven for 12 to 14 minutes. Mix sugar and lemon juice together to form glaze. Remove and brush tops immediately with lemon glaze.

Yield: 2½ dozen cookies

Grandma Ide's Ginger Snaps

Lilian Gray learned to bake these cookies from her mother, Kathrine Ide. Doubled, this recipe makes enough cookies to feed a wheat harvest crew.

> ½ cup shortening
> ½ cup white sugar
> ½ cup molasses
> ¼ cup cold water
> 1½ cups flour
> 1 teaspoon ginger
> 1 teaspoon cinnamon
> ½ teaspoon allspice
> ½ teaspoon nutmeg
> ¼ teaspoon clove
> ½ teaspoon baking soda
> 1½–3 cups additional flour

Preheat the oven to 375°. Cream the shortening and the sugar well, then add the molasses and cold water. Mix 1½ cups flour with the spices and baking soda, then add to the shortening mixture. Add more flour until dough no longer sticks to hands, around 2 cups. Chill dough for 1 hour. Roll out one portion at a time to preferred thickness. Cut with cookie cutters. Bake in the oven for 10 to 15 minutes, depending on thickness of dough.

Yield: 8 dozen cookies

Snickerdoodles

The classic cookie. Crisp and crunchy. With a bowl of fresh berries
and cream—the perfect Pacific Northwest picnic ending.

> *1 cup shortening*
> *1½ cups sugar*
> *2 eggs*
> *2½ cups all-purpose flour*
> *2 teaspoons cream of tartar*
> *1 teaspoon baking soda*
> *¼ teaspoon salt*

> Cinnamon Sugar:
> *1 cup sugar*
> *2 teaspoons cinnamon*

Preheat the oven to 350°. Cream shortening and sugar until light
and fluffy. Add eggs, one at a time.

Mix together flour, cream of tartar, baking soda and salt. Add to
creamed mixture. Form into golf ball-sized balls and roll in mixture
of cinnamon and sugar. Placed on greased cookie sheet. Flatten
with bottom of a glass. Bake in the oven for 15 minutes.

Yield: 24 cookies

Salted Peanut Cookies

Firm, crisp, and peanut-flavored. The salted peanuts contrast with
the sweet cookie dough.

> *1 cup butter*
> *2 eggs*
> *1 cup brown sugar*
> *1 cup white sugar*
> *1 teaspoon vanilla*
> *2 cups all-purpose flour*
> *2 teaspoons baking soda*
> *3 cups corn flakes*
> *2 cups salted peanuts*

Preheat the oven to 350°. Cream together butter, eggs, sugars and vanilla. Mix in flour, baking soda, and corn flakes. Stir in peanuts.

Drop onto greased cookie sheet and bake in the oven for 12 to 15 minutes.

Yield: 2½–3 dozen cookies

Pecan Tea Cookies

A rich butter cookie that's perfect to offer after dinner as an accompaniment to a special ice cream.

> *1 cup butter*
> *1 cup sugar*
> *½ teaspoon salt*
> *1 egg*
> *1 teaspoon vanilla*
> *2 cups flour*
> *1 teaspoon baking powder*
> *2–3 whole pecans*

Preheat the oven to 350°. Cream together butter, sugar, and salt. Add egg and beat well. Add vanilla. Stir in flour and baking powder. Knead well. Shape into 1½- to 2-inch rolls and chill well. Slice into ½-inch slices and top each slice with one whole pecan. Bake in the oven for 8 to 10 minutes on a greased baking sheet until a small golden brown ring forms around edge. Remove from cookie sheet while still warm.

Yield: 2–3 dozen cookies

Brown Sugar–Hazelnut Shortbread Cookies

Kim Smith is a wonderful cook and baker, and serves these cookies at her restaurant, C'est Cheese, on Mercer Island.

> *2 cups all-purpose flour*
> *1 cup hazelnuts, toasted and skins removed*
> *1 cup butter, at room temperature*
> *¾ cup packed brown sugar*

Preheat the oven to 300°. Grind flour and nuts together in food processor until mixture becomes a fine powder.

Cream together butter and sugar in a mixer until smooth and creamy. Add in the flour–hazelnut mixture. Wrap and chill for 2 hours or more.

When ready to roll out cookies, remove from refrigerator and let sit at room temperature for 20 to 30 minutes to soften slightly. Roll out dough ¼-inch thick and cut into 1-inch squares. Bake on teflon-coated baking sheet in the oven for 20 to 25 minutes, or until lightly colored.

Yield: 4 dozen cookies

Laughing Horse Theater Chocolate Chip Cookies

Still my family's favorite. This is a weekly commitment at our house. Laughing Horse Summer Theater in Ellensburg, Washington, serves these cookies, crisp on the outside and soft on the inside, at each play.

> *½ pound butter*
> *1 teaspoon salt*
> *1 teaspoon vanilla*
> *¾ cup white sugar*
> *¾ cup brown sugar*
> *2 eggs, beaten*

1 teaspoon baking soda dissolved in 1 teaspoon water
2¼ cups flour
12 ounces chocolate chips
8 ounces walnuts

Preheat the oven to 375°. Cream together in an electric mixer the butter, salt, vanilla, and sugars until light and fluffy. Add eggs and continue beating for several minutes. Stir in dissolved baking soda. Add flour. Fold in chocolate chips and nuts.

Form dough into 1¾-inch balls. Place on cookie sheet and flatten to ½-inch thickness. Bake in the oven for 15 minutes. Remove from baking sheet and let cool. Store in airtight tins.

Yield: 3 dozen cookies

Eve's Shortbread Cookies

A crisp, buttery, light-colored cookie that's just right with a cup of tea. The cornstarch makes this a more delicate shortbread.

1 pound butter
1 cup granulated sugar
1 cup cornstarch
3 cups flour

Preheat the oven to 350°. Cream together butter and sugar in an electric mixer for 5 minutes until light and fluffy. Mix in the cornstarch and flour. Turn out onto a board that is lightly dusted with cornstarch. Divide dough in half. Press into two square 8-inch pans. Flatten dough with hands to about ½-inch thick. Thoroughly prick the surface with a fork to prevent blistering during baking.

Bake in the oven for 30 minutes. Remove from oven and cut into small squares while still hot. Let cool in pan. Remove when cool.

Yield: 3 dozen cookies

Sugar Cookies

Serve with homemade ice cream, or lemonade, these are my favorite summer cookies.

3 eggs	*4 cups all-purpose flour*
1 cup butter, softened	*1 teaspoon baking soda*
1 cup sugar	*2 teaspoons cream of tartar*
1 teaspoon vanilla	*Sugar*

Preheat the oven to 375°. Beat eggs for 5 minutes until lemon-colored and creamy. Whip in butter, sugar and vanilla. When very light and fluffy, mix in flour, baking soda and cream of tartar.

Roll into walnut-sized balls and dip in sugar. Flatten with bottom of a glass. Place on greased baking sheet and bake in the oven for 10 to 12 minutes.

Yield: 3 dozen cookies

Nina's Torchetti Cookies

One of the reasons to leave I-90 and enter Cle Ellum when driving across Washington State is to buy these cookies at the bakery. They're made from an old Italian recipe, though Nina is a friend, not the Cle Ellum baker. This is a cookie for grownups to enjoy while drinking coffee, not for the lunchbox.

2 packages yeast	*½ cup sugar*
1¼ cups warm water	*2 teaspoons salt*
5½ cups all-purpose flour	*1 pound butter, at room temperature*

Preheat the oven to 375°. Mix yeast in water. Let sit 10 minutes. Add 1 cup of the flour, then the sugar and salt. Mix well and let sit 15 minutes. Add remaining flour and mix in butter. Refrigerate 4 to 6 hours.

Pinch off golf ball-sized pieces of dough and roll into pencil-shaped strips, 6 inches long, on a board lightly sprinkled with granulated sugar. Shape into horseshoes with ends barely touching. Bake in the oven for 8 to 10 minutes. Place briefly under broiler to glaze.

Yield: 18–24 cookies

Lunchbox Oatmeal Cookies

Big, chewy cookies with a snap.

1 cup solid shortening	*2 cups all-purpose flour*
1 cup brown sugar	*1 teaspoon salt*
1 cup white sugar	*1 teaspoon baking soda*
2 eggs	*3 cups quick oatmeal*
1 teaspoon vanilla	

Preheat the oven to 375°. Cream well the shortening, sugars, eggs and vanilla. Mix in flour, salt and baking soda. Add oatmeal.

Drop onto greased cookie sheet and bake in the oven for 12 minutes.

Yield: 2–3 dozen cookies

Old-fashioned Peanut Butter Cookies

A crisp, delicious cookie that's not too sweet.

1 cup butter	*2 eggs*
1 cup white sugar	*3 cups flour*
1 cup brown sugar	*2 teaspoons baking soda*
1 cup peanut butter	*1 teaspoon salt*

Preheat the oven to 375°. Cream together butter and sugars until light and fluffy. Beat in peanut butter and add eggs, one at a time. Mix together flour, baking soda and salt. Add to sugar–egg mixture. Roll into walnut-sized balls, and place on a lightly greased and floured baking sheet. Flatten with a fork dipped in cold water, making a crisscross pattern. Bake in the oven for 20–25 minutes.

Yield: 6 dozen cookies

Dark Chocolate Brownies

These are chocolaty and soft rather than cake-like.

> *3 squares unsweetened chocolate*
> *⅔ cup shortening*
> *4 eggs, beaten*
> *2 cups sugar*
> *1½ cups flour*
> *1 teaspoon baking powder*
> *1 teaspoon vanilla*

Preheat the oven to 375°. Melt chocolate and shortening together over low heat. Let cool to room temperature.

Beat eggs and sugar together until well blended and creamy. Stir in melted chocolate. Mix in dry ingredients and vanilla. Spread in greased baking pan. Bake in the oven for 30 minutes.

Note: The brownies can be frosted with Dover Judy Frosting (recipe follows).

Yield: 24 squares

Dover Judy Frosting

My Aunt Louise always uses this frosting on her cakes. A rich, shiny chocolate frosting, it also works well on brownies.

> *1 cup powdered sugar*
> *1 tablespoon butter, softened*
> *¼ cup milk*
> *1 egg*
> *2 squares unsweetened chocolate, melted*

In a bowl, mix together powdered sugar and butter. Add milk and egg and beat well. Slowly add melted chocolate, stirring continuously. Set bowl in ice water and beat until mixture thickens.

Yield: enough frosting for 1 pan of brownies

1, 2, 3 Banana Bread

A moist quickbread with a good banana flavor. It keeps well and slices easily.

½ cup margarine	1 teaspoon baking soda
1 cup sugar	¼ teaspoon salt
2 eggs	¼ cup chopped nuts
3 over-ripe bananas, mashed well	
2 cups flour	

Preheat the oven to 350°. Cream together margarine and sugar. Add eggs, one at a time. Mix in bananas. Stir in flour, baking soda, salt and chopped nuts. Bake in a greased 9- x 5- x 3-inch bread pan for 1 hour. Cool in pan for 15 minutes, then remove from pan and finish cooling on a rack.

Yield: 1 loaf

Rhubarb Nut Bread

As virtually all rhubarb sold commercially in this country is grown in the shadow of Mount Rainier, this recipe embodies the Pacific Northwest in content as well as spirit.

2 cups finely chopped rhubarb	1 cup milk
1½ cups sugar	2 eggs, beaten
2 cups all-purpose flour	3 tablespoons vegetable oil
1 teaspoon salt	½ cup chopped nuts
4 teaspoons baking powder	
1 teaspoon cinnamon	

Preheat the oven to 375°. Mix rhubarb with sugar; let stand for 30 minutes. Put dry ingredients in large mixing bowl, then stir in milk, eggs and oil. Fold in rhubarb and nuts. Pour into greased 9- x 5-inch loaf pan. Bake in the oven for 1 hour.

Yield: 1 loaf

Blueberry–Orange Bread

Serve this bread directly from the oven, with the juices from the berries flowing and mingling with the orange-scented crumbs.

> *2 tablespoons butter*
> *¼ cup hot water*
> *½ cup orange juice*
> *1 tablespoon orange zest*
> *1 teaspoon vinegar*
> *1 egg*
> *1 cup sugar*
> *2 cups all-purpose flour*
> *1 teaspoon baking powder*
> *¼ teaspoon baking soda*
> *2 cups blueberries*

Preheat the oven to 325°. Melt butter in hot water. Add orange juice, zest and vinegar.

Beat egg with sugar until light and fluffy.

Mix together flour, baking powder and baking soda. Add to eggs alternately with orange juice mixture. Combine completely but do not overmix. Fold in blueberries.

Put into well-greased 9- x 5- x 3-inch pan. Bake in the oven for 1 hour and 10 minutes.

Yield: 1 loaf

Zucchini and Black Walnut Bread

This is a Labor Day ritual if you have zucchini in your garden. By that time of year the squash is usually too big to simply sauté. Next time, don't break the rule: one plant per family of five.

> *3 cup flour*
> *2 cups sugar*
> *3 teaspoons cinnamon*

1 teaspoon salt
2 teaspoons baking soda
3 teaspoons vanilla
1 cup vegetable oil
3 eggs, beaten
2 cups zucchini, peeled and grated
½–1 cup chopped black walnuts

Preheat the oven to 325°. Mix together all ingredients in a bowl, being careful not to overmix. Put into 2 small lightly greased loaf pans. Bake in the oven for 45 minutes.

Yield: 2 loaves

Fresh Cranberry–Orange Bread

You'll find that this bread slices best the next day.

1 cup raw cranberries, chopped
1 tablespoon orange zest
2 tablespoons plus ¾ cup sugar
2 cups flour
1 teaspoon baking soda
¾ teaspoon salt
1 egg, beaten
½ cup orange juice
½ cup water
3 tablespoons shortening, melted
1 cup chopped pecans

Preheat the oven to 375°. Combine cranberries, orange zest and 2 tablespoons sugar. Mix together flour, baking soda, salt and ¾ cup sugar.

Combine egg, juice and water. Add to flour mixture along with melted shortening, cranberry mixture and pecans. Stir just until blended. Put into 9- x 5-inch bread pan and bake in the oven for 1 hour.

Yield: 1 loaf

Carpie's Graham Bread

A coarse-textured quick bread that's very moist, and especially good for breakfast.

> 1½ cups brown sugar
> 2 cups graham flour
> 1 cup all-purpose flour
> 1 teaspoon baking soda
> 1 teaspoon baking powder
> 1 teaspoon salt
> 2 cups buttermilk
> 3 tablespoons shortening, melted

Preheat the oven to 350°. Mix sugar, flours, baking soda, baking powder and salt. Make a well in the middle and pour in buttermilk and melted shortening. Mix lightly. Put in a lightly greased 9- x 5- x 3-inch bread pan. Bake in the oven for 1 hour.

Yield: 1 loaf

Warm Gingerbread Cake

This moist, sweet bread has a pronounced ginger and molasses flavor.

> 1 cup butter
> 1 cup sugar
> 1 cup molasses
> 2 eggs
> 3 cups flour
> ½ teaspoon salt
> 1 teaspoon baking soda
> 1 teaspoon cinnamon
> 1½ teaspoons ginger
> 1 teaspoon allspice
> 1¼ cups buttermilk
> Whipping cream, whipped and lightly sweetened

Preheat the oven to 350°. Cream together the butter and sugar, then add the molasses and eggs.

Mix together the dry ingredients and alternately add them and the buttermilk to the creamed butter and sugar. Mix well and pour into greased and floured 9- x 13-inch cake pan. Bake in the oven for 35 to 45 minutes. Serve warm, topped with lightly sweetened whipped cream.

Yield: 1 sheet cake

Buttermilk Chocolate Cake

You need a large sheet pan for this cake, which is thinner than a standard cake.

> *2 cups all-purpose flour*
> *2 cups sugar*
> *½ cup butter*
> *½ cup shortening*
> *3 tablespoons cocoa*
> *1 cup water*
> *2 eggs, beaten*
> *½ cup buttermilk*
> *1 teaspoon baking soda*
> *½ teaspoon cinnamon*
> *1 teaspoon vanilla*
> *½ teaspoon salt*
>
> Glaze:
> *½ cup butter*
> *6 tablespoons milk*
> *3 tablespoons cocoa*
> *1 pound powdered sugar*

Preheat the oven to 350°. Put flour and sugar in large mixing bowl and mix well.

Combine butter, shortening, cocoa, and water in medium-sized saucepan and bring to a boil. Pour it over flour–sugar mixture. Mix lightly and add eggs, buttermilk, baking soda, cinnamon, vanilla and salt. Mix well and pour into greased and floured 11- x 14- x 1½-inch pan. Bake in the oven for 20 to 25 minutes.

To make the glaze: Put butter, milk, and cocoa in a medium-sized saucepan and bring to a boil. Let it cool a bit and then put in mixing bowl with powdered sugar and beat until mixture thickens. Spread over cake while still warm.

Yield: 1 sheet cake

Kelly's Cream Cheese Pound Cake

Pound cake is a good dessert when topped with sugared fresh berries and lightly whipped extra-thick cream poured over. The cream cheese makes this pound cake particularly moist.

> *1½ cups butter, softened*
> *8 ounces cream cheese, at room temperature*
> *3 cups sugar*
> *6 eggs*
> *1 teaspoon vanilla extract*
> *1 teaspoon almond extract*
> *3 cups all-purpose flour*

Preheat the oven to 325°. Cream together butter and cheese. Add sugar. Beat in eggs, one at a time. Add flavorings. Stir in flour. Pour into greased and floured tube pan and bake in the oven for 1 hour and 15 minutes. Let cool in pan on cake rack for 10 minutes.

Yield: 1 cake

Kitty's Applesauce Cake

A moist summertime square-pan cake.

> ½ *cup shortening*
> 1½ *cups sugar*
> 2 *eggs, beaten*
> 1 *cup thick, unsweetened applesauce*
> 2 *cups flour*
> ¼ *teaspoon salt*
> 1 *teaspoon baking powder*
> ½ *teaspoon baking soda*
> 1 *teaspoon cinnamon*
> ½ *teaspoon cloves*
> 1 *cup raisins*
>
> Frosting:
> 2 *cups brown sugar*
> 1 *cup white sugar*
> 2 *tablespoons white corn syrup*
> ⅔ *cup whipping cream*

Preheat the oven to 350°. Cream shortening and sugar together, add eggs and beat well. Fold in applesauce and dry ingredients. Mix well. Stir in raisins. Bake in a waxed paper-lined 8-inch square pan in the oven for 45 to 50 minutes. Remove from oven when done and let cool to room temperature before frosting.

Cook frosting ingredients over low heat until sugar dissolves. Cover saucepan 2 to 3 minutes to dissolve sugar crystals. Uncover and cook to soft ball stage (238°). Cool to lukewarm, then beat to a spreading consistency and spread over cake.

Yield: 1 8-inch cake

Oatmeal Crackers

I like to serve these crisp, nutty-flavored crackers with cranberry quince jelly.

> *1 cup shortening*
> *1 cup sugar*
> *3 cups all-purpose flour*
> *4 cups quick oatmeal*
> *2 teaspoons salt*
> *1 teaspoon baking soda, dissolved in 1 cup warm water*

Preheat the oven to 350°. Cream together shortening and sugar. Mix in flour, oatmeal, salt and baking soda water.

Roll dough out on lightly floured board to ¼-inch thickness and cut into 2-inch squares. Bake in the oven on a greased baking sheet for 15 minutes.

Yield: 2½–3½ dozen crackers

Sharon's Tips for Better Yeast Bread Baking

1. When I use a bread recipe for the first time I always use ½ cup less flour than is called for. You can always knead in more flour if the dough is too sticky. But too much flour will lead to a dry, crumbly loaf. There are many variables in bread baking that can't be met in a recipe, like the kind of flour used or the humidity in the kitchen, both of which can affect the end result. To prevent over-rising on hot summer days, use water at room temperature, rather than hot water.

2. When working with yeast dough I knead the dough for two or three minutes on a lightly floured board, then cover it with the bowl while cleaning up. That takes about five minutes and gives the dough a chance to rest and the gluten a chance to relax, which makes the dough much easier to knead to a smooth, elastic consistency. This technique also prevents the dough from absorbing too much flour during the kneading process.

3. For the first rising, I always use a large plastic Tupperware-style bowl with a tight-fitting lid. It provides a warm, moist, draft-free environment for the dough to rise in. I can guarantee that in this kind of bowl the first rising will usually be complete within 45 minutes.

4. If you consistently have trouble getting dough to rise, change your brand of yeast. I find that Red Star Yeast works well.

Granny's 100-year-old Oatmeal Bread

I love this bread for its moist, full texture, and for the ease with which it comes together. Great toast. Betsy Piper's grandmother passed on this recipe to her family.

> 2 cups boiling water
> 1 cup oatmeal (quick or regular)
> 2 tablespoons shortening
> ½ cup honey
> 1 package dry yeast
> 2 teaspoons salt
> 5–6 cups all-purpose flour

Preheat the oven to 375°. In a large bowl, pour boiling water over oatmeal and stir to blend. Mix in shortening and honey. Let cool until warm and no longer hot. Blend in yeast. Let stand 5 minutes. Add salt and 4 cups flour and beat until blended.

Let dough rest 10 minutes on floured board, then knead in remaining flour a bit at a time until dough is smooth and elastic. Let rise 1 hour, or until doubled in bulk. Shape into 2 loaves, place in small, oiled bread pans, and let rise for 1 hour. Bake in the oven for 40 minutes.

Yield: 2 loaves

Pumpernickel Bread with Orange Zest

For the soup and salad dinner, this is the bread to serve. It has a special flavor, unlike anything you can buy.

> *2 packages dry yeast*
> *¼ cup warm water*
> *½ cup light molasses*
> *1 tablespoon plus 1½ teaspoons grated orange zest*
> *2 teaspoons crushed fennel seed*
> *1½ teaspoons salt*
> *2 cups buttermilk*
> *3 cups pumpernickel or rye flour*
> *2½–3½ cups all-purpose flour*

Glaze:
¼ cup water
1 tablespoon molasses

Preheat the oven to 350°. In large mixing bowl, dissolve yeast in water.

In medium-sized saucepan heat molasses, orange zest, fennel and salt. Bring to boil, stirring constantly. Remove from heat, stir in buttermilk, and cool to lukewarm. Stir buttermilk mixture into yeast, then gradually stir in pumpernickel or rye flour. Mix in all-purpose flour. Knead for 15 minutes. Cover and let rise for 1 hour.

Punch down dough, divide in half, shaping each half into a ball. Place on greased baking sheet. Slightly flatten loaves, cut an "X" across their tops with a sharp knife, and let rise for 1 hour. Mix together water and molasses to form glaze. Brush loaves with glaze. Bake in the oven for 45 to 50 minutes. Remove from pans. Brush with glaze a second time while loaves are still hot. Cool bread on wire racks.

Yield: 2 loaves

Basic Sourdough Starter

You can't achieve the flavor or the texture of sourdough without a starter.

> *1 package dry yeast*
> *1 tablespoon sugar*
> *2 cups warm potato water*
> *2 cups all-purpose flour*
> *2 cups warm water*

Combine the first 3 ingredients in a glass or porcelain bowl. Cover lightly with cheesecloth and let stand at room temperature for 24 hours (stir mixture occasionally).

After 24 hours, add flour and warm water, cover lightly and let sit out overnight. This is your basic starter. Always keep the starter in a glass or porcelain container with a lid in the refrigerator each time after using.

Note: To replenish the starter, add to it 1½ cups flour and 1 cup warm water, beating until smooth. Cover with cheesecloth and leave out overnight, then stir down and refrigerate.

Yield: 1 quart

Alfred Schissel's Sourdough Rye Bread

We first tasted this bread on a skiing vacation at Crystal Mountain. Alfred's daughter Dody baked it for us, and I have linked its lovely flavor with the Cascade Mountains ever since.

> *1 cup all-purpose flour*
> *3 tablespoons sugar*
> *2½ teaspoons salt*
> *1 package dry yeast*
> *1 cup milk*
> *2 tablespoons butter*
> *1½ cups Basic Sourdough starter (above)*
>
> *¼ cup rye flour*
> *2½ cups whole wheat flour*
> *Cornmeal*
> *Eggwhite*
> *Caraway seeds*

Preheat the oven to 350°. Combine the all-purpose flour, sugar, salt and yeast in a large bowl.

In a small saucepan, warm milk and butter to 110°. Gradually add to dry ingredients and beat for several minutes by hand until well blended, or 2 minutes at medium speed in a mixer.

Add starter and rye flour and mix well. Stir in the wheat flour. Turn dough out onto a floured board, knead into a ball, and cover with bowl for about 5 minutes. Continue to knead until smooth and elastic (10 minutes). Place in greased bowl. Cover. Let rise in warm place until doubled in size (1 hour).

Punch dough down and turn onto lightly floured board. Divide in half. Let rest for 15 minutes.

Shape into 2 loaves and place seam-side down on greased baking sheets sprinkled with cornmeal. Let rise 1 hour, until doubled in bulk. Just before baking, carefully slash tops of loaves on diagonal with sharp knife.

Brush the loaves with water and egg white. Sprinkle with caraway seeds. Bake in the oven for 40 to 50 minutes.

Yield: 2 loaves

Sourdough White Bread

This bread has a smooth texture, a nice crust, and that characteristic sourdough flavor.

> *1 cup Basic Sourdough Starter (p. 333)*
> *1 cup water*
> *5–6 cups all-purpose flour*
> *1 package dry yeast*
> *1 cup warm water*
> *1 tablespoon salt*
> *Egg white, beaten with 1 tablespoon water*

Preheat the oven to 450°. Mix starter, water and 2 cups flour, and let sit overnight.

In large bowl, dissolve yeast in water. Let stand 10 minutes, then stir in starter mixture. Add salt and remaining flour. Turn out onto lightly floured board and knead for 10 minutes. Cover and let rise for 1½ hours.

Punch down dough and divide in half. Shape into 2 round loaves. Let rise for 1 hour. Cut slashes across top of each loaf. Brush lightly with beaten egg white. Bake in the oven for 25–30 minutes.

Yield: 2 loaves

Honey–Whole Wheat Bread

This is our "house" bread; it makes great toast, is wonderful with bacon, lettuce and tomato sandwiches, and makes a good dinner bread, too. To serve warm, simply reheat in oven.

> 4 cups warm water
> 1 cup honey
> 2 packages dry yeast
> 4 cups whole wheat flour
> 1 cup wheat germ
> 1 cup butter, melted
> 5–6 cups all-purpose flour
> 1 tablespoon kosher salt

Preheat the oven to 375°. Combine water, honey and yeast in a large bowl and let sit for 5 minutes. Add whole wheat flour, wheat germ, and salt. Mix well. Add butter and 4 cups of white flour. Beat with a wooden spoon until well mixed. Dough will be sticky at this point. Stir in the remaining white flour, ½ cup at a time, until dough no longer sticks to sides of bowl. Turn out on well-floured board and cover with bowl.

Let rest for 10 minutes, then knead dough, adding more flour if necessary, until smooth and elastic. Cover and let rise in lightly greased bowl for 1 hour.

Punch down and divide into 3 equal pieces. Shape into loaves and place in buttered 9- x 5-inch bread pans. Let rise, uncovered, until dough comes above edge of pan (at least 1–1½ hours). Bake loaves in the oven for 40–50 minutes. Remove from pans and let cool on racks.

Yield: 3 loaves

Whole Wheat Nut–Raisin Yeast Bread

This recipe comes from Moore's Flour Mill near Portland, Oregon, where the flour is stone-ground.

> *2 packages dry yeast*
> *½ cup plus 2 cups warm water*
> *1 cup regular oatmeal*
> *½ cup molasses*
> *2 tablespoons butter*
> *1 tablespoon salt*
> *½ cup milk*
> *1 cup chopped walnuts*
> *2 cups raisins (soften in boiling water)*
> *3 cups whole wheat flour*
> *3 cups all-purpose flour*

Preheat the oven to 375°. Soften yeast in ½ cup warm water.

Bring 2 cups water to a boil and gradually pour in oatmeal, stirring constantly for 1 minute. Add molasses, butter and salt. Mix well. Stir in milk and cool to lukewarm.

Add dissolved yeast. Stir in nuts and raisins. Add 2 cups whole wheat flour. Let rest for 30 minutes.

Add remaining flour. Turn out on floured board and knead for 15 minutes. Divide in half and place each into a 9- x 5-inch greased baking pan. Let rise for 1 hour. Bake in the oven for 50 minutes, remove the pans and cool.

Yield: 2 loaves

Manor Farm Bread

Taking the ferry from Seattle to Poulsbo to reach the Manor Farm Inn gives you a real sense of Seattle, the water around it and the feeling of easy escape to the country. A trip to the 30-acre farm tucked into the hillsides of the Kitsap Peninsula is a great getaway. Breakfast and dinner, with this wonderful freshly baked bread, are served to guests.

> *1 tablespoon yeast*
> *1 teaspoon sugar*
> *¼ plus 2½ cups hot water (110°)*
> *4 cups whole wheat flour*
> *3 cups white flour*
> *½ cup 8-grain cereal*
> *⅓ cup salad oil*
> *⅔ cup honey*
> *1 tablespoon salt*
> *1 cup walnuts, chopped*

Preheat the oven to 325°. Dissolve yeast and sugar in ¼ cup water. Let rest for 5 minutes. Transfer to large mixing bowl. Add remaining ingredients. Mix well. Turn out onto well-floured board and knead well. Lightly grease mixing bowl and put in the dough. Cover and let rise until doubled in size (1½ hours).

Punch down and let rise again for 1 hour.

Shape into 4 small round loaves. Make a crosscut on the top of each loaf. Place on lightly greased baking sheets and bake in the oven for 35 minutes. Shut oven off and leave baking sheets in for 5 minutes. Remove baking sheets and place loaves on baking racks to cool.

Yield: 4 small loaves

Squaw Bread

At Sun River, Oregon, people line up early in the morning at the bakery to buy their favorite baked goods and at least two loaves of squaw bread. This is a version that I make at home, when I don't have any loaves left in the freezer. A slightly sweet, moist bread that makes wonderful toast and sandwiches.

> 2½ cups water
> ⅓ cup salad oil
> ¼ cup honey
> ⅓ cup light molasses
> 2 packages yeast
> ¼ cup warm water
> 3 cups whole wheat flour
> 2 teaspoons salt
> 1½ cups rye flour
> 2½ cups all-purpose flour
> ½ cup cornmeal

Preheat the oven to 375°. Combine water, salad oil, honey and molasses. Mix well. Soften yeast in warm water.

Mix together whole wheat flour, salt, rye flour, one cup of all-purpose flour, and cornmeal. Add oil and honey mixture and the yeast to the flour mixture. Mix on low speed in mixer for several minutes. Gradually add enough of the remaining all-purpose flour to make a soft dough. Turn out onto a floured board. Cover with mixing bowl for 5–10 minutes. Knead for 10 minutes until smooth. Cover and let rise for 1 hour.

Punch down. Shape into 3 round loaves and place on lightly greased baking sheets. Let rise 50–60 minutes. Bake in the oven for 40 minutes. Cool on racks.

Yield: 3 loaves

Mrs. Bastrom's Good Hot Dinner Rolls

This is the perfect hot dinner roll, a recipe handed down by my mother-in-law. A panful is a thing to behold. Pull them apart, watch the steam rise, and add the butter.

> *2 packages dry yeast*
> *1 cup warm water*
> *1 cup warm milk*
> *6 tablespoons sugar*
> *2 teaspoons salt*
> *¼ cup shortening*
> *1 egg*
> *6 cups all-purpose flour*
> *Melted butter*

Preheat the oven to 325°. Combine all ingredients except flour and melted butter. Add flour, mix, turn out on board, cover with bowl, and let rest for 10 minutes. Knead dough for 10 minutes. Let rise 1 hour.

Punch down. Pinch off 24 equal-sized pieces of dough. Shape into balls. Place each one on the bread board, cover with cupped hand, and roll with a circular motion. You'll feel the ball tighten up under your palm. If you've done it right, the balls will have a smooth surface and a crease on the bottom. Evenly space rolls in a 9- x 13-inch greased baking pan and let rise 1 hour. Bake in the oven for 45 to 50 minutes. Remove from oven and brush with melted butter.

Yield: 24 rolls

Raised Whole Wheat Buns

Here's a nice bun to serve with your favorite soup and a tray of fruit and cheese for a simple dinner.

2 packages dry yeast
2 cups warm water
½ cup vegetable oil
¼ cup molasses
¼ cup honey
1 tablespoon salt
¼ cup sunflower seeds
¼ cup wheat germ
6 cups whole wheat flour

Preheat the oven to 375°. Dissolve yeast in ¼ cup warm water in mixing bowl. Add oil, the remaining water, molasses, honey, salt, sunflower seeds, wheat germ and 4 cups flour. Mix well. Let rest for 30 minutes. Add remaining 2 cups flour. Turn out on floured board and knead 15 minutes. Cover and let rise 1 hour.

Punch down dough. Roll out ½-inch thick on floured board. Cut with 2-inch biscuit cutter. Place on greased baking sheet. Let rise for 45 minutes. Bake in the oven for 20 minutes.

Yield: approximately 3½ dozen buns

Gretchen Driver's Orange Rolls

A lovely, sweet breakfast roll with a wonderful orange flavor.

> *5 cups all-purpose flour*
> *2 packages dry yeast*
> *1¼ cups milk*
> *½ cup shortening*
> *⅓ cup sugar*
> *1 tablespoon grated orange zest*
> *¼ cup orange juice*
> *1 teaspoon salt*
> *2 eggs*
>
> Orange Glaze:
> *1 cup powdered sugar*
> *1 teaspoon orange zest*
> *2 tablespoons orange juice*

Preheat the oven to 375°. In a large mixing bowl combine 2 cups flour and the yeast.

Warm the milk, shortening, sugar, orange zest, orange juice and salt in a saucepan over low heat just until shortening melts. Let cool to lukewarm and add to flour and yeast mixture. Mix well. Beat in eggs.

Stir in 2½ cups flour. Knead on floured board 10 minutes, adding remaining ½ cup flour if necessary. Cover and let rise 1 hour.

Punch down. Let rest 10 minutes. Roll into rectangle 18- x 10 inches x ½-inch thick. Cut into strips ¾-inch wide and 10 inches long. Loosely tie each strip into a knot. Place on greased baking sheet. Let rise 30 minutes. Bake in the oven for 20 to 25 minutes, until golden brown.

While rolls are baking, make orange glaze by mixing sugar, zest and juice together. Remove rolls from oven and brush with glaze.

Yield: 18 rolls

Mary Alice's Rhubarb Crunch

It's hard to call rhubarb a vegetable once you add the sugar and bake as lovely a dessert as this one. It's the first sign of spring, and this is a dessert everyone looks forward to.

Crumb Mix:
1 cup flour
¾ cup oatmeal
½ cup butter, melted
1 cup brown sugar
1 teaspoon cinnamon

Syrup:
1 cup white sugar
1 cup cold water
1 teaspoon vanilla
1 tablespoon cornstarch

4 cups raw rhubarb, diced

Vanilla ice cream

Preheat the oven to 350°. Blend ingredients for crumb mixture until crumbly.

Combine ingredients for syrup and cook over medium heat until clear.

Put one half of the crumb mixture into an 8- x 8- x 2-inch pan, add rhubarb, pour on the syrup, and top with the rest of the crumb mixture. Bake in the oven for 1 hour. Serve warm, topped with vanilla ice cream.

Serves 6

Marta's Almond Roca Candy

In Tacoma, Washington, the Brown and Haley Company has become known for its Almond Roca candy. I like to make this for a Christmas sweet.

1 pound butter
2 cups sugar
5 ounces blanched almonds, chopped fine
1 large package of milk chocolate chips

Cook butter and sugar over moderate heat until the temperature on a candy thermometer registers 300°, stirring constantly. Remove from heat. Add ¾ of the chopped almonds. Spread in buttered 12- x 18-inch buttered cookie sheet. Sprinkle with chocolate chips and spread them as they melt. Sprinkle remaining almonds on top. Cool. Break into pieces.

Store in airtight container.

Yield: approximately 2 pounds of candy

Christmas Peanut Brittle

I like to make candy at Christmastime for our sweet bar. Everyone looks forward to helping himself to "one of these and two of those."

2 cups sugar
1 cup corn syrup
½ cup water
2 teaspoons baking soda
2 cups peanuts
1 teaspoon vanilla
1 teaspoon butter

Mix sugar, corn syrup and water in a large enamel saucepan and cook over moderate heat until the temperature on a candy thermometer registers 280°, or until syrup is light golden brown. Stir in baking soda and remove from the heat at once (soda causes syrup to bubble and foam up, and produces the foamy appearance of the hardened candy). Add peanuts, vanilla and butter.

Pour candy onto a large buttered marble slab or into a 12- x 18-inch shallow buttered pan and spread quickly in a thin layer. When cold, break into pieces.

Yield: approximately 2 pounds of peanut brittle

SAUCES AND CONDIMENTS

Krueger Pepper Farm's Salsa

At Krueger Pepper Farm in Zillah, Washington, a wide variety of peppers is available. They are in season from mid-August through September, the same time we get ripe red beefsteak tomatoes. As a result, salsa has become a mainstay of our late summer meals; it's especially good with grilled fish and meats.

> *6 vine-ripened tomatoes*
> *2 fresh tomatillos (or 1 green tomato)*
> *2 cloves garlic*
> *3 Anaheim peppers*
> *3 tablespoons red wine vinegar*
> *1–2 jalapeño peppers*
> *1 small white onion*
> *½ cup fresh cilantro leaves*
> *1–2 tablespoons lime juice, to taste*
> *Salt and pepper to taste*

Cut tomatoes in half, gently squeeze out seeds and discard. Dice tomatoes. Finely chop the tomatillos and add to the tomatoes. Mince garlic and mix with tomatoes and tomatillos.

Roast Anaheim peppers under broiler until skins blister and put them into plastic bag while still warm. Let cool. Remove as much skin as possible. Dice and add to tomatoes. Stir in vinegar.

Cut jalapeños in half. Remove seeds. Finely dice and add.

Chop onion and mix with tomatoes. Just before serving, add cilantro leaves and lime juice, and season to taste with salt and pepper.

Yield: 2½ cups

Auntie Alma's
Mustard Sauce for Vegetables

This sauce is delicious on cooked cauliflower, brussels sprouts, or sautéed cabbage.

> ½ cup butter
> 2 tablespoons dry mustard
> ¾ teaspoon salt
> 1 teaspoon Worcestershire sauce

Melt butter and add the rest of the ingredients. Pour over hot vegetables.

Yield: 2½ cups

Tartar Sauce

I like the taste of dill pickle in tartar sauce much better than the traditional sweet pickle. The tartness works better with fish.

> ½ medium white onion
> 1 cup chopped dill pickle
> 1 cup mayonnaise, preferably homemade
> 2 tablespoons lemon juice
> 2 tablespoons minced parsley
> 1 tablespoon chopped fresh dill

Finely chop the white onion; you should have ½ cup. Rinse with cold water and pat dry. Mix with dill pickle, mayonnaise, lemon juice, parsley and dill. Refrigerate for several hours to let flavors blend.

Yield: 2½ cups

Butter Cream Sauce

A light, creamy sauce that you can flavor with brandy or rum and serve warm over apple cake, steamed pudding or bread pudding.

> *1 cup brown sugar*
> *1 cup butter*
> *½ cup half-and-half*
> *1½ teaspoons vanilla*
> *Dash of nutmeg*
> *Brandy, rum or orange juice*

Put sugar, butter and half-and-half in a saucepan. Simmer gently for 15 minutes. Add vanilla and nutmeg. Just before serving, stir in the brandy, rum or juice.

Yield: 1½ cups

Herb Sauce

This is a nice sauce to serve with the Stuffed Flank Steak (p. 127).

> *2 tablespoons butter*
> *2 tablespoons flour*
> *½ cup white wine*
> *1 cup rich beef broth*
> *1 tablespoon chopped parsley*
> *½ teaspoon orange zest*
> *1 tablespoon capers*

Melt butter in small pan. Stir in flour and cook slowly for several minutes. Stir in the wine and blend well. Add the beef broth. Sprinkle in parsley, orange zest and capers. Simmer until thickened and the alcohol taste of wine has evaporated.

Yield: 1½ cups

Rhubarb–Chutney Sauce

In the early spring, the Puyallup Valley yields a large rhubarb crop, a popular and easy plant to grow in the Northwest. The first asparagus from eastern Washington usually arrives just at the peak of the rhubarb season; together, they herald the arrival of spring. My mother made a rhubarb pie from the garden every March. Rhubarb is also known as the "pie plant." The rhubarb completely breaks down in this recipe, forming a delicious sauce to serve with spring lamb or roast pork.

> 1 cup white vinegar
> 2 cups white sugar
> ½ cup dried currants
> 2 cloves garlic, finely chopped
> 3 tablespoons candied ginger
> 1 teaspoon crushed coriander seed
> ½ teaspoon red pepper flakes
> 6 cups rhubarb, finely chopped (about 2 pounds)

In a heavy saucepan bring all the ingredients except the rhubarb to a boil. Add rhubarb and simmer gently for 30 minutes, stirring occasionally until the mixture thickens to the desired consistency.

Yield: 1 quart

Cranberry–Horseradish Sauce

In the Aberdeen–Hoquiam area of Washington State—near the Olympic Rain Forest, a beautiful part of the state and very damp—there are many cranberry bogs. My best friend grew up in Aberdeen, and while traveling in New England this past fall, someone suggested that she might enjoy touring the cranberry bogs. She quickly declined!

My sister-in-law serves this for Christmas dinner with an old-fashioned bone-in baked ham, beautifully glazed, and a steaming hot dish of scalloped potatoes. It's the perfect condiment for ham.

> *2 cups fresh cranberries*
> *1 small white onion*
> *½ cup sugar*
> *¾ cup sour cream*
> *2 tablespoons creamy-style horseradish*

Chop the cranberries and onion in the food processor. Add the remaining ingredients and process until smooth. Refrigerate.

Yield: 3 cups

Fresh Horseradish Sauce

Fresh horseradish is delicious with roast beef or baked tongue.

> *1 pound horseradish root*
> *White vinegar*
> *3 tablespoons sugar*

Wash the horseradish, remove the thick peel, and grate. Mix well with the white vinegar to cover. Add the sugar, mix well and refrigerate. Keeps well.

Yield: 2 cups

Sweet and Sour Plum Sauce for Pork and Duck

We have an Italian plum tree that we harvest late in the summer. We shake the tree, gather the plums and then freeze them as follows:

> *5 quarts plums*
> *2 cups water*
> *1 cup granulated sugar*

Place plums in a 5-quart enamel saucepan. Pour in the water. Cover and steam briefly, just until skins begin to split. Remove from heat. Sprinkle sugar over plums. Let cool. With a slotted spoon, place plums in freezer bags and freeze.

> Sauce:
> *3 cups frozen, sugared plums (remove seeds)*
> *¼ cup red wine vinegar*
> *1 teaspoon fresh ginger, minced*
> *Pinch of powdered cloves*

Place plums, vinegar, ginger and cloves in a 1½- or 2-quart saucepan. Cover and simmer over medium heat, stirring occasionally, for 15 minutes. Serve warm.

Yield: 3 cups

John's Sweet Hot Mustard

John Ludtka—editor of the Ellensburg, Washington, newspaper—makes this mustard every Christmas and gives it out as gifts. It has a tangy sweetness that complements smoked meats and corned beef.

> *1 cup Colman's dry mustard*
> *1 cup white vinegar*
> *2 eggs, beaten*
> *1 cup brown sugar*

Mix dry mustard and white vinegar in a small bowl and let sit overnight.

Next day, mix the eggs and sugar together with the mustard–vinegar mixture in a small heavy saucepan. Cook, stirring continuously, over low heat until mixture thickens.

Remove from heat immediately and transfer to a bowl. Continue stirring to cool mixture so that it doesn't overcook the eggs.

Yield: enough for 4–5 small jars

Paul's Sour Dills

10 1-quart canning jars

Fresh small pickling cucumbers
20 whole cloves garlic
Fresh dill
3 quarts water
1 cup pickling salt
2 quarts white vinegar (5% acidity)
6 tablespoons pickling spice
Hot red pepper (optional)

Sterilize 10 1-quart canning jars and their lids.

Fill each jar with cucumbers, 2 garlic cloves and 1 sprig of dill.

Bring water, salt, vinegar and pickling spice to a boil and boil 3 minutes to form the hot brine. Immediately fill jars with hot brine and seal. Jars will seal on their own. (If you like hot dills, you can add 1 small hot red pepper to each jar.)

Yield: enough for 10 1-quart canning jars

Pickled Asparagus Spears

Pickled asparagus spears are the perfect thing to serve with smoked salmon. They are tart and complement the richness of the fish.

8–10 1-quart canning jars

8–10 cloves garlic, peeled
3–4 pounds asparagus (depending on the size of the spears)
½ cup plus 2 tablespoons pickling salt
3 quarts water
2 quarts white vinegar (5% acidity)
1 tablespoon pickling spice (cloves removed)

Sterilize 8–10 1-quart canning jars and their lids.

Put 1 garlic clove in each jar. Cut asparagus to fit into jars. Add to jars.

Bring salt, water, vinegar and pickling spice to a boil to form the hot brine. Boil 3 minutes. Immediately fill jars with hot brine and seal.

Yield: enough for 8–10 1-quart canning jars

THE WINES AND SPIRITS
OF THE PACIFIC NORTHWEST

S tephen McCarthy's family has been in the fruit business since the turn of the century when his grandfather, a Yale forestry graduate, came west to Oregon with others who sought fresh opportunity, bought land, and put in orchards. While the others made the kinds of fortunes that established them among the prominent families of Portland, Stephen McCarthy's grandfather somehow lost it all. The family bought back into the fruit business, however, in the 1960s near Parkdale, Oregon, halfway between Mount Hood and the Columbia River, high up in the Hood River Valley at an altitude of 1,800 feet. Stephen and his brother bought orchard land, and so did their parents. The McCarthys grow Bartlett pears.

The connection between fruit production and Northwest wine may not be apparent at first. The lesson here isn't so much that the McCarthys grow pears, but that Stephen McCarthy turns the harvest into *eau de vie de poire,* or pear brandy. Had there not been twenty years of struggling wine production preceding his efforts with fermented fruits and copper pot stills, it is unlikely Stephen McCarthy would have dreamed of advancing from wine to brandy. Twenty years ago no one really believed that the production of fine wine was possible in the Pacific Northwest, a bias caused by too much California sun. Such notions have proved false. The potential of the wine industry in the Pacific Northwest determined by the kinds of grapes now grown and wines being made is compared today not as much to California as it is to France. So Stephen McCarthy is not falling all that far from the tree when he makes his leap from fine wine to fine brandy, marc, and possibly cognac. A France without calvados, poire and cognac is as unimaginable as a France without fine Bordeaux wines and champagne. A similar future awaits the Pacific Northwest, if Stephen McCarthy has his way.

At harvesttime McCarthy transports the family pear crop to Portland, crushes it all at his Clear Creek Distillery, dumps ten tons of fruit at a time into three twenty-foot-high stainless steel water-cooled tanks—each with capacities of over 2,000 gallons—adds Red Star Champagne yeast, lets the fruit ferment for a month to bring the sugar level down to zero, then pumps the mash into sixty-gallon copper pot stills, to which he applies indirect heat. The valves and gauges and pipes that loop out of the stills look like the dive controls on an early submarine. McCarthy must adjust heat levels and pressure levels and cooling systems throughout the distilling process, called a "run." He plays his stills like instruments in an all-brass ensemble. Out the other end drips an *eau de vie de poire* that can hold up to the best of its kind distilled in France and Switzerland. It takes thirty runs to pass the contents of a single fermenting tank through a pot still. Each sixty-gallon run fills a five-gallon glass carboy about three-quarters full.

In his second commercial year McCarthy distilled only 1,000 cases of Clear Creek Williams Pear Brandy. Williams is a name associated with the finest pear brandy, and what the Bartlett pear is called in Europe, a fact that caught McCarthy's attention a dozen years ago and set him on a course that has resulted in a two-still operation in downtown Portland. When it came to designing the label for his poire, McCarthy decided to prominently display the Williams Pear name as a way to alert knowledgeable customers that this was a first-class European-style distilled product and not another vodka flavored with fruit extract.

Stephen McCarthy lifts a small glass of his pear brandy to his nostrils. The fragrance of pear occupies the free air space in the glass while the slight flavor of pear, the distilled essence of the fruit, takes up residence in the clear, slightly viscous liquid. Even at 80 proof, smoothly sliding down the back of the throat, pear brandy feels like it could revive the dead. "This has to be the greatest way to sell fruit," McCarthy says with palpable satisfaction. "This is the tail that wags the dog."

He is a businessman first, then a distiller. Initially trained as a lawyer, Stephen McCarthy acquired a small manufacturing business that produced specialty items for the hunting and shooting trades, things like rifle slings and sling swivels, cartridge belts and pouches, holsters, black powder reaming irons. After nine years of steady growth he was able to sell the company for $15 million, cash. The next day he was a full-time distiller, though he had started small, three years before, with a single still.

McCarthy owns the building that houses Clear Creek Distillery in Portland, and he owns the considerable range of equipment that fills the open, high-ceilinged interior, from the forklift to the fruit crusher to the three enormous fermentation tanks to the two copper pot stills built for him by Arnold Holstein, the man who, in McCarthy's opinion, designs and manufactures the best pot stills in Germany. Each still costs $50,000, an expense McCarthy didn't cover without considerable thought and study. "People were getting tired of hearing me talk all the time about the possibility of producing *eau de vie* like this," McCarthy says, raising his glass of *eau de vie de poire* to the light. "I decided I had to either stop talking or prove it could be done."

He could have gone into wine production, but thought that the last thing the Northwest needed was another small premium wine producer. In the near future in the Pacific Northwest the competition among wine producers is bound to be fierce. The growth of the wine industry in Oregon and Washington in the last twenty years has been phenomenal. In 1960 there were four wineries in Oregon making sweet wines of a kind favored by tramps and hoboes, fruity wines that had been produced in the Northwest since the fall of Prohibition. In the 1930s nearly thirty such wineries had been in operation. Then in 1961 Richard Sommer established Hillcrest Vineyard and planted vinifera wine grapes on land near Roseburg in southern Oregon in the Umpqua Valley, selecting the Riesling grape that has since become the backbone of the Oregon wine industry. David Lett followed with Eyrie Vineyards in 1965, settling in the Dundee Hills near Portland in the Willamette Valley despite dire warnings from his contemporaries at the University of California at Davis wine program that he was being foolish to plant vinifera grapes—let alone pinot noir—in a region with such inclement weather. Today Lett's pinot noirs are the class act of the Oregon wine industry and have brought the region to the attention of the wine world. Lett proved that what might be true in California isn't necessarily the case in the Northwest. Lett and Sommer have been followed by some fifty other vineyards and wineries in Oregon, nearly all of them small.

A similar story can be told of the wine industry in Washington State, though the first real winery there was established by a group of University of Washington professors in the early 1960s. They hired a winemaker. Washington State growers have since gone on to plant various vinifera grapes in such profusion that only California harvests more wine grapes. As a result there were seventy wineries in Washington in 1987, up from twenty-eight in 1983, with more likely to go into production.

The Northwest is as ideally suited to wine production as it is to fruit production, though that realization has been a long time coming, with many misconceptions about the Northwest having to fall by the wayside. The process is still fermenting. The Northwest wine industry has been a diffident stepchild of California wine production. The majority of the people making and growing wine in the Northwest either come from, or were trained in, California. It is only natural that people in a state known for its sun would think that anything as far north as the Northwest must be butt up against North Pole icebergs, or covered in thick, wet moss. Rieslings and Gewürztraminers, the wines of Germany and Austria, were thought best for Northwest climactic conditions. But in fact the land where the majority of Oregon and Washington wine grapes grow parallels the great wine regions of France, from Bordeaux north to the Loire Valley, not the Rhine Valley. And the rain forest is out on the coast, not in the interior of the Pacific Northwest.

The storms that cluster and build out in the Pacific Ocean off the north coast of Hawaii or in the Gulf of Alaska follow the Japanese Current into the Washington and Oregon coasts. Rarely does just one big storm sail through. More often it is one storm after another, pounding away, dropping rain, obscuring the sun behind gray skies from fall through spring with little glorious one-day and two-day respites, when the land shakes off its wet coat and stands up on its hind legs to embrace the sun. The storms are forced up over mountain ranges before they can ever move east. They drop their water on the windward side of the Olympic Mountains on Washington's Olympic Peninsula, and on the Coastal Range in Oregon, before confronting the 12,000-foot wall that is the Cascade Mountain Range, stretching from Canada down into southern Oregon. These mountains cast an eastward shadow, a rain shadow, where little water falls. Driving from west to east across the Cascade passes, the forest changes from mossy primeval to scrubby pine as dry as mouse-nest tinder. Then the trees give out altogether and what's left is bitter brush and bunch grass and lava flows. Anywhere a man has chosen to irrigate, of course, the land blooms like nowhere else in the nation.

Of the many pockets of wine grape cultivation in the Northwest, the two bound for most glory are Washington's Columbia Valley and Oregon's Willamette Valley. The Columbia Valley is a desert brought to life by those who care to water and farm its soil. The days are hot and long—each one a full hour longer than any growing day farther south in California—and the nights are cool. The Columbia River directs ocean air up its gorge and spills it across the land, moderating the climate. In the Willamette Valley, the climate is a gentle, maritime affair, the land protected from wet weather by the Coastal Range. Again, ocean air can funnel into the valley, calming down the hottest days, preventing fall and spring frosts and winter freezes. When the right vinifera grapes are selected for the climate, the soil, and the long growing season, they couldn't be happier. The growing conditions in the Columbia Valley can produce grapes both high in sugar and acidity, while the grapes grown in cooler climates in Oregon ripen with a lower sugar content than might be expected. It has taken time to shrug off old viticulture assumptions brought north from California and to settle on what works.

"In Oregon they are finding that maybe they have the wrong chardonnay, a clone that was brought up from California," says Ron Irvine, co-owner of Pike and Western Wines in Seattle's Pike Place Market. Though he is built like a light middleweight and has the kind of piercing brown-eyed stare that could easily un-man an opponent in the ring, Irvine is a gentle sort whose wine shop has grown in step with the ever-evolving Northwest wine trade. Like the Californians who thought growing grapes in the Northwest was a dandy idea only to be met with hoots of derision from their contemporaries, Irvine was told he and his partner, Jack Bagdade, were making a big mistake by opening a wine shop in Seattle's Pike Place Market at a time in the early 1970s when the Market was scruffy and under-appreciated by the sort of customers in Seattle who are interested in fine wine. The Market today is the spiritual center of Pacific Northwest small-scale food production, and there could be no better place to pair Northwest wines with Northwest produce. It has been one big learning experience, the Pacific Northwest food revolution and wine revolution bursting out of adolescence like two ripe teenagers rubbing against each other at a Grange Hall dance, then becoming slightly more self-assured citizens of the world as the maturation process kicks in. The food revolution in the Northwest today is shaky in high heels, the wine revolution still trying to knot a bow tie. Irvine is used to advising his customers, educating them as he educates himself. Since he has a business to run he isn't blind to the inadequacies of Northwest wines—there are many—and doesn't tout them at the expense of any others of interest. But he does see the future evolving in the vineyards and the wineries today as experience takes hold and old errors of judgment and technique give way.

"The chardonnay clone first planted in Oregon," Irvine explains, "was developed for California, which harvests between August and mid-September. In Oregon they can sometimes harvest into November, but usually between mid-September and mid-October. So the conditions in Oregon are just opposite the conditions that the clone was developed to meet. There's talk now of importing cooler climate chardonnay vines from France." In the meantime Oregon's pinot noirs have brought to the region the serious attention of the wine connoisseur, and the trade developing there leans more to quality wines than is the case in eastern Washington. The physical capacities of the vineyards have a lot to do with the chosen style. Willamette Valley vineyard land is expensive and the vineyards are small. So too is the production. Land in eastern Washington is wide open and comparatively cheap, so quantity easily wins out.

The temptation is to lump Northwest wines together, but Irvine eschews such simplicity. The climactic differences between the wine regions of Oregon and Washington (or, for that matter, between those of eastern and western Washington) are as dramatic as differences between the Napa and Sonoma valleys in California, let alone the differences between California and all of the Pacific Northwest. "Grapes are so site-specific, and we are dealing with so many different micro-climates in Washington and Oregon," Irvine says. "Just in the Willamette Valley, when you get to know the pinot noir produced there, you can feel and taste the difference between a wine grown in the Dundee Hills and one grown closer to the Coast Range, where the pinot becomes more like a burgundy. For the consumer, in the long term, there will be some distinct differences as winemakers tune in to that."

Irvine sees winemaking in the Pacific Northwest as a fledgling enterprise riding on California's coattails, but an enterprise that in the next twenty years will define itself and capitalize on its strengths. The wines for which he feels the Pacific Northwest will become known include the following:

In western Washington

Pinot noir: It has a wonderful delicacy with an assertive flavor. It can be peppery and spicy with raspberry and fruit flavors lingering underneath. The grape only produces well in great years, and it remains to be seen how many of those will occur in a decade. A good example is the 1986 Salishan Vineyards Pinot Noir.

Chardonnay: A light wine with higher acidity than its Oregon or California counterpart. A ripe, subtle flavor closely aligned with the Oregon style, in which the chardonnay ranges from a well-defined fresh, appley flavor to a full, buttery flavor that retains a delicacy against the oak. A good western Washington example is the 1984 Salishan Vineyards Chardonnay.

Muller–Thurgau: A grape not well known in this country, but widely planted in Germany. It shows promise in western Washington. Closely aligned with the Riesling and the Sylvaner grapes from which it has been crossed, the wine has a delicate, yet assertive flavor characterized as appley with a slightly muscat aroma. It is finished off dry—with a little sweetness. The typical ten percent alcohol makes this a light wine alternative for the consumer. A good example is the 1987 Mount Baker Vineyards Muller-Thurgau.

There is as yet an unexplored potential in western Washington to grow English and French cider apple varieties to produce a distinctive and exciting hard cider. We should see strong advances in the next twenty years.

In eastern Washington

Cabernet sauvignon: A bolder wine than is known in California with flavors that range from full raspberry to the classically described black currant, with an underlying herbaceousness. The flavor balances with a higher acidity, giving the effect of a big wine without the high alcohol content. The wine is consistent and ages well. The best years are 1983 and 1985. Good examples come from the David Lake Signature Series of Columbia Winery, Leonetti Cellar, and Quilceda Creek Vintners.

Sauvignon blanc and Sémillon: Sauvignon blanc has a stronger, grassier, fresher flavor than one might expect, an expression of the eastern Washington climate. It's a wine that comes right at you and doesn't need any oak from aging in oak casks. Flavor ranges from a fresh hay undercarriage to a leafy quality with intense fruitiness. That, in turn, is balanced by good acidity. The flavor hangs on. Sémillon can be softer, rounder, and often is blended with sauvignon blanc. These wines will distinguish eastern Washington. It is interesting that these grapes, like the cabernet sauvignon, are Bordeaux grapes. Good examples include the Hogue Cellars Fumé

Blanc, Arbor Crest Sauvignon Blanc, and Columbia Winery Sémillon.

In Oregon

The grapes of Burgundy—pinot noir, chardonnay, pinot gris— have proven themselves in Oregon's protected maritime climate.

Pinot noir: Quality, not quantity will always be a hallmark. The wines have a wide character range that can be traced through the Willamette Valley as the soil changes. The flavor can move from a cherry fruit through raspberry to blackberry, all the time exhibiting what the British like to call a "boiled beet" vegetative flavor. On the palate the wines range from delicate to a medium-range weight, but with assertive, distinctive flavor. It takes a cool, long harvest with plenty of sun to increase the sugar in the grapes to bring out the best in pinot noir, a tough combination for Oregon. Some good examples include the Bethel Heights Vineyard 1986 Pinot Noir, Knudsen Erath Winery 1986 Pinot Noir, the Ponzi Vineyards 1986 Pinot Noir, and Eyrie Vineyards 1985 Pinot Noir.

Chardonnay: Oregon is searching for the clone best adapted to the growing conditions. The chardonnay produced tends to be of medium weight, wonderfully balanced, with a slightly higher acidity and a buttery undercurrent. It can be too appley when first released and needs more time to age than people are used to, but it does settle down. Good examples include the Elk Cove Vineyards 1985 Chardonnay, the Bethel Heights Vineyards 1986 Chardonnay, which is made from a different clone than is typical, the Tualatin Vineyards 1986 Chardonnay, and the Adelsheim Vineyard 1986 Chardonnay.

Pinot gris: A grape in the pinot noir family that shows potential. It has character, balance, and a unique, though light flavor. It goes well with oily fish, like salmon and black sea bass, and has the ability to pull flavors out of a dish it accompanies. Eyrie Vineyard has a 1986 Pinot Gris, as does Adelsheim Vineyard. The Ponzi Vineyard 1987 Pinot Gris is a good example of this wine's potential.

Riesling: Oregon produces a fully ripened, beautifully balanced dry Riesling that retains its fruity flavor. The Tualatin Vineyard 1986 White Riesling and the Ponzi Vineyard 1986 Riesling are good examples. The Knudsen Erath 1986 White Riesling is slightly sweeter.

When David Lett at Eyrie Vineyards finished pressing his merlot grapes last fall, Stephen McCarthy took the pulp that was left back to Portland to distill marc. It sits unfinished in a five-gallon glass carboy, a clear liquid that clocks in at 130 proof. A sip forces a cough from the most leathery throat. When McCarthy has finished with the marc, the proof will be much more acceptable. But even in so raw a state it is indeed a smooth distillation with the distinct fragrance of the merlot grape and a stain of its flavor. "To tell you the truth," McCarthy says, "I think I make a better marc from Lett's merlot pressings than he makes a wine." A sip brings to mind haunting M.F.K. Fisher ramblings about an occasion at table highlighted by the dusty bottle of marc appearing from the closet at the back of the tiny French restaurant. One sip today, and the reason a writer would fix on the occasion becomes clear. Marc has the ability to intensify the reality of the moment. Great marc, the kind that Stephen McCarthy is likely to produce given the grapes at hand, has the power to leave an indelible blot on one's memory, or to erase it altogether.

Two dozen enormous oak casks line one wall, casks that once contained cognac. They are now filled with apple brandy. McCarthy is experimenting as yet, and isn't satisfied with his product. But he thinks he is on the right trail. He doesn't speak of his apple brandy as a true Calvados for the simple reason that it has the smell and flavor of apples. "In Normandy," he says, "the distillation of the rough apple wine that drips into the carboys has no smell and no taste. You would never know it came from apples. That distillation is then oaked for five to eight years before it is bottled. My *eau de vie de pomme* smells like apples. It taste like apples. So I don't call it Calvados."

McCarthy tried to determine which apple varieties were being used in Calvados production in Normandy and finally decided that the French distillers didn't have a clear idea what varieties they crush and in what combination or quantities. McCarthy uses Red and Golden Delicious apples, a fruit he belittles as an eating apple for its sugar confection quality. "I should be given an award simply for taking those apples off the fruit market," he says. He has experimented with batches of pure Red Delicious crushings and pure Golden Delicious crushings, as well as a 50–50 mix, and he thinks that he may only have to oak his brandy for eighteen months. Time will tell.

He has also experimented with distilling dry land plums as well as distilling framboise from raspberries. His success has been limited, he admits, but each run of the still moves him closer to the perfection he has achieved with his *eau de vie de poire*. "It's the fruit that makes up half the product. You start with good fruit and you are halfway there. That's why I say this is the tail that wags the dog. We are surrounded by wonderful fruit here in the Northwest. Fields of plums drop on the ground and rot. They can't give their apples away, so many have been harvested. It could all go into a product like mine. Hard liquor sales are off and there's no reason to think they will ever come back. Restaurants need a new product to sell. They can sell a table a bottle of wine. And now they have my poire to sell at the end of the meal. It's perfect. The demand is so great I could produce and sell 20,000 cases a year and never have to advertise."

Given time, the fruit of the vine and the fruit of the field and orchard will help define the culinary magnificence of the Pacific Northwest. How nice it will be to stop by a winery at the end of a long day of pheasant shooting in the Yakima Valley to pick up a bold red wine that can hold up to the game at hand. How nice, at the end of the meal, to toast the success of the hunter and the skill of the cook with the essence of fall picked from the tree and transformed into a liquid as clear as light fading fast behind the last line of ragged mountains to the west.

A WORD ABOUT TOOLS

I t must be nice to be a cook with the talent, the training, and the experience of Sharon Kramis. Give her the ingredients, the fire, and a Boy Scout mess kit and she will turn out a feast. I would turn out a meal that tasted like it had been cooked in a mess kit over fire by a Boy Scout. While proper tools will not make the cook, they certainly help.

Sharon's indispensable cookware list includes a ten-inch black cast-iron skillet. You can't make good Dutch babies without one. And no other pan cooks sausages, hash, pork chops, or hash browns half as well. She uses a seven-quart enamel-coated iron pot for soups, stocks, chili, and the like. The pot cooks evenly without burning. Sharon selects a frypan that doesn't get a hot spot over high heat, a ten- or twelve-inch Silverstone pan. Such pans get scratched after a while, but are inexpensive enough to replace. Her other favorite is a small 6-to-8-cup enamel-clad iron pan with a pour spout that she can use as a double boiler, thus eliminating the need to stand watch and carefully stir over low heat. This is a good pan for cooking scrambled eggs. Because of the high sides, the eggs steam and get much fluffier than in a frypan.

I had the good fortune ten years ago to stumble onto a line of copper cookware called Copper Chef, which has a copper exterior, a pure aluminum core, and a stainless steel cooking surface. I have been unable to damage these pans in the ensuing years, though I long ago gave up on any ideas about keeping the copper clean. The cooking qualities are wonderful: no hot spots; fast, even heat; and a cooking surface that doesn't react with acids in foods. I recently eliminated the oddball pots and pans in my kitchen and filled in with another line of cookware by the same company (All-Clad of Canonsburg, Pennsylvania), called All-Clad. The pans have the same cooking surface, a layer of stainless steel no thicker than three sheets of paper, bonded to a pure aluminum core for the best possible heat conductivity. The exterior is an extra-hard, anodized aluminum oxide that is both attractive and impossible to scratch. I find I constantly use frypans and sauté pans, though I do Dutch babies in a black cast-iron skillet. All-Clad also produces a commercial line popular with chefs called Master Chef. It has an industrial look, but with all the fine qualities of the copper and the anodized aluminum line, and at a third the cost.

For baking, there is no point in starting without an accurate oven thermometer. Measuring cups for dry ingredients that can be leveled with the straight edge of a spatula or with a knife are also essential. While cooking allows plenty of leeway, baking demands accuracy for good results. Sharon bakes bread and pies in glass dishes. There is less of a tendency toward overbrowning. She has a big Kitchen-Aid mixer on call. But I have found in my own kitchen that a small Sunbeam mixer that fits neatly on a counter fulfills all my needs.

Good sharp knives are essential, if not to success, then to safe, quick labor. A ten-inch chef's knife has the weight and blade shape for the majority of slicing, chopping, and mincing tasks. A small Japanese cleaver used for vegetables is also a nice addition. A boning knife, a fillet knife, a carving set, and several paring knives round out the list. For sharpening I rely on a diamond stone— diamond dust set in a plastic block. I never have to fiddle with oil on stone, and it's right there in the drawer. A good sharpening steel is all you need to maintain a keen edge. Not enough can be said about sharp knives. Cutting tasks are easy and relaxed when the blade cuts with no effort. As soon as you start to force a knife to cut because it is dull, you are asking for an accident.

My one eccentric piece of kitchen equipment is a sausage stuffer. There is nothing like fresh sausage, or home-cured sausage like salami, and a stuffer eliminates all the labor. I first made sausage with a Kitchen-Aid grinder attachment, loved the results—and never repeated the task. It was too much trouble, too much fiddling around. The Kitchen-Aid grinder/stuffer does, however, allow you to make sausages in small batches. I found the cleanup trouble enough that I am happy to make sausage in big batches, ten to twenty pounds at a time, and to leave the grinding to my butcher. The Tre Spade sausage stuffer is a beautifully designed Italian product that attaches to a table. I can stuff 5 pounds of sausage in a couple of minutes, from bulk meat to finished links. And then the stuffer comes apart for easy cleaning in the dishwasher.

Finally, the tool that has changed my life: the instant-read thermometer. Stick this baby into $75 worth of roasting meat and it will tell you, instantly and accurately, what the internal temperature might be. No more guessing. No more stomach-wrenching stress and worry about overcooking meat. No more tapping loaves of bread on the bottom for that hollow sound. Baked bread should read 190°. And with an instant-read thermometer, when the bread is done, that's just what it does.

INDEX